T0320318

METHODS FOR
ESTIMATION
AND INFERENCE
IN MODERN
ECONOMETRICS

METHODS FOR ESTIMATION AND INFERENCE IN MODERN ECONOMETRICS

STANISLAV ANATOLYEV
NIKOLAY GOSPODINOV

CRC Press
Taylor & Francis Group
Boca Raton   London   New York

CRC Press is an imprint of the
Taylor & Francis Group, an informa business

A CHAPMAN & HALL BOOK

Chapman & Hall/CRC
Taylor & Francis Group
6000 Broken Sound Parkway NW, Suite 300
Boca Raton, FL 33487-2742

© 2011 by Taylor and Francis Group, LLC
Chapman & Hall/CRC is an imprint of Taylor & Francis Group, an Informa business

No claim to original U.S. Government works

International Standard Book Number: 978-1-4398-3824-2 (Hardback)

Visit the Taylor & Francis Web site at
http://www.taylorandfrancis.com

and the CRC Press Web site at
http://www.crcpress.com

To our families:

Masha and Olga

Alexandra, Victoria and Tzvetana

Contents

Preface

The book covers several interesting and important topics that have recently been developed in the econometrics literature. In particular, the book discusses methods for efficient estimation in models defined by unconditional and conditional moment restrictions, inference in possibly misspecified models, the class of generalized empirical likelihood estimators and alternative asymptotic approximations.

The first chapter provides a general overview of the well-established nonparametric and parametric approaches to estimation and now conventional (asymptotic and bootstrap) frameworks for statistical inference. The next three chapters are concerned with estimation of models based on moment restrictions implied by economic theory. These chapters review various method-of-moments estimators for unconditional and conditional moment restriction models and develop the asymptotic theory for correctly specified and misspecified models. The last two chapters cover non-conventional asymptotic tools that lead to improved finite sample inference. One set of such tools uses higher-order asymptotic analysis that allows for more accurate approximations via various asymptotic expansions. Another asymptotic device is based on a drifting parameter framework and offers substantial improvements over the standard asymptotics in approximating the finite sample behavior of estimators and test statistics. The book addresses several problems that often arise in the analysis of economic data, such as weakly informative but potentially large number of instrumental variables, near-nonstationarity and low signal-to-noise ratio. In order to make the book self-contained, a separate appendix provides a review of some basic concepts and results from linear algebra, probability theory and statistics that are used throughout the book.

To the best of our knowledge, this book is the first to provide a comprehensive introduction to a wide range of recently developed topics that are not discussed in detail outside highly technical research papers. They include generalized empirical likelihood estimators, estimation in models with conditional moment restrictions and inference under drifting parameterizations. The book offers a unified approach to studying these problems using first- and higher-order asymptotic theory and the theory of misspecified models. This book is structured as a monograph but it will be appropriate also as a graduate textbook in advanced econometric courses as well as a reference book for econometricians, statisticians and practitioners. While there are some excellent monographs on some econometrics topics (nonparametric econometrics, finite sample econometrics, nonstationary econometrics), our book links most of the existing estimation and inference methods in a general framework which is expected to benefit readers in synthesizing various aspects of modern econometric theory. To help readers and instructors using the book, we include various theoretical exercises with suggested solutions.

Notation and Abbreviations

FOC	first-order condition(s)
CDF	cumulative distribution function, typically denoted as F
EDF	empirical distribution function, typically denoted as F_n
PDF	probability density function, typically denoted as f
(U)LLN	(uniform) law of large numbers
(F)CLT	(functional) central limit theorem
OLS	ordinary least squares
IV	instrumental variables
2SLS	two-stage least squares
GMM	generalized method of moments
(G)EL	(generalized) empirical likelihood
(V)AR	(vector) autoregression
MA	moving average
HAC	heteroskedasticity and autocorrelation consistent
$\mathbb{I}\{A\}$	indicator function returning 1 if event A holds, 0 otherwise
$\Pr\{A\}$	probability of event A
$E[y\vert x]$	mathematical expectation (mean) of y conditional on x
$\mathrm{var}[y\vert x]$	variance of y conditional on x
$\mathrm{var}(x)$	variance of x
$\mathrm{cov}(x,y)$	covariance between x and y
$\mathrm{corr}(x,y)$	correlation coefficient between x and y
$\mathcal{F}, \mathcal{F}_t$	information set, filtration
$\bar{x}$	sample average of x
log	natural logarithm
plim	probability limit
tr	trace operator
rk	matrix rank
vec	matrix vectorizing operator
det	matrix determinant
$\mathbb{R}$	real line
$\mathbb{R}^k$	k-dimensional real space
$\mathbb{N}$	set of natural numbers
$\xrightarrow{p}$	convergence in probability
$\xrightarrow{d}$	convergence in distribution
$\xrightarrow{a.s.}$	almost sure convergence
$\Rightarrow$	weak convergence
$o_P(c_n)$	order (in probability) smaller than c_n
$O_P(c_n)$	order (in probability) at most c_n
$\varnothing$	null set
$\subset$	subset
$\otimes$	Kronecker product
$\forall$	for all
sup	supremum
inf	infimum
arg max	argument of the maximum
arg min	argument of the minimum

$\langle \cdot, \cdot \rangle$	inner product of two vectors
$\lvert \cdot \rvert$	Euclidean norm of a vector
$\lVert \cdot \rVert$	Euclidean (Frobenius) norm of a matrix
$\partial a / \partial b'$	matrix of derivatives of vector a with respect to vector b
$\operatorname{diag} \{a_j\}$	diagonal matrix with a_j's on the main diagonal
$a^{(i)}$	i^{th} element of vector a
I_k	$k \times k$ identity matrix
$0_{\ell \times k}$	$\ell \times k$ matrix of zeros
1_k	$k \times 1$ vector of ones
$\sim$	distributed as
$\mathcal{N}$	normal (Gaussian) distribution
$\mathcal{E}$	exponential distribution
χ_k^2	chi-square distribution with k degrees of freedom
$W(r)$	standard Brownian motion (Wiener process)
IID	independently and identically distributed
$\varphi(\lambda)$	characteristic function
$\mathbb{K}(\lambda)$	cumulant generating function
n	sample size
k	number of parameters in parametric models
ℓ	number of instruments or moment conditions
θ, θ_0	parameter vector and its true value
Θ	parameter space for θ
$Q(\cdot), Q_n(\cdot)$	population and sample objective functions
$m(\cdot, \cdot)$	moment function
$g(\cdot, \cdot)$	regression function
M_{xz}, M_{zz}	expectations of xz' and zz'
M	$E[\partial g(\theta_0)/\partial \theta]$ for some function $g(\theta)$
V	$E[\partial g(\theta_0)/\partial \theta \, \partial g(\theta_0)/\partial \theta']$ for some function $g(\theta)$
Ω	variance matrix of parameter estimates
K	kernel function
b	bandwidth
$\mathcal{KLIC}$	Kullback–Leibler information criterion
$\mathcal{W}$	Wald test statistic
$\mathcal{LR}$	likelihood ratio test statistic
$\mathcal{DM}$	distance metric test statistic
$\mathcal{LM}$	Lagrange multiplier (score) test statistic
$\mathcal{J}$	test statistic for overidentifying restrictions

Part I

Review of Conventional Econometric Methods

Chapter 1

Standard Approaches to Estimation and Statistical Inference

1.1 Introduction

This chapter provides a brief review of some popular parametric and nonparametric estimation methods as well as some approaches to statistical inference. While these methods are now well known and are the subject of comprehensive treatment in various textbooks and monographs, they provide a natural starting point for the material that is introduced and discussed later in the book. Since most of the topics covered in this book are extensions and generalizations of the more conventional econometric methodology, it proves useful to develop the proper context for the subsequent analysis.

We start the chapter with a discussion of methods for estimating unknown parameters or functions that describe the behavior of a particular economic phenomenon or process. The choice of an estimation method is determined to a large degree by information about the underlying data generation process provided by economic theory. Another important criterion in selecting an appropriate estimation method is its asymptotic properties, which are the main subject of discussion for each estimation method considered in this book. As a result, the econometrician is often faced with a trade-off between optimality and robustness of the candidate estimation method.

In the first part of the chapter, we provide an overview of extremum estimators that comprise a general class which includes the maximum likelihood estimator, generalized method of moments, minimum distance estimators, etc. These methods are based on information that allows us to fully parameterize the model of interest (maximum likelihood) or on limited information obtained only from a set of conditional or unconditional moment restrictions (method of moments). Furthermore, if economic theory does not provide sufficient information about the shape of the conditional mean function, researchers often resort to nonparametric methods for estimation. In addition, we briefly discuss robust estimation such as quantile regressions.

In the second part of the chapter, we review the fundamentals for testing parametric restrictions, specification testing in overidentified models and confidence interval construction by test inversion. The practical implementation of these inference procedures requires knowledge of the exact or approximate distribution of the statistic of interest. Most of this book is concerned with first- or higher-order asymptotic inference. This approach is based on the large sample theory and gives approximate distributional results that are easy to implement for hypothesis testing and construction of confidence intervals. There are cases, however, when these large sample approximations can deviate substantially from the actual distribution that is the object of interest. There are other approaches to statistical inference that may be better suited when the sample size is relatively small. The exact distribution theory, for example, is designed to handle small-sample problems but its validity depends crucially on some strong assumptions that are rarely satisfied by non-experimental economic data. One relatively new and easy-to-implement inference method is the bootstrap, which, in many situations, tends to deliver a smaller approximation error than the first-order asymptotics. This chapter introduces the theoretical underpinnings and computational aspects of the bootstrap, while later in the book we discuss its higher-order asymptotic properties.

1.2   Parametric Estimators

Let θ be a $k \times 1$ vector of unknown parameters with a parameter space Θ, $\{w_i\}_{i=1}^n$ be a random sample of observed variables, where $w_i = (y_i, x_i)$ or $w_i = (y_i, x_i, z_i)$, and $Q_n(\theta)$ denote an objective (criterion) function that satisfies certain conditions. The index n indicates the dependence of $Q_n(\theta)$ on the sample. The *extremum estimator* is defined as

$$\hat{\theta} = \arg\min_{\theta \in \Theta} Q_n(\theta).$$

The true value of θ, denoted by θ_0, is the value of θ that minimizes $Q(\theta) = \text{plim}_{n \to \infty} Q_n(\theta)$. The class of extremum estimators includes the M-estimators, minimum distance, generalized empirical likelihood and generalized method of moments estimators. For the *M-estimators*, the objective function takes the form

$$Q_n(\theta) = \frac{1}{n} \sum_{i=1}^n q(w_i, \theta),$$

where $q(w_i, \theta)$ is a function only of the ith observation of the data and the parameter θ.

The most celebrated member of the class of M-estimators is the *maximum likelihood (ML) estimator* for which

$$q(w, \theta) = -\log f(y|x, \theta)$$

and

$$Q_n\left(\theta\right) = -\frac{1}{n}\sum_{i=1}^{n}\log f\left(y_i|x_i,\theta\right),$$

where $f\left(y|x\right)$ is the conditional density of y given x. To make the ML proce-
dure operational, it is typically assumed that $f\left(y|x\right)$ comes from a particular
parametric family of density functions. For this reason, we refer to the ML as
a parametric estimation method.

By contrast, the *generalized method of moments (GMM) estimator* does not
fully specify the conditional density and is based only on partial information
provided by a set of moment restrictions. Let

$$E\left[m\left(w,\theta_0\right)\right] = 0$$

be a population moment condition implied by economic theory, where $m\left(w,\cdot\right)$
is a given moment function from $\mathbb{R}^k$ to $\mathbb{R}^\ell$ with $\ell \geq k$. Then, the GMM estimator (Hansen, 1982) minimizes a quadratic form in the sample counterparts of
these moment conditions. The quadratic form is constructed using a positive
definite matrix and has the form

$$Q_n\left(w,\theta\right) = m_n\left(\theta\right)' W_n m_n\left(\theta\right),$$

where

$$m_n\left(\theta\right) = \frac{1}{n}\sum_{i=1}^{n} m\left(w_i,\theta\right),$$

and W_n is an $\ell \times \ell$ symmetric positive definite weighting matrix.

For many econometric models the moment conditions do not have a tractable
analytical form. In this case, $m_n\left(\theta\right)$ can be replaced by an approximation
based on simulations from the model of interest. This is the idea behind the
simulation-based methods of moments. The *simulated method of moments estimator* of Duffie and Singleton (1993) is an example of a *minimum distance
(MD) estimator* and is defined to minimize the quadratic form

$$\hat{\theta} = \arg\min_{\theta\in\Theta} D_n(\theta)' W_n D_n(\theta)$$

with

$$D_n(\theta) = \frac{1}{n}\sum_{i=1}^{n} m\left(w_i,\theta\right) - \frac{1}{nN}\sum_{i=1}^{nN} m\left(\tilde{w}_i\left(\theta\right),\theta\right)$$

and some weighting matrix W_n. In these expressions, $n^{-1}\sum_{i=1}^{n} m\left(w_i,\theta\right)$ is
a vector of empirical moments based on the data $\{w_i\}_{i=1}^{n}$, $\{\tilde{w}_i\left(\theta\right)\}_{i=1}^{nN}$ denotes a simulated sample path of length nN from the model for a candidate
value of the parameter vector θ and $(nN)^{-1}\sum_{i=1}^{nN} m\left(\tilde{w}_i\left(\theta\right),\theta\right)$ is an approximation to the population moments of the structural model. The indirect

inference estimator of Gourieroux, Monfort and Renault (1993), which is another simulation-based method of moments estimator, also has the structure of a minimum distance estimator.

In the next subsections, we will describe in more detail the properties of the ML, GMM and robust estimators.

1.2.1   Asymptotic Properties of M-Estimators

Establishing the asymptotic properties of parametric estimators follows similar arguments and structure for various estimators. This section discusses some main concepts and tools that can be easily adapted to the different estimation frameworks that we consider later in the book. For this reason, it is instructive to introduce these concepts in a more familiar parametric framework such as ML or GMM in order to gain some intuition about the basic regularity conditions for consistency, asymptotic normality and efficiency of the estimators.

To show the consistency of M- and extremum estimators, we need to impose conditions on $Q_n(\theta)$ which would ensure that the *uniform weak law of large numbers* (U-WLLN) holds. U-WLLN states that $Q_n(\theta)$ converges in probability uniformly to $Q(\theta)$ over $\theta \in \Theta$ if

$$\sup_{\theta \in \Theta} |Q_n(\theta) - Q(\theta)| \xrightarrow{p} 0 \text{ as } n \to \infty,$$

where sup denotes the supremum (least upper bound) operator.

Converting the pointwise convergence into uniform convergence requires that some sufficient regularity is imposed on the objective function $Q_n(\theta)$. For this purpose, it is assumed that $Q_n(\theta)$ is continuous in θ, Θ is compact, and the dominance condition $E[\sup_{\theta \in \Theta} |Q_n(\theta)|] < \infty$ is satisfied. These assumptions imply that the stochastic equicontinuity condition for uniform convergence holds. The function $Q_n(\theta)$ is said to be *stochastically equicontinuous* if there exists a uniformly bounded random sequence $B_n = O_P(1)$ and a non-negative deterministic function $\xi(\cdot)$ such that $\xi(s) \to 0$ as $s \to 0$ and

$$|Q_n(\theta_1) - Q_n(\theta_2)| \le B_n \xi(|\theta_1 - \theta_2|) \text{ for all } \theta_1, \theta_2 \in \Theta,$$

where $|\theta_1 - \theta_2|$ denotes the Euclidean norm of the vector $\theta_1 - \theta_2$. In what follows, we denote the Euclidean (or Frobenius) norm of a matrix A as $\|A\|$. For more detail regarding U-WLLN and stochastic equicontinuity, see Andrews (1994) and Newey and McFadden (1994).

We can now specialize the above results to provide more primitive conditions that ensure the consistency of the ML estimator (MLE). In particular, if we assume that Θ is compact, $f(y|x,\theta)$ is continuous in $\theta \in \Theta$, $E[\sup_{\theta \in \Theta} |\log f(y|x,\theta)|] < \infty$ and $\Pr\{f(y|x,\theta) \ne f(y|x,\theta_0)\} > 0$ for all $\theta \ne \theta_0$, then $\hat{\theta} \xrightarrow{p} \theta_0$ as $n \to \infty$. The first three conditions imply that $Q_n(\theta) \xrightarrow{p}$

$Q(\theta)$ uniformly on Θ while the last condition ensures that $-E\left[\log f\left(y|x,\theta\right)\right]$ is minimized uniquely at θ_0.

The proof of the asymptotic normality of the MLE is based on a first-order Taylor series (mean value) expansion of $\partial Q_n(\hat{\theta})/\partial\theta$ about θ_0. For this reason, it is required that θ_0 be in the interior of Θ and $f(y|x,\theta)$ be twice continuously differentiable in θ. Furthermore, combined with the above conditions, $E\left[\sup_{\theta\in\mathbf{N}}\left\|\partial^2\log f\left(y|x,\theta\right)/\partial\theta\partial\theta'\right\|\right]<\infty$ for some neighborhood $\mathbf{N}$ of θ_0 guarantees that

$$H_n(\theta) = -\frac{1}{n}\sum_{i=1}^{n}\frac{\partial^2\log f\left(y_i|x_i,\theta\right)}{\partial\theta\partial\theta'}$$

converges uniformly to

$$H = -E\left[\frac{\partial^2\log f\left(y|x,\theta_0\right)}{\partial\theta\partial\theta'}\right].$$

Finally, assuming that $E\left\|\partial\log f\left(y|x,\theta_0\right)/\partial\theta\cdot\partial\log f\left(y|x,\theta_0\right)/\partial\theta'\right\|<\infty$ and H is of full rank, we have

$$\sqrt{n}(\hat{\theta}-\theta_0)\xrightarrow{d}\mathcal{N}\left(0,H^{-1}VH^{-1}\right),$$

where

$$V = E\left[\frac{\partial\log f\left(y|x,\theta_0\right)}{\partial\theta}\frac{\partial\log f\left(y|x,\theta_0\right)}{\partial\theta'}\right].$$

If the model is correctly specified, the information matrix equality holds

$$-E\left[\frac{\partial^2\log f\left(y|x,\theta_0\right)}{\partial\theta\partial\theta'}\right] = E\left[\frac{\partial\log f\left(y|x,\theta_0\right)}{\partial\theta}\frac{\partial\log f\left(y|x,\theta_0\right)}{\partial\theta'}\right]$$

and

$$\sqrt{n}(\hat{\theta}-\theta_0)\xrightarrow{d}\mathcal{N}\left(0,H^{-1}\right),$$

i.e., the estimator of θ attains the Cramér–Rao lower bound.

Interestingly, the Cramér–Rao lower bound can be attained in cases even when the density $f(y|x,\theta)$ is not fully parameterized. This possibility is referred to in the literature as *adaptive estimation*. Suppose that the parameter vector of interest is θ and f is described by the nuisance parameter vector η with the true value η_0, which can be estimated nonparametrically by kernel methods described in section 1.4 below. Let

$$H_{\theta\theta} = E\left[\frac{\partial^2\log f\left(y|x,\theta_0,\eta_0\right)}{\partial\theta\partial\theta'}\right],$$

$$H_{\theta\eta} = H'_{\eta\theta} = E\left[\frac{\partial^2\log f\left(y|x,\theta_0,\eta_0\right)}{\partial\theta\partial\eta'}\right]$$

and

$$H_{\eta\eta} = E\left[\frac{\partial^2\log f\left(y|x,\theta_0,\eta_0\right)}{\partial\eta\partial\eta'}\right].$$

When η_0 is known, the Cramér–Rao lower bound of estimating θ_0 is given by $H_{\theta\theta}^{-1}$ as shown above. If η_0 is not known and has to be estimated, the Cramér–Rao lower bound is given by

$$\left(H_{\theta\theta} - H_{\theta\eta}H_{\eta\eta}^{-1}H_{\eta\theta}\right)^{-1} \geq H_{\theta\theta}^{-1}.$$

Then, an estimator $\hat{\theta}_{AE}$ is said to be adaptive if

$$\sqrt{n}(\hat{\theta}_{AE} - \theta_0) \xrightarrow{d} \mathcal{N}(0, H_{\theta\theta}^{-1}).$$

The necessary condition for adaptive estimation is $H_{\theta\eta} = 0$. This condition implies that η is asymptotically irrelevant for the estimation of θ or the matrix

$$\begin{pmatrix} H_{\theta\theta} & H_{\theta\eta} \\ H_{\eta\theta} & H_{\eta\eta} \end{pmatrix}$$

is block diagonal. In linear regression models, for example, the slope parameters are typically adaptively estimable without any strong conditions on the distributional properties of regression errors.

Exercise 1.1. Let (y, x) have a joint density of the form

$$f(y, x|\theta_0) = f_c(y|x, \gamma_0, \delta_0)f_m(x|\delta_0),$$

where $\theta_0 \equiv (\gamma_0, \delta_0)$, γ_0 and δ_0 are scalar parameters, and f_c and f_m denote the conditional and marginal distributions, respectively. Let $\hat{\theta}_c \equiv (\hat{\gamma}_c, \hat{\delta}_c)$ be the ML estimator of γ_0 and δ_0 based on the conditional density f_c, and $\hat{\delta}_m$ be the ML estimator of δ_0 based on the marginal density f_m. For a random sample $\{(y_i, x_i)\}_{i=1}^n$, define

$$\tilde{\gamma} = \arg\max_{\gamma} \sum_{i=1}^{n} \log f_c(y_i|x_i, \gamma, \hat{\delta}_m)$$

to be a two-step estimator of parameter γ_0 which uses the preliminary estimator $\hat{\delta}_m$ of δ_0. Find the asymptotic distribution of $\tilde{\gamma}$. How does it compare to that for $\hat{\gamma}_c$?

Exercise 1.2. Represent the nonlinear least squares estimator of θ_0 in the mean regression model

$$E[y|x] = g(x, \theta_0)$$

as an M-estimator, and derive its asymptotic properties under random sampling.

1.2.2 GMM Estimator

As mentioned above, the GMM estimator is based on the unconditional moment restriction $E[m(w, \theta_0)] = 0$. Often, however, the moment restriction implied by the model takes the form of a conditional restriction

$$E[h(y, x, \theta_0)|z] = 0 \qquad (1.1)$$

for some scalar function $h(\cdot)$. It is common practice to apply the law of iterated expectations and obtain the unconditional moment restriction

$$E[h(y, x, \theta_0)z] = 0.$$

Thus, (1.1) can be rewritten as $E[m(w, \theta_0)] = 0$, where $m(w, \theta) = h(y, x, \theta)z$. In general, the function $h(y, x, \theta)$ could be a vector, in which case $m(w, \theta) = h(y, x, \theta) \otimes z$ is an $\ell \times 1$ vector ($\ell = \dim(h)\dim(z)$), where $\otimes$ is the Kronecker product. We will see in Chapter 3 how this approach can result in a loss of efficiency and even inconsistent estimation.

When $\ell = k$, we refer to this case as the just-identified case. While we show later that the weighting matrix W_n plays a critical role for the efficiency of the estimator in overidentified models, the choice of W_n is irrelevant in just-identifed models. Since the GMM objective function $Q_n(\theta)$ is a positive definite quadratic form, $Q_n(\theta) = 0$ if and only if $m_n(\theta) = 0$. Therefore, in the just-identified case, the method of moments estimator solves the equation $m_n(\hat{\theta}) = 0$.

Typically, the number of moment conditions ℓ exceeds the number of parameters k and $m_n(\hat{\theta})$ cannot be set exactly to zero. In this overidentified case ($\ell > k$), the GMM estimator $\hat{\theta}$ is set to minimize the squared distance of $m_n(\theta)$ from 0 measured by the quadratic form

$$Q_n(\theta) = m_n(\theta)' W_n m_n(\theta).$$

Several popular estimation methods can be considered to be special cases of the GMM for different choices of moment functions $m(w, \theta)$. For example, in the maximum likelihood framework, if the estimating function is the score function $m(w, \theta) = \partial \log f(y|x, \theta)/\partial\theta$, the method of moments estimator coincides with the maximum likelihood estimator. Also, the instrumental variables estimator is a method of moments estimator if $m(w, \theta) = z(y - x'\theta)$ for some instrumental variable z. The OLS estimator is a special case of this framework when $z = x$. Finally, for the α-quantile estimator, $m(w, \theta) = xh(y - x'\theta)$, where $h(u) = \alpha\mathbb{I}\{u > 0\} - (1 - \alpha)\mathbb{I}\{u \leq 0\}$, which simplifies to $m(w, \theta) = x\operatorname{sgn}(y - x'\theta)$ for the least absolute deviation estimator ($\alpha = 1/2$).

The consistency of the GMM estimator can be established using similar conditions as in the previous section that ensure the stochastic equicontinuity of the GMM objective function $Q_n(\theta)$. They typically involve the continuity of $m(w, \theta)$ in θ, dominance condition $E[\sup_{\theta \in \Theta} |m(w, \theta)|] < \infty$ and compactness of the parameter space $\Theta \subset \mathbb{R}^k$, which, combined with the identification condition and convergence in probability of W_n to a nonstochastic symmetric positive definite matrix W, guarantee the consistency of the GMM estimator.

In the overidentified case, the efficiency properties of the GMM estimator depend crucially on the choice of the weighting matrix W_n. Let

$$M_n(\theta) = \frac{\partial m_n(\theta)}{\partial \theta'} = \frac{1}{n} \sum_{i=1}^{n} \frac{\partial m(w_i, \theta)}{\partial \theta'}.$$

Under some further regularity conditions which require that $\partial m(w, \theta) / \partial \theta$ is continuous in θ, $E[m(w, \theta_0) m(w, \theta_0)']$ exists and is finite, $M = E[\partial m(w, \theta_0) / \partial \theta']$ is of full rank and $E[\sup_{\theta_0 \in \mathbf{N}} \|\partial m(w, \theta_0) / \partial \theta'\|] < \infty$ for some neighborhood $\mathbf{N}$ of θ_0, we have

$$\sqrt{n} \left(\hat{\theta} - \theta\right) \xrightarrow{d} \mathcal{N}(0, \Omega),$$

where

$$\Omega = (M'WM)^{-1} M'WVWM (M'WM)^{-1}$$

and

$$V = E\left[m(w, \theta_0) m(w, \theta_0)'\right].$$

The optimal GMM estimator $\hat{\theta}$, which attains the lowest variance bound in the class of estimators based only on information contained in $E[m(w, \theta_0)] = 0$, sets $W = V^{-1}$. In this case,

$$\Omega_0 = (M'V^{-1}M)^{-1} M'V^{-1}VV^{-1}M (M'V^{-1}M)^{-1}$$
$$= (M'V^{-1}M)^{-1}.$$

To show that $\Omega - \Omega_0$ is a positive semi-definite matrix, note that

$$\Omega - \Omega_0 = (M'WM)^{-1} M'WVWM (M'WM)^{-1} - (M'V^{-1}M)^{-1}$$
$$= (M'WM)^{-1} \left[M'WVWM - M'WM (M'V^{-1}M)^{-1} M'WM\right]$$
$$\times (M'WM)^{-1}$$
$$= (M'WM)^{-1} M'WV^{\frac{1}{2}} \left[I_\ell - V^{-\frac{1}{2}}M (M'V^{-1}M)^{-1} M'V^{-\frac{1}{2}}\right]$$
$$\times V^{\frac{1}{2}} WM (M'WM)^{-1}.$$

It is easy to verify that the matrix $I_\ell - V^{-\frac{1}{2}}M (M'V^{-1}M)^{-1} M'V^{-\frac{1}{2}}$ is idempotent and idempotent matrices are positive semi-definite. Since the above expression is a quadratic form in an idempotent (and hence positive semi-definite) matrix, it is also positive semi-definite.

Exercise 1.3. Consider GMM estimation based on the moment function

$$m(w, \theta) = \begin{pmatrix} m_1(w, \theta) \\ m_2(w) \end{pmatrix},$$

where the second part does not depend on the parameters. Determine under what conditions the second restriction helps in reducing the asymptotic variance of the GMM estimator of θ_0.

Exercise 1.4. Suppose we want to estimate a parameter $\theta_0 \in \Theta$ implicitly defined by $\phi_0 = \varphi(\theta_0)$, where $\varphi : \mathbb{R}^k \to \mathbb{R}^\ell$ with $\ell \geq k$, and we have a consistent estimator $\hat{\phi}$ of ϕ_0 with an asymptotic distribution $\sqrt{n}(\hat{\phi} - \phi_0) \xrightarrow{d} \mathcal{N}(0, V)$. The minimum distance (MD) estimator is defined as

$$\hat{\theta}_{MD} = \arg\min_{\theta \in \Theta} \left(\hat{\phi} - \varphi(\theta) \right)' W_n \left(\hat{\phi} - \varphi(\theta) \right),$$

where W_n is some symmetric, positive definite, data-dependent matrix that converges in probability to a symmetric, positive definite weighting matrix W. Assume that Θ is compact, $\varphi(\theta)$ is continuously differentiable with full rank matrix of derivatives $\partial\varphi(\theta)/\partial\theta'$ on Θ, θ_0 is unique and all needed moments exist. Give an informal argument for the consistency of $\hat{\theta}_{MD}$ and derive its asymptotic distribution. Find the optimal choice for the weighting matrix W and suggest its consistent estimator.

Minimizing the GMM criterion function $Q_n(\theta)$ typically involves numerical optimization using standard gradient-type (for instance, quasi-Newton) methods. The efficient GMM sets $W_n = V_n(\bar{\theta})^{-1}$, where $V_n(\bar{\theta})$ is a sample analog of V using some consistent estimator $\bar{\theta}$ of θ_0. The two-step GMM estimator that is most commonly used in applied work involves (i) estimating the model with some arbitrary symmetric and positive definite weighting matrix (for example, the identity matrix $W_n = I_\ell$) which produces a consistent but not necessarily efficient estimator $\bar{\theta}$ and (ii) setting $W_n = V_n(\bar{\theta})^{-1}$ and re-estimating θ_0 by minimizing $Q_n(\theta) = m_n(\theta)' V_n(\bar{\theta})^{-1} m_n(\theta)$. The obtained estimator, denoted by $\hat{\theta}_{GMM}$, is asymptotically efficient.

The efficient two-step GMM estimator $\hat{\theta}_{GMM}$ solves k first-order conditions

$$0 = \frac{\partial m_n(\theta)' V_n(\bar{\theta})^{-1} m_n(\theta)}{\partial \theta}\bigg|_{\hat{\theta}_{GMM}} \tag{1.2}$$
$$= M_n(\hat{\theta}_{GMM})' V_n(\bar{\theta})^{-1} m_n(\hat{\theta}_{GMM}).$$

Equation (1.2) shows that the two-step GMM estimator takes a linear combination of the sample moment conditions and sets it equal to zero. Thus, the two-step GMM estimator solves

$$a_n^{GMM} m_n(\hat{\theta}_{GMM}) = 0,$$

where the weights are

$$a_n^{GMM} = M_n(\hat{\theta}_{GMM})' V_n(\bar{\theta})^{-1}.$$

A drawback of this estimator is that it is not invariant to linear transformations of the moment functions of the form $Am(w, \theta)$ for some fixed, non-singular $\ell \times \ell$ matrix A. This suggests that the two-step GMM estimator is affected by simple scaling of the data and the moment conditions.

An alternative estimator is the iterated GMM estimator (Hansen, Heaton and Yaron, 1996) with the same two steps as in the two-step estimator but instead of stopping at the second step, it keeps iterating until convergence of both W_n and θ. This estimator can be expressed as a just-identified GMM estimator with a moment function

$$\begin{pmatrix} V - m(w, \theta)m(w, \theta)' \\ M - \partial m(w, \theta)/\partial \theta' \\ M'V^{-1}m(w, \theta) \end{pmatrix}$$

(Imbens, 1997). Unlike the two-step GMM estimator, the iterated GMM estimator is invariant to transformations of the form $Am(w, \theta)$ but not to $A(\theta)m(w, \theta)$ where $A(\theta)$ depends on the unknown parameter θ.

An estimator that is invariant to both types of transformations considered above is the continuously updated (CU) GMM estimator (Hansen, Heaton and Yaron, 1996). This estimator, denoted by $\hat{\theta}_{CU}$, does not require a preliminary estimate and directly minimizes the objective function

$$Q_n(\theta) = m_n(\theta)' V_n(\theta)^{-1} m_n(\theta).$$

Note that in this case, the weighting matrix also depends on the parameter vector θ, and the form of the first-order conditions is more complicated. In particular, when θ is a scalar, the first-order conditions are given by (Donald and Newey, 2000)

$$M_n(\hat{\theta}_{CU})' V_n(\hat{\theta}_{CU})^{-1} m_n(\hat{\theta}_{CU})$$

$$- m_n(\hat{\theta}_{CU})' V_n(\hat{\theta}_{CU})^{-1} \frac{\partial V_n(\hat{\theta}_{CU})}{\partial \theta} V_n(\hat{\theta}_{CU})^{-1} m_n(\hat{\theta}_{CU}) = 0$$

(1.3)

using that

$$\frac{\partial V_n(\theta)^{-1}}{\partial \theta} = -V_n(\theta)^{-1} \frac{\partial V_n(\theta)}{\partial \theta} V_n(\theta)^{-1}.$$

Since $V_n(\theta) = n^{-1} \sum_{i=1}^{n} m(w_i, \theta) m(w_i, \theta)'$, we have

$$\frac{\partial V_n(\hat{\theta}_{CU})}{\partial \theta} = \frac{1}{n} \sum_{i=1}^{n} m(w_i, \hat{\theta}_{CU}) \frac{\partial m(w_i, \hat{\theta}_{CU})'}{\partial \theta}$$

(1.4)

$$+ \frac{1}{n} \sum_{i=1}^{n} \frac{\partial m(w_i, \hat{\theta}_{CU})}{\partial \theta} m(w_i, \hat{\theta}_{CU})'.$$

Let

$$p_i^{CU} = \frac{1 - m_n(\hat{\theta}_{CU})' V_n(\hat{\theta}_{CU})^{-1} m(w_i, \hat{\theta}_{CU})}{n}, \quad i = 1, ..., n.$$

Then, substituting (1.4) into (1.3) yields

$$\sum_{i=1}^{n} p_i^{CU} \frac{\partial m(w_i, \hat{\theta}_{CU})'}{\partial \theta} V_n(\hat{\theta}_{CU})^{-1} m_n(\hat{\theta}_{CU}) = 0, \tag{1.5}$$

or

$$a_n^{CU} m_n(\hat{\theta}_{CU}) = 0,$$

where the weights are

$$a_n^{CU} = \sum_{i=1}^{n} p_i^{CU} \frac{\partial m(w_i, \hat{\theta}_{CU})'}{\partial \theta} V_n(\hat{\theta}_{CU})^{-1}.$$

This implies that the CU estimator is using p_i^{CU} in the construction of the weights a_n^{CU} for optimal selection of the moment conditions $m_n(\hat{\theta}_{CU})$. In comparison, the two-step GMM estimator uses $p_i = n^{-1}$ and does not incorporate efficiently the conditional information contained in the moment restrictions. Furthermore, the first-order conditions of the standard two-step GMM estimator, evaluated at the true values of the parameters, are non-zero. This gives rise to an important source of bias which is exacerbated if the number of instruments increases. By contrast, the first-order conditions for the continuously updated GMM, evaluated at the true values of the parameters, are centered at zero (Donald and Newey, 2000). As a result, the CU estimator is approximately median unbiased although it has a larger variance and fatter tails than the two-step GMM estimator.

Despite the different form of the first-order conditions, the two-step and CU estimators are asymptotically equivalent. We show in Chapter 2 that the first-order conditions (1.5) coincide with the first-order conditions of the Euclidean likelihood estimator which is derived from a completely different point of departure. This equivalency proves useful in inferring some properties of the CU estimator that are derived more conveniently in the generalized empirical likelihood framework.

It is instructive to inspect more closely the structure of the GMM first-order conditions that are based on

$$M'V^{-1}E[m(w, \theta_0)] = 0$$

or

$$\bar{M}'V^{-1/2}E[m(w, \theta_0)] = 0, \tag{1.6}$$

where $\bar{M} = V^{-1/2}E[\partial m(w, \theta_0)/\partial \theta']$.

Equation (1.6) implies that the columns of $\bar{M}$ are orthogonal to $V^{-1/2}E[m(w, \theta_0)]$ or, equivalently, that $V^{-1/2}E[m(w, \theta_0)]$ is in the null space of $\bar{M}$ so that a projection of $V^{-1/2}E[m(w, \theta_0)]$ on $\bar{M}$ is zero (Sowell, 1996; Hall, 2005). Hence, $V^{-1/2}E[m(w, \theta_0)]$ can be decomposed into two orthogonal components

$$V^{-1/2}E[m(w, \theta_0)] = \bar{M}(\bar{M}'\bar{M})^{-1}\bar{M}'V^{-1/2}E[m(w, \theta_0)]$$
$$+ [I_\ell - \bar{M}(\bar{M}'\bar{M})^{-1}\bar{M}']V^{-1/2}E[m(w, \theta_0)],$$

where

$$\bar{M}(\bar{M}'\bar{M})^{-1}\bar{M}'V^{-1/2}E[m\,(w,\theta_0)] = 0, \qquad (1.7)$$

$$[I_\ell - \bar{M}(\bar{M}'\bar{M})^{-1}\bar{M}']V^{-1/2}E[m\,(w,\theta_0)] = 0, \qquad (1.8)$$

and

$$\bar{M}(\bar{M}'\bar{M})^{-1}\bar{M}'[I_\ell - \bar{M}(\bar{M}'\bar{M})^{-1}\bar{M}'] = 0.$$

As a result, the ℓ-dimensional vector of normalized population moment conditions $V^{-1/2}E[m\,(w,\theta_0)]$ is decomposed into k identifying restrictions used for estimation of θ and $(\ell - k)$ overidentifying restrictions (Sowell, 1996; Hall, 2005). In particular, equation (1.7) places k (equal to the rank of $\bar{M}(\bar{M}'\bar{M})^{-1}\bar{M}'$) restrictions on the normalized moment conditions that characterize the space of identifying restrictions and equation (1.8) places $(\ell - k)$ restrictions that characterize the space of overidentifying restrictions which could be used for testing the validity of the model.

In a similar vein of reasoning, Gospodinov, Kan and Robotti (2010) introduce an $\ell \times (\ell - k)$ orthonormal matrix P with columns that are orthogonal to $\bar{M}$ and

$$PP' = I_\ell - \bar{M}(\bar{M}'\bar{M})^{-1}\bar{M}'.$$

Then, the (properly standardized) sample analog of the $(\ell - k)$-dimensional vector $P'V^{-1/2}E[m\,(w,\theta_0)]$ has a non-degenerate asymptotic distribution that proves convenient for studying and testing the validity of the population moment conditions.

A comprehensive treatment of the theoretical and empirical properties of the GMM estimators considered in this section is provided in Hall (2005).

1.2.3   Robust Estimation

Many interesting economic problems are based on the conditional prediction problem (Manski, 1991)

$$\min_{y_p} E[L(y - y_p)|x],$$

where $L(.)$ is a loss function, y_p is a predictor for y based on information in x, and $E[L(y - y_p)|x]$ is the expected loss conditional on x. For a given loss function, the best predictor depends only on the distribution of y conditional on x. In particular, for the square loss function $L(u) = u^2$, the best predictor is the conditional mean of y given x. In the case of absolute loss function $L(u) = |u|$, the best predictor is the conditional median of y given x. More generally, for the α-absolute loss function $L(u) = |u|(\alpha\mathbb{I}\{u > 0\} + (1-\alpha)\mathbb{I}\{u \leq 0\})$, where $\alpha \in (0,1)$ is a specified constant, the best predictor is given by the conditional α-quantile of y given x. Hence, the conditional quantiles can prove extremely useful for asymmetric loss functions and studying the tails of the conditional distribution. Given the robustness properties of the conditional median and the conditional quantiles, we refer to these estimators as *robust estimators*.

To introduce the concept of quantile regression, consider the model

$$y = x'\theta_0 + e, \quad Q_\alpha(e|x) = 0, \tag{1.9}$$

where $Q_\alpha(e|x)$ denotes the α-quantile[1] of the conditional distribution of e given x. This quantile restriction implies $Q_\alpha(y|x) = x'\theta_0$, where θ_0 is the value of θ which ensures that $\Pr\{e \le 0|x\} = \Pr\{y \le x'\theta_0|x\} = \alpha$ and $\Pr\{e > 0|x\} = \Pr\{y > x'\theta_0|x\} = 1 - \alpha$.
Let

$$\rho_\alpha(u) = u\left(\alpha\mathbb{I}\{u > 0\} - (1-\alpha)\mathbb{I}\{u \le 0\}\right) = u\left(\alpha - \mathbb{I}\{u \le 0\}\right)$$

and $\{(y_i, x_i)\}_{i=1}^n$ be a random sample. Then, the quantile estimator of θ_0 in the general regression model (1.9) can be defined as

$$\hat{\theta} = \arg\min_{\theta \in \Theta} \frac{1}{n} \sum_{i=1}^n \rho_\alpha(y_i - x_i'\theta) \tag{1.10}$$

which solves the first-order condition

$$\frac{1}{n} \sum_{i=1}^n x_i h(y_i - x_i'\hat{\theta}) = 0,$$

where

$$h(u) = \alpha\mathbb{I}\{u > 0\} - (1-\alpha)\mathbb{I}\{u \le 0\}.$$

Since the quantile regression model has a linear programming representation, the unknown parameter vector θ_0 is typically estimated using linear programming methods.

The asymptotic theory for the quantile estimator is non-standard due to non-differentiability of the objective function. For details on the asymptotic analysis see Koenker and Bassett (1978, 1982), Newey and McFadden (1994) and Andrews (1994). It can be shown that, under some regularity conditions,

$$\frac{1}{\sqrt{n}} \sum_{i=1}^n x_i h(y_i - x_i'\theta_0) \xrightarrow{d} \mathcal{N}(0, E[h(e)^2 xx'])$$

and

$$\sqrt{n}(\hat{\theta} - \theta_0) \xrightarrow{d} \mathcal{N}(0, M^{-1}VM^{-1}),$$

where $M = E\left[f_e(0|x)xx'\right]$, $V = E[h(e)^2 xx'] = \alpha(1-\alpha)E[xx']$ and $f_e(0|x)$ is the conditional density of e evaluated at zero. Note that if the density of e

---

[1] The α-quantile of the distribution $F(u) = \Pr\{z \le u\}$ of a random variable z is defined as $Q_\alpha(u) = \inf\{u : F(u) \ge \alpha\}$.

evaluated at zero is independent of x, then $f_e(0|x) = f_e(0)$ and the asymptotic variance of the quantile estimator simplifies to

$$\frac{\alpha(1-\alpha)}{f_e(0)^2} E\left[xx'\right]^{-1}$$

so that the differences in the variances of the parameter estimates at different quantiles are driven by the differences in $\alpha(1-\alpha)$ and $f_e(0)$ for various α.

When $\alpha = \frac{1}{2}$, the objective function in (1.10) specializes to $n^{-1}\sum_{i=1}^{n} |y_i - x_i'\theta|$ and the corresponding estimator is the least absolute deviation (LAD) estimator. The LAD estimator provides an estimate of the conditional median of y given x and is equivalent to the maximum likelihood estimator of θ_0 in (1.9) when the regression errors follow a Laplace (double exponential) distribution.

1.3   Long-Run Variance

Most of the parametric estimation methods reviewed so far continue to apply when the data are stationary and ergodic time series and thus are possibly serially correlated (the basic concepts and results for dependent processes are reviewed in Appendix A at the end of the book). The reason is that for such data, the large sample theory also holds, with some minimal though important corrections. These corrections require certain changes in the algorithms of estimation and inference.

To denote that we work with time series data, we change the indexing of the data from i to t so that w_i becomes w_t, etc. Let w_t be vector valued, and consider its population mean $E\left[w_t\right]$ whose sample analog is $\bar{w} = n^{-1}\sum_{t=1}^{n} w_t$. When the series w_t is strict white noise (that is, zero mean IID), the CLT implies $n^{1/2}\bar{w} \xrightarrow{d} \mathcal{N}\left(0, V_w\right)$, where $V_w = \text{var}\left(w\right)$. When the series w_t exhibits serial dependence but is a martingale difference with respect to its own past, another version of the CLT also implies $n^{1/2}\bar{w} \xrightarrow{d} \mathcal{N}\left(0, V_w\right)$, where again $V_w = \text{var}\left(w\right)$. However, if the series w_t exhibits serial correlation, the asymptotic normality still holds, but the asymptotic variance becomes

$$V_w = \lim_{n\to\infty} \text{var}\left(\sqrt{n}\bar{w}\right),$$

which in general differs from var (w). Indeed,

$$
\begin{aligned}
V_w &= \lim_{n\to\infty} \mathrm{var}\left(\sqrt{n}\bar{w}\right) \\
&= \lim_{n\to\infty} E\left[\left(\sqrt{n}\bar{w}\right)\left(\sqrt{n}\bar{w}\right)'\right] \\
&= \lim_{n\to\infty} E\left[\frac{1}{n}\sum_{t=1}^{n}\sum_{s=1}^{n} w_t w_s'\right] \\
&= \lim_{n\to\infty} \frac{1}{n}\sum_{t=1}^{n}\sum_{s=1}^{n} E\left[w_t w_s'\right].
\end{aligned}
$$

Denote the autocovariance of w_t at delay j by $\rho(j) = E[w_t w_{t-j}']$. Using that $\rho(-j) = \rho(j)'$ and the Toeplitz lemma, we obtain

$$
\begin{aligned}
V_w &= \lim_{n\to\infty} \frac{1}{n}\left[n\rho(0) + \sum_{j=1}^{n-1}(n-j)\left(\rho(j) + \rho(j)'\right)\right] \\
&= \lim_{n\to\infty}\left[\rho(0) + \sum_{j=1}^{n-1}\left(1 - \frac{j}{n}\right)\left(\rho(j) + \rho(j)'\right)\right] \\
&= \sum_{j=-\infty}^{\infty} \rho(j).
\end{aligned}
$$

The above expression for V_w is termed the *long-run variance*. If instead of zero $E[w_t]$ we consider possibly non-zero $E[m(w_t)]$ for some function $m(\cdot)$, the long-run variance $V_m = \lim_{n\to\infty} \mathrm{var}\left(\sqrt{n}\sum_{t=1}^{n} m(w_t)\right)$ has the same representation as before, but the autocovariance of $m(w_t)$ at delay j takes the form $\rho(j) = E[(m(w_t) - E[m(w_t)])(m(w_{t-j}) - E[m(w_t)])']$.

The *long-run covariance* between, say, $m(w_t)$ and $\mu(w_t)$ is defined similarly as

$$
\begin{aligned}
C_{m,\mu} &= \lim_{n\to\infty} \mathrm{cov}\left(\frac{1}{\sqrt{n}}\sum_{t=1}^{n} m(w_t), \frac{1}{\sqrt{n}}\sum_{t=1}^{n}\mu(w_t)\right) \\
&= \sum_{j=-\infty}^{\infty} \gamma(j),
\end{aligned}
$$

where $\gamma(j) = E[(m(w_t) - E[m(w_t)])(\mu(w_{t-j}) - E[\mu(w_t)])']$ is the cross-covariance between $m(w_t)$ and $\mu(w_t)$ at delay j.

Consistent estimation of the long-run variance is not straightforward. Each autocovariance $\rho(j)$ can be consistently estimated by

$$
\widehat{\rho(j)} = \frac{1}{n}\sum_{t=j+1}^{n}\left(m(w_t) - \frac{1}{n}\sum_{s=1}^{n} m(w_s)\right)\left(m(w_{t-j}) - \frac{1}{n}\sum_{s=1}^{n} m(w_s)\right)'
$$

for non-negative j, and by $\widehat{\rho(j)} = \left(\widehat{\rho(-j)}\right)'$ for negative j. A natural estimator of V_m is

$$\hat{V}_m^0 = \sum_{j=-(n-1)}^{n-1} \widehat{\rho(j)}.$$

However, this estimator is not consistent because it is constructed using co-variance estimates whose number increases proportionately with the sample size. One possible solution is to truncate the summation at $-p$ and p, where $p < n - 1$, getting rid of the least informative autocovariances:

$$\hat{V}_m^{HH} = \sum_{j=-p}^{p} \widehat{\rho(j)}.$$

This is the *Hansen–Hodrick estimator* (Hansen and Hodrick, 1980), which is consistent as $n \to \infty$ and the serial correlation is of order p or less. When the serial correlation has unknown or infinite order, $\hat{V}_m^{HH}$ can be made consistent by letting $p \to \infty$ as $n \to \infty$, with a suitable rate such as $n^{1/3}$.

Unfortunately, the Hansen–Hodrick estimator is not guaranteed to be a positive semi-definite matrix, while positive semi-definiteness is a highly desirable feature of a reasonable estimate of a variance matrix. Newey and West (1987) proposed the following judicious modification:

$$\hat{V}_m^{NW} = \sum_{j=-p}^{p} \left(1 - \frac{|j|}{p+1}\right) \widehat{\rho(j)},$$

where the weights ensure that this *Newey–West estimator* is positive semi-definite.

Andrews (1991) showed that the Newey–West estimator can be generalized to a whole class of nonparametric variance estimators that are consistent and positive definite by construction. The *Andrews estimator* is given by

$$\hat{V}_m^A = \sum_{j=-(n-1)}^{n-1} \omega(j) \widehat{\rho(j)},$$

where $\omega(j)$ is a sequence of weights such that $\omega(j) = K(j/b)$, $K(.)$ is a symmetric and continuous at 0 *kernel function* with $K(0) = 1$, and b is a *bandwidth* that satisfies $b \to \infty$ as $n \to \infty$ with a suitable rate. The kernel function may be nonnegative and defined on a bounded support (e.g., the uniform, Bartlett and Parzen kernels), but either property is not necessary (e.g., the Quadratic spectral kernel violates both). A subset of such kernels generates long-run variance estimators that are positive definite by construction. This subset includes, in particular, the Bartlett, Parzen and Quadratic spectral kernels but not the uniform kernel.

Andrews (1991) specifies conditions (for the growth rate of b, in particular) under which the estimator is consistent, even if the object whose long-run variance is of interest, $m(w_t)$, depends on a parameter θ which has to be estimated. Andrews (1991) also derives an optimal rate of growth of b (that depends on the smoothness of $K(\cdot)$ at zero) and an optimal kernel (the Quadratic spectral kernel) by minimizing the asymptotic mean squared error of the estimator. Alternative approaches to long-run variance estimation can be found in den Haan and Levin (1997), Kiefer, Vogelsang, and Bunzel (2000) and Smith (2005).

The application of the long-run variance estimators is widespread in estimation and inference for models with dependent data. For example, in the GMM context of section 1.2.2, the optimal weighting matrix is given by $V_n(\bar{\theta})^{-1}$, where $V_n(\bar{\theta})$ is a consistent estimator of the long-run variance of the moment function $m(w_t, \theta_0)$

$$V_m = \lim_{n\to\infty} \text{var}\left(\sqrt{n}\, m_n(\theta_0)\right) = \sum_{j=-\infty}^{\infty} E\left[m(w_t, \theta_0)\, m(w_{t-j}, \theta_0)'\right].$$

The feasible optimal weighting matrix is then an estimate of V_m which also uses a preliminary estimator $\bar{\theta}$ in place of θ_0. Similarly, for the least squares estimator in a linear time series regression $y_t = x_t'\theta_0 + e_t$, $E[e_t|x_t] = 0$, the asymptotic variance of $\hat{\theta}$ can be estimated using the long-run variance estimator of $x_t\hat{e}_t$, where $\hat{e}_t$ are the OLS residuals of the model. Because the long-run variance estimators automatically take into account the serial correlation and conditional heteroskedasticity in e_t, these estimators are often referred to in the literature as *Heteroskedasticity and Autocorrelation Consistent* (HAC) estimators.

1.4 Nonparametric Regression

In this section we review the nonparametric estimation of mean regression that avoids making parametric assumptions about the functional form of the conditional expectation function. Most of the discussion is focused around kernel regression methods although some other nonparametric methods (splines, sieves, etc.) are also briefly introduced. Other comprehensive reviews of these methods include the surveys of Härdle and Linton (1994) and Racine (2008), as well as books by Härdle (1990), Pagan and Ullah (1999) and Li and Racine (2007). Although the conventional objects of interest are the mean regression and density, there is also a related literature on local quasi-likelihood estimation (e.g., Fan, Heckman and Wand, 1995) and nonparametric estimation under asymmetric loss (e.g., Anatolyev, 2006).

Let $\{(x_i, y_i)\}_{i=1}^n$ be a random sample from the population of (x, y). We are interested in estimating the mean regression function $g(x) = E[y|x]$ assuming that it exists for all x in its support. The most common approach to performing this task is a parametric approach that assumes a known functional form and a finite number of unknown parameters. The estimation of these parameters automatically yields estimates of $g(x)$. However, misspecification of the functional form may lead to serious distortions in the estimation and inference procedures in often unpredictable ways.

We assume for now that there is only one single regressor x. Later, we will extend the discussion to the case of a multivariate regression.

1.4.1   Construction

Consider first the case of discrete regressors. Let x have a discrete distribution with support $a_{(1)}, \ldots, a_{(k)}$, where $a_{(1)} < \ldots < a_{(k)}$. Fix $a_{(j)}, j = 1, \ldots, k$, and observe that

$$g(a_{(j)}) = E\left[y|x = a_{(j)}\right] = \frac{E\left[y\mathbb{I}\left\{x = a_{(j)}\right\}\right]}{E\left[\mathbb{I}\left\{x = a_{(j)}\right\}\right]}$$

using

$$E\left[\mathbb{I}\left\{x = a_{(j)}\right\}\right] = \Pr\{x_i = a_{(j)}\}$$

and

$$E\left[y\mathbb{I}\left\{x = a_{(j)}\right\}\right] = E\left[y|x = a_{(j)}\right]\Pr\{x = a_{(j)}\}.$$

According to the analogy principle, we can construct $\hat{g}(a_{(j)})$ as

$$\hat{g}(a_{(j)}) = \frac{\sum_{i=1}^{n} y_i\, \mathbb{I}\left\{x_i = a_{(j)}\right\}}{\sum_{i=1}^{n} \mathbb{I}\left\{x_i = a_{(j)}\right\}}. \tag{1.11}$$

This is interpreted as an average over observations that fall onto the vertical line $x = a_{(j)}$.

In the case of continuous regressors, the estimator above does not work as no observations (except for possibly only one observation) can be found on the vertical line $x = a$ even though $f(a) \neq 0$, where $f(a)$ is the density $f(x)$ of the regressor evaluated at $x = a$. Therefore, the information needed for estimation of the unknown function $g(a)$ has to be collected from alternative sources. For example, if the regression line is continuous, the observations falling in the vicinity of a are highly informative about the regression function at a and can be employed for constructing an estimator of $g(a)$.

Let b denote a *bandwidth* or *window width*, and generalize (1.11) as

$$\hat{g}(a) = \frac{\sum\limits_{i=1}^{n} y_i \, \mathbb{I}\{a - b \leq x_i \leq a + b\}}{\sum\limits_{i=1}^{n} \mathbb{I}\{a - b \leq x_i \leq a + b\}}. \tag{1.12}$$

The estimator in (1.12) takes an average over observations that fall into the window $[a - b, a + b]$. When one varies a, the estimator $\hat{g}(a)$ tracks the estimated regression curve. Note that this procedure exhibits jumps because of new observations falling in and old observations dropping from the window.

The information from the observations in the window $[a - b, a + b]$ is used uniformly. That is, all observations falling into this window are assigned equal weights, and the observations outside of the window receive zero weights. A natural extension of this approach is to utilize a weighting scheme that depends on the distance from x_i to a, and possibly accounts for information in all observations. For that purpose, let us introduce a symmetric *kernel function* $K(u)$ that integrates to one, i.e., $\int K(u)\, du = 1$, where the integral is taken over the whole domain, which may be a bounded symmetric interval, usually $[-1, 1]$, or the whole real line. Some popular kernels are:

$$\text{Uniform:} \quad K(u) = \frac{1}{2}\mathbb{I}\{|u| \leq 1\},$$

$$\text{Triangular:} \quad K(u) = (1 - |u|)\,\mathbb{I}\{|u| \leq 1\},$$

$$\text{Epanechnikov:} \quad K(u) = \frac{3}{4}\left(1 - u^2\right)\mathbb{I}\{|u| \leq 1\},$$

$$\text{Gaussian (normal):} \quad K(u) = \frac{1}{\sqrt{2\pi}}\exp\left(-\frac{u^2}{2}\right).$$

The first three kernel functions have bounded domain $[-1, 1]$, while the last one has infinite support. This means that the estimator based on the uniform, triangular and Epanechnikov kernels uses information in the bounded neighborhood of a, while the estimator based on the Gaussian kernel uses information contained in all sample points. Note that a kernel may not be necessarily nonnegative everywhere.

Furthermore, let us define

$$K_b(u) = \frac{1}{b}K\left(\frac{u}{b}\right),$$

where the normalization by b in the definition of $K_b(u)$ does not affect the estimator's numerical value and is made for convenience. Now we generalize

(1.12) to

$$\hat{g}(a) = \frac{\sum\limits_{i=1}^{n} y_i K_b \left(x_i - a \right)}{\sum\limits_{i=1}^{n} K_b \left(x_i - a \right)}. \tag{1.13}$$

The estimator (1.13) is known in the literature as the *Nadaraya–Watson regression estimator* (Nadaraya, 1965; Watson, 1964).

Many kernels (including the triangular, Epanechnikov and Gaussian) ensure that the estimated regression curve is continuous as the old and new sample observations enter the formula in a smooth way when a varies. The kernel functions assign more weight to points near a as the weights decline when x_i gets farther away from a. The distance from a is determined by the bandwidth parameter b, which plays a crucial role in the kernel estimation. If b is too big, too much irrelevant information will be used by the estimator, which will increase the bias and will lead to *oversmoothing*. An oversmoothed estimator is "too linear" and may lead to significant distortions in the shape of the true regression function. If instead b is too small, too few sample observations will be used by the estimator, which will increase the variance and will lead to *undersmoothing*. An undersmoothed estimator follows the observations too closely and can be "too wiggly" since there are not enough points for averaging or smoothing.

1.4.2   Asymptotic Properties

In the discrete regressor case, it is easy to show, using the and central limit theorem (CLT), that

$$\sqrt{n} \left(\hat{g}(a_{(j)}) - g(a_{(j)}) \right) \xrightarrow{d} \mathcal{N} \left(0, \frac{\mathrm{var} \left(y | x = a_{(j)} \right)}{\Pr\{x = a_{(j)}\}} \right).$$

Note that the accuracy of estimation is positively related to how often the observations fall onto the vertical line $x = a_{(j)}$, and inversely related to how scattered they are along it. Note the parametric rate of convergence $\sqrt{n}$. Indeed, the problem may be considered as parametric because the parameter vector $\left(a_{(1)}, \ldots, a_{(k)} \right)'$ is in fact finite dimensional (or countable at most).

In the continuous case, the bandwidth parameter has to be asymptotically shrinking, otherwise the bias arising from too much irrelevant information in the neighboring observations will make the estimator inconsistent, i.e., we have to set $b \to 0$ as $n \to \infty$. On the other hand, the bandwidth should not go to zero too fast since too little information used for smoothing will make the variance too large. More precisely, as the variance is inversely proportional to the effective number of participating observations which in turn is proportional to nb, we set $nb \to \infty$ as $b \to 0$ and $n \to \infty$.

Let us denote

$$\sigma_K^2 = \int u^2 K(u)\, du$$

and

$$R_K = \int K(u)^2\, du.$$

These two constants depend only on the chosen kernel, and are assumed to be finite. Next, let us set an additional requirement for the rate of shrinkage of the bandwidth:

$$\lambda = \lim_{n \to \infty} \sqrt{nb^5},$$

assuming $\lambda < \infty$. Note that λ may or may not be zero. We also assume continuity and boundedness of $g(x)$, $g'(x)$, $g''(x)$, $f(x)$ and $f'(x)$ everywhere except possibly at a finite number of points.

Consider the difference between the estimate and the estimand:

$$\hat{g}(a) - g(a) = \frac{\hat{r}_1(a) + \hat{r}_2(a)}{\hat{f}(a)},$$

where

$$\hat{r}_1(a) = \frac{1}{n}\sum_{i=1}^{n} e_i K_b(x_i - a),$$

$$\hat{r}_2(a) = \frac{1}{n}\sum_{i=1}^{n} (g(x_i) - g(a)) K_b(x_i - a),$$

$$\hat{f}(a) = \frac{1}{n}\sum_{i=1}^{n} K_b(x_i - a).$$

The denominator $\hat{f}(a)$ is called the *Nadaraya–Watson density estimator* of the regressor density $f(x)$ at $x = a$. It is straightforward to show that this estimator is consistent for $f(a)$. Next, the first term in the numerator $\hat{r}_1(a)$ is a kernel-weighted average of regression errors. As in the parametric analysis, this yields asymptotic normality. Indeed, one can show that $\sqrt{nb}\,\hat{r}_1(a) \xrightarrow{d} \mathcal{N}\left(0, \sigma^2(a) f(a) R_K\right)$. Finally, the second term in the numerator $\hat{r}_2(a)$ is a weighted average of deviations of the regression function evaluated at the sample points from the regression function evaluated at a. These deviations induce a bias, and one can show that $\sqrt{nb}\,\hat{r}_2(a) \xrightarrow{p} \lambda f(a) \mathcal{B}(a) \sigma_K^2$, where

$$\mathcal{B}(a) = \frac{g'(a) f'(a)}{f(a)} + \frac{g''(a)}{2}.$$

Collecting these results, we obtain that

$$\sqrt{nb}\,(\hat{g}(a) - g(a)) \xrightarrow{d} \mathcal{N}\left(\lambda \mathcal{B}(a) \sigma_K^2, \frac{\sigma^2(a)}{f(a)} R_K\right). \tag{1.14}$$

Two interesting features of this asymptotic result deserve some remarks. First, the nonparametric rate of convergence $\sqrt{nb}$ is slower than the parametric rate $\sqrt{n}$ because $b \to 0$ asymptotically. This reflects the lower precision of estimation of infinite dimensional objects compared to finite dimensional ones. Second, although the asymptotic distribution is normal, it is not centered at zero. The asymptotic bias reflects the fact that the information used for estimation is not entirely relevant.

The asymptotic variance formula is similar to that in the discrete regressor case as it involves the skedastic function in the numerator and the "probability mass" in the denominator. The asymptotic bias depends on many features of the shapes of the regression and density functions incorporated in $\mathcal{B}(a)$. One part of the asymptotic bias is proportional to $g'(a)f'(a)$, reflecting the bias arising when the slope of the regression curve is nonzero and there is asymmetry in how many observations fall to the left and to the right of a. The other part of the asymptotic bias is proportional to $g''(a)$, reflecting the bias arising when the regression curve is locally nonlinear because the observation ordinates are non-symmetrically scattered above and below $g(a)$ even when the observation abscissas are symmetrically distributed around a. Note that both the variance and the bias are generally inversely related to the density $f(a)$, which reflects the fact that the precision of estimating $g(a)$ is low near the boundaries of the support of x where the density approaches zero.

The asymptotic result also implies that the optimal rate of shrinkage for b is $b \propto n^{-1/5}$ because in this case, $\lambda > 0$ and the asymptotic bias and asymptotic variance are balanced. On the other hand, setting $b = o\left(n^{-1/5}\right)$ makes λ equal to zero and the asymptotic bias disappears. Of course, this is convenient from the point of view of implementation (one does not have to estimate $\mathcal{B}(a)$, which is quite involved), but this conceals the actual biasedness property and leads to a poor asymptotic approximation.

Exercise 1.5. Derive the asymptotic distribution of the Nadaraya–Watson estimator of the density of a scalar random variable x having a continuous distribution. Provide an interpretation on how the expressions for the asymptotic bias and asymptotic variance depend on the shape of the density.

The asymptotic result in (1.14) implies that approximately

$$\hat{g}(a) \sim \mathcal{N}\left(g(a) + \frac{\sqrt{nb^5}\mathcal{B}(a)\sigma_K^2}{\sqrt{nb}}, \frac{\sigma^2(a)}{f(a)}\frac{R_K}{nb}\right).$$

As usual, the asymptotic distribution can be used for testing statistical hypotheses and constructing confidence intervals for $g(a)$. For example, the $100\left(1-\alpha\right)\%$ equal-tailed confidence interval, where α is the significance level, is

$$\hat{g}(a) - b^2\hat{\mathcal{B}}(a)\sigma_K^2 \mp \tau_{1-\alpha/2}\sqrt{\frac{\hat{\sigma}^2(a)}{\hat{f}(a)}\frac{R_K}{nb}},$$

where $\tau_{1-\alpha/2}$ is the $(1 - \alpha/2)$-quantile of the standard normal distribution, and $\hat{f}(a)$, $\hat{\mathcal{B}}(a)$ and $\hat{\sigma}^2(a)$ are nonparametric estimates of the corresponding population functions evaluated at a. Moreover, the construction of confidence intervals for $g(a)$ on a fine grid of values for a leads to a *pointwise confidence band* for $g(x)$.

1.4.3 Bandwidth Selection

From the asymptotic result in (1.14), it follows that the asymptotic mean squared error is

$$\mathcal{AMSE}(a) = b^4 \mathcal{B}(a)^2 \sigma_K^4 + \frac{\sigma^2(a)}{f(a)} \frac{R_K}{nb}.$$

If we minimize this with respect to b, we get the *plug-in rule* for the *(locally) optimal bandwidth*

$$b^*(a) = \left(\frac{\sigma^2(a)}{4f(a) \mathcal{B}(a)^2} \frac{R_K}{\sigma_K^4} \right)^{1/5} n^{-1/5}.$$

Note that the rate of shrinkage is optimal, as established earlier.

The practical implementation of the plug-in rule requires (nonparametrically) estimating the functions $f(a)$, $f'(a)$, $g'(a)$, $g''(a)$, $\sigma^2(a)$, computing R_K, σ_K^4, and plugging these into the formula for $b^*(a)$. Furthermore, this already cumbersome routine gives a numerical value of an optimal bandwidth for only one design point a, and hence should be repeated for all a's. As this procedure is rather tedious, applied researchers would naturally prefer only one *globally optimal bandwidth* b^* which is common for all a's of interest.

The globally optimal bandwidth obtains easily if one uses as a criterion the integrated asymptotic mean squared error

$$\mathcal{IAMSE}(x) = \int \mathcal{AMSE}(x) dx = b^4 \sigma_K^4 \int \mathcal{B}(x)^2 \, dx + \frac{R_K}{nb} \int \frac{\sigma^2(x)}{f(x)} dx.$$

Of course, one may want to introduce a more complex weighting scheme if uniform weighting is deemed restrictive. Under uniform weighting, the optimal bandwidth is given by

$$b^* = \left(\frac{\int \dfrac{\sigma^2(x)}{f(x)} dx}{4 \int \mathcal{B}(x)^2 \, dx} \frac{R_K}{\sigma_K^4} \right)^{1/5} n^{-1/5}.$$

This strategy, however, does not relieve the researcher from estimating $f(x)$, $f'(x)$, $g'(x)$, $g''(x)$ and $\sigma^2(x)$, and it is as inconvenient as using the local optimal bandwidth. Bernard Silverman derived a universal formula that is applicable under certain "benchmark" circumstances, including, for example, the normal density f.[2] This universal formula is called *Silverman's rule*:

$$b^S = 1.364 \left(\frac{R_K}{\sigma_K^4} \right)^{1/5} \hat{\sigma}_x n^{-1/5},$$

where $\hat{\sigma}_x^2$ is the regressor's sample variance. In particular, the formula reduces to $b^S = 1.06 \hat{\sigma}_x n^{-1/5}$ for the Gaussian kernel. When used in practice, Silverman's rule usually produces reasonable results except possibly near the boundaries of the support of x. There are cases, however, where the estimated regression curve is not satisfactory, and Silverman's rule is used as a benchmark for finding a more suitable bandwidth.

A principally different bandwidth selection rule is *cross validation (CV)*. It is based on measuring the quality of fit rather than on asymptotic arguments. A reasonable goodness-of-fit criterion to be minimized is the *cross validation function*

$$CV(b) = \frac{1}{n} \sum_{i=1}^{n} \left(y_i - \hat{g}_{-i}(x_i) \right)^2,$$

where $\hat{g}_{-i}(x_i)$ is a Nadaraya–Watson estimator at location x_i obtained from leaving out observation i and fitting a kernel regression using all the remaining $(n-1)$ points, i.e.,

$$\hat{g}_{-i}(x_i) = \frac{\displaystyle\sum_{j=1, j \neq i}^{n} y_i K_b \left(x_j - x_i \right)}{\displaystyle\sum_{j=1, j \neq i}^{n} K_b \left(x_j - x_i \right)}.$$

The optimal bandwidth, in terms of CV, is the bandwidth b^{CV} that minimizes $CV(b)$. The ith point is removed from the computation to prevent explanation of an observation solely by itself; otherwise, interpolation by setting b to a very low value would be optimal. Unfortunately, in actual applications, this bandwidth often leads to severe undersmoothing, and in such cases it also may be used only as a benchmark.

1.4.4   Multivariate Kernel Regression

Up to now, we considered kernel regression estimation with only a single regressor x. Below, we describe how to generalize the Nadaraya–Watson estimator to a multiple regressors setting.

Let us denote by s the dimensionality of x. The kernel will now have s-dimensional argument, mapping the distance between each x_i and a in the

---

[2] Silverman used an optimal bandwidth for the Nadaraya–Watson estimator of the density.

s-dimensional space to a scalar weight: $K : \mathbb{R}^s \to \mathbb{R}$. Define an $s \times s$ symmetric and positive definite *bandwidth matrix* B and

$$K_B(u) = \frac{1}{\det B} K\left(B^{-1}u\right).$$

The multivariate Nadaraya–Watson estimator has a similar form as before:

$$\hat{g}(a) = \frac{\sum\limits_{i=1}^{n} y_i K_B(x_i - a)}{\sum\limits_{i=1}^{n} K_B(x_i - a)}.$$

There are many ways of organizing the structure of K and B but two main approaches are commonly used in practice.

The first approach uses the decomposition of the s-dimensional space into the product of s one-dimensional ones:

$$K_B(u) = \prod_{j=1}^{s} K_{b_j,j}(u_j) = \prod_{j=1}^{s} \frac{1}{b_j} K_j\left(\frac{u_j}{b_j}\right),$$

where K_j and b_j are kernel and bandwidth in the jth dimension. Such $K_B(u)$ is called the *product kernel*. The K_j's may potentially be different across dimensions. The bandwidth matrix is $B = \text{diag} \{b_j\}_{j=1}^{s}$, and each b_j is selected separately.

The product kernel ignores the dependence structure among the regressors. Moreover, the selection of s separate bandwidths is not particularly appealing. The second method does not have these drawbacks. The bandwidth matrix has the following structure:

$$B = b \hat{\Sigma}^{1/2},$$

where b is a single bandwidth, $\hat{\Sigma}$ is the sample variance matrix of regressors, and $\hat{\Sigma}^{1/2}$ denotes its square root (for example, from the Choleski decomposition).

Unfortunately, the precision of estimation for high values of s is greatly reduced. This phenomenon is called the *curse of dimensionality*. The reason is that typically the s-dimensional hyper-window has fewer observations than the one-dimensional analog, and the variance of the estimator increases rapidly with s. In particular, the rate of convergence (under the second scheme) is $\sqrt{nb^s}$, and the optimal bandwidth is $O\left(n^{-1/(s+4)}\right)$. In practice, nonparametric estimation is usually feasible only for very small s, and requires very big samples for the estimation to be reliable.

1.4.5   Local Polynomial Regression

We now return to the case of a single regressor x. Note that the Nadaraya–Watson estimator may be represented as a weighted least squares minimization problem:

$$\hat{g}(a) = \arg\min_{\beta_0} \sum_{i=1}^{n} (y_i - \beta_0)^2 K_b (x_i - a).$$

This means that the Nadaraya–Watson estimation is a local (in the sense that it involves weighting based on the locality of points to a) regression on a constant. There is no compelling reason to restrict the estimation to a regression on a constant and it seems natural to extend it to a linear regression on a constant and x. Then, the resulting estimator is the *local linear regression* estimator:

$$\hat{g}_1(a) = (1,0) \arg\min_{(\beta_0,\beta_1)'} \sum_{i=1}^{n} (y_i - \beta_0 - \beta_1 (x_i - a))^2 K_b (x_i - a).$$

The vector $(1,0)$ selects the first element of a 2×1 vector. As a by-product, the second element yields the local linear regression estimate of the slope of the regression curve at a, i.e., the first derivative $g'(a)$.

The local linear regression estimator has an advantage over the Nadaraya–Watson estimator since it takes into account the slope of the regression line, which makes a difference if the observations are asymmetrically concentrated around a, and hence reduces the bias. This is reflected in the asymptotic properties, which are the same as those of the Nadaraya–Watson estimator except that now

$$B(a) = \frac{g''(a)}{2}.$$

As this bias expression suggests, the local linear regression estimator is unbiased when $g(a)$ is linear while the Nadaraya–Watson estimator is typically not. Also, the local linear estimator tends to alleviate the boundary effect bias of the kernel estimator that arises from inherent sparsity of data near the boundary.

The local linear regression can be further generalized to the *local polynomial regression of order* p:

$$\hat{g}_p(a) = (1,0,\ldots,0) \quad \arg\min_{(\beta_0,\beta_1,\ldots,\beta_p)}$$

$$\sum_{i=1}^{n} (y_i - \beta_0 - \beta_1 (x_i - a) - \ldots - \beta_p (x_i - a)^p)^2 K_b (x_i - a).$$

This estimator takes into account not only the slope but also other curvature properties of the regression function at a and produces, as a by-product, estimates of p derivatives of $g(x)$ at a. It can also be conveniently written in a closed form as a weighted least squares estimator

$$\hat{g}_p(a) = (1,0,\ldots,0) (X'WX)^{-1} X'WY,$$

where $Y = (y_1, \ldots, y_n)'$, $X = (X_1, \ldots, X_n)'$, $X_i = (1, x_i - a, \ldots, (x_i - a)^p)'$, and $W = \text{diag} \{K_b (x_i - a)\}_{i=1}^{n}$. If $p > 1$, the bias term $\mathcal{B}(a)$ is zero, which means that the optimal bandwidth and the resulting rate of convergence of the estimator are different from those discussed above.

In practice, there is a serious shortcoming in using local polynomial regression. The use of information in local nonparametric methods is very limited, and increasing p leads to a loss of degrees of freedom. As an extreme example, consider the uniform kernel and a rather narrow bandwidth so that only 2 points are inside the window. Then, the Nadaraya–Watson estimator takes an average of y's of these two points, the local linear regression connects them with a straight line and reads off an ordinate of the intersection with the vertical line $x = a$, and the local polynomial regression with $p > 1$ is not defined at all.

1.4.6   Other Nonparametric Methods

Any nonparametric method can be classified into one of two groups: local and global. The Nadaraya–Watson estimator, local linear and local polynomial regressions are local because the estimation of $g(x)$ at a uses information from the sample points in a vicinity of a. The global nonparametric methods instead try to fit the whole curve to all sample points at the same time. Here, the influence of one observation is less limited, and its value affects not only the estimated regression in its neighborhood but also the position and the shape of the whole estimated regression curve. Irrespective of whether the method is global or local, it always requires a *smoothing parameter* that controls the degree of smoothing and has to be chosen by the researcher. The smoothing parameter in the methods already discussed is the bandwidth.

Another local nonparametric method is the *N-nearest neighbors estimator*

$$\hat{g}_{NN}(a) = \frac{1}{N} \sum_{i-1}^{n} y_i \, \mathbb{I} \{ x_i \text{ is one of } N \text{ nearest neighbors to } a \},$$

where the neighborhood is judged by how close the sample point abscissas are to a. Here, N is the smoothing parameter and the consistency of the estimator requires that $N \to \infty$ and $N/n \to 0$ as $n \to \infty$. Another version is the *symmetrized N-nearest neighbors estimator*

$$\hat{g}_{SNN}(a) = \frac{1}{N} \sum_{i=1}^{n} y_i \, \mathbb{I} \left\{ \begin{array}{l} x_i \text{ is one of left } N/2 \text{ or right} \\ N/2 \text{ nearest neighbors to } a \end{array} \right\},$$

assuming that N is even. The asymptotic properties of these estimators are similar to those of the Nadaraya–Watson estimator.

One of the advantages of the nearest neighbors estimation over the kernel method is the guaranteed existence of the estimator. In the nearest neighbor estimator, any point always has neighbors in the sample whereas the window in the kernel estimator may not contain any observations. Furthermore, the number of points being averaged is fully controlled. The idea of nearest neighbors can also be combined with the idea of kernel weighting.

Series estimation, or *sieves*, is a global method which is based on the expansion of a smooth function in the functional space. Suppose that there is a (preferably orthogonal) ordered basis $\{\psi_j(x)\}_{j=0}^{\infty}$ such that

$$g(x) = \sum_{j=0}^{\infty} \gamma_j \psi_j(x).$$

The term "ordered" means that $\psi_0(x)$ is most important, $\psi_1(x)$ is of less importance, etc. For example, these could be Hermite, Legendre or Laguerre polynomials, or trigonometric (Fourier) series. If we choose a truncation parameter J such that asymptotically $J \to \infty$ and $J/n \to 0$ as $n \to \infty$, then

$$\hat{g}_S(x) = \sum_{j=0}^{J} \hat{\gamma}_j \psi_j(x),$$

where $(\hat{\gamma}_0, \ldots, \hat{\gamma}_J)'$ is a vector of OLS estimates in a "linear regression" of y on $(\psi_0(x), \ldots, \psi_J(x))'$. This method is often called semi-nonparametric, since it is nonparametric in essence, but parametric in its technical implementation. For details, see the survey article by Chen (2007).

The idea of *artificial neural networks* (ANN) is similar to that of sieves and is used to approximate a nonlinear function by a linear combination of some basis functions. A typical choice of basis functions for the ANN estimation is the logistic function in which case

$$\hat{g}_{ANN}(x) = \hat{\phi}_{0,0} + \hat{\phi}_{1,0}x + \sum_{j=1}^{J} \frac{\hat{\gamma}_j}{1 + \exp(\hat{\phi}_{0,j} + \hat{\phi}_{1,j}x)},$$

where the coefficients are estimated by nonlinear least squares instead of OLS as in the sieve estimation. Another popular choice of basis functions is the hyperbolic tangent function. Extended versions of ANN estimation include interesting hierarchical structures (see Chapter 5 in Franses and van Dijk, 2000, and the references therein).

Yet another global method is the estimation by *splines*. Suppose we want to fit the regression curve using the sum of squared errors as a goodness-of-fit criterion. This, of course, will immediately lead to interpolation, i.e., extreme undersmoothing, as it tends to fit every data point exactly. However, we can add a penalty term which penalizes for the lack of smoothness. Since the lack of smoothness of an interpolating function is often manifested in a large second derivative in absolute value, we can consider the following *spline estimator*:

$$\hat{g}_{CS}(x) = \arg\min_{\hat{g}(x)} \sum_{i=1}^{n} (y_i - \hat{g}(x))^2 + \lambda \int (\hat{g}''(u))^2 \, du,$$

where λ denotes the smoothing parameter. If λ approaches zero, the solution gets closer to an interpolating curve, while if λ is very big, the solution is close to the least squares linear predictor. The index CS stands for "cubic spline," which means that the solution is a piecewise cubic polynomial with continuously differentiable transitions at the observation abscissas. A comprehensive treatment of splines is provided in Wahba (1990).

1.5   Hypothesis Testing and Confidence Intervals

Let T denote a scalar test statistic (a real-valued function of the sample) and θ be the parameter of interest in the parameter space Θ. The testing problem divides the parameter space into two sets, Θ_0 and Θ_1, that are mutually exclusive ($\Theta_0 \cap \Theta_1 = \varnothing$) and exhaustive ($\Theta_0 \cup \Theta_1 = \Theta$). The *null hypothesis* $H_0 : \theta \in \Theta_0$ is the conjecture (e.g., restriction implied by economic theory) to be tested, and the *alternative hypothesis* is $H_1 : \theta \in \Theta_1$.

The classical testing procedure divides the possible values of T into two regions: acceptance region $\mathcal{A}$ and rejection region $\mathcal{R}$. The *size* (also called *significance level* or *type I error probability*) of the test is the probability that the test statistic will reject the null hypothesis when H_0 is true,

$$\alpha = \Pr \left\{ T \in \mathcal{R} \, | \, \theta \in \Theta_0 \right\}.$$

The *power* of the test is the probability that the test statistic will reject the null hypothesis when H_0 is not true,

$$\begin{aligned} \pi &= \Pr\{T \in \mathcal{R} \, | \, \theta \in \Theta_1\} \\ &= 1 - \Pr \left\{ T \in \mathcal{A} \, | \, \theta \in \Theta_1 \right\}, \end{aligned}$$

where $\Pr \left\{ T \in \mathcal{A} \, | \, \theta \in \Theta_1 \right\}$ is the *type II error probability*. The test is said to be *consistent* against alternatives in Θ_1 if $\pi \to 1$ as $n \to \infty$.

Assigning the test to the acceptance or the rejection region requires knowledge of the distribution of T under the null hypothesis. Since the exact distribution of the test statistic T is typically known only in a limited number of special cases, researchers often resort to an asymptotic approximation of this distribution. This is the approach we follow in this section. In the next section, we discuss an alternative method for approximating the unknown distribution of T based on repeated resampling of the observed data (bootstrap method).

Now let $Q_n (\theta)$ denote the criterion function of an extremum estimator $\hat{\theta} = \arg \min_{\theta \in \Theta} Q_n (\theta)$ considered in section 1.2, and θ_0 be the true value of the $k \times 1$ parameter vector θ. The null hypothesis of q (possibly nonlinear) restrictions on the parameter vector θ_0 can be expressed as $H_0 : d (\theta) = 0$, where $d\left(\cdot\right) : \mathbb{R}^k \to \mathbb{R}^q$ is continuous and twice differentiable in a region about θ_0.

Let $R\left(\theta\right) = \partial d\left(\theta\right)/\partial \theta'$. If $\sqrt{n}(\hat{\theta} - \theta_0) \overset{d}{\to} \mathcal{N}\left(0, \Omega\right)$, the distribution of $d(\hat{\theta})$ under the null hypothesis $H_0 : d\left(\theta\right) = 0$ can be obtained by the Delta method as

$$\sqrt{n}d(\hat{\theta}) \overset{d}{\to} \mathcal{N}\left(0, R\Omega R'\right),$$

where $R \equiv R\left(\theta_0\right)$. The *Wald* statistic is constructed as a quadratic form of $d(\hat{\theta})$

$$\mathcal{W} = nd(\hat{\theta})' \left(\hat{R}\hat{\Omega}\hat{R}'\right)^{-1} d(\hat{\theta}),$$

where $\hat{R} \equiv R(\hat{\theta})$, and $\hat{\Omega}$ is a consistent (possibly, HAC) estimator of Ω. Under the null hypothesis $H_0 : d\left(\theta\right) = 0$ and as $n \to \infty$,

$$\mathcal{W} \overset{d}{\to} \chi_q^2.$$

One serious problem that arises with the Wald test is that it is not invariant to reparameterization of the null hypothesis (Gregory and Veal, 1985). The Lagrange multiplier and the distance metric tests that we consider next do not share this shortcoming.

The Lagrange multiplier ($\mathcal{LM}$) test employs the restrictions imposed on the model by the null hypothesis $H_0 : d\left(\theta\right) = 0$. Let $\tilde{\theta} = \arg\min_{\theta \in \Theta} Q_n\left(\theta\right)$ subject to $d\left(\theta\right) = 0$, and $\hat{\gamma}$ denote a $q \times 1$ vector of Lagrange multipliers associated with the constraints. It can be shown that, under the null hypothesis,

$$\sqrt{n}\hat{\gamma} \overset{d}{\to} \mathcal{N}\left(0, (R\Omega R')^{-1}\right).$$

The $\mathcal{LM}$ statistic measures the distance of the estimated Lagrange multipliers $\hat{\gamma}$ from zero and is given by the quadratic form

$$\mathcal{LM} = n\hat{\gamma}' \tilde{R}\tilde{\Omega}\tilde{R}'\hat{\gamma},$$

where $\tilde{R} \equiv R(\tilde{\theta})$, and $\tilde{\Omega}$ is a consistent (possibly, HAC) estimate of Ω under the null hypothesis.

Equivalently, the $\mathcal{LM}$ test can be expressed as

$$\mathcal{LM} = n\frac{\partial Q_n(\tilde{\theta})}{\partial \theta'}\tilde{\Omega}\frac{\partial Q_n(\tilde{\theta})}{\partial \theta}.$$

If $Q_n(\theta)$ is a likelihood function, $\partial Q_n(\theta)/\partial \theta$ is the score function and the $\mathcal{LM}$ test is often referred to as the score test. The $\mathcal{LM}$ test is asymptotically equivalent to the $\mathcal{W}$ test and under the null hypothesis $H_0 : d\left(\theta\right) = 0$,

$$\mathcal{LM} \overset{d}{\to} \chi_q^2.$$

In addition to being invariant to reparameterizations of the null hypothesis, the $\mathcal{LM}$ test is characterized by good size properties and can offer computational advantages over the $\mathcal{W}$ test. Since the $\mathcal{LM}$ test is based only on the estimates under the null hypothesis, it is often the case (in testing the linearity of the model, for example) that the estimation of the null model is much more convenient than the estimation of the unrestricted model.

Unlike the $\mathcal{W}$ and $\mathcal{LM}$ statistics, the distance metric ($\mathcal{DM}$) test uses information contained in both the unrestricted and restricted estimates and is defined (up to a possible multiplication constant) as

$$\mathcal{DM} = n\left(Q_n(\tilde{\theta}) - Q_n(\hat{\theta})\right).$$

In a maximum likelihood framework, this is the familiar likelihood ratio ($\mathcal{LR}$) test based on the differences in the likelihood functions for the unconstrained and constrained estimators. By expanding $Q_n(\tilde{\theta})$ and $\partial Q_n(\tilde{\theta})/\partial\theta$ about $\hat{\theta}$, it follows that the $\mathcal{DM}$ and $\mathcal{LM}$ tests are asymptotically equivalent, $\mathcal{DM} = \mathcal{LM} + o_P(1)$, so that

$$\mathcal{DM} \overset{d}{\to} \chi_q^2.$$

Exercise 1.6. Show that $\mathcal{DM} = \mathcal{LM} + o_P(1)$ in the general extremum estimation framework. Derive the $\mathcal{LR}$ test statistic in the ML framework.

Next, we exploit the duality between confidence intervals and hypothesis testing using one of the statistics introduced above and discuss the construction of interval estimators, which are a convenient and informative way of reporting estimation results. Suppose that under the null hypothesis, the test statistic T ($\mathcal{W}$, $\mathcal{LM}$ or $\mathcal{DM}$) has a sampling distribution,

$$G_n(\tau) = \Pr\{T \leq \tau \mid H_0\}.$$

For a fixed confidence level $(1 - \alpha)$, there exists a unique $\tau(1 - \alpha)$ such that

$$\Pr\{T < \tau(1 - \alpha) \mid H_0\} > 1 - \alpha,$$

where $\tau(1 - \alpha)$ is the $(1 - \alpha)$-quantile of the distribution of T which can be obtained by inverting G_n. Then, the $100(1 - \alpha)\%$ confidence interval (set) is given by the set of values of θ satisfying $T \leq \tau(1 - \alpha)$,

$$C_{1-\alpha}(\theta) = \{\theta \in \Theta : T \leq \tau(1 - \alpha)\},$$

or equivalently

$$C_{1-\alpha}(\theta) = \{\theta \in \Theta : \theta \in \mathcal{A}\},$$

where Θ is the parameter space of θ and $\mathcal{A}$ is the acceptance region of the test T. The endpoints of the confidence interval (set) are the infimum and supremum over $C_{1-\alpha}(\theta)$ given by

$$\theta_L = \inf\{\theta \in \Theta : \Pr\{T \leq \tau(1 - \alpha) \mid H_0\} \geq 1 - \alpha\},$$
$$\theta_U = \sup\{\theta \in \Theta : \Pr\{T \leq \tau(1 - \alpha) \mid H_0\} \geq 1 - \alpha\}.$$

In general, the endpoints of the confidence interval (set) need to be calculated numerically by computing the test statistic T for a sequence of hypotheses $H_0 : d(\theta) = 0$ on a (possibly multi-dimensional) grid of points for θ. In the case when θ is a vector, confidence intervals for each element of θ can be constructed by projection methods.

Finally, we discuss one of the most popular specification tests in overidentified moment condition models. This test is known in the literature as the $\mathcal{J}$ (or Sargan–Hansen) test and tests for compatibility of the moment conditions. The $\mathcal{J}$ test is based on the criterion function of the efficient GMM estimator, evaluated at the parameter estimates, and as $n \to \infty$,

$$\mathcal{J} = n\, Q_n(\hat{\theta}) \xrightarrow{d} \chi^2_{\ell-k},$$

where $\ell - k$ is the degree of overidentification. One important implication of rejecting the null hypothesis is that the asymptotic variance of the GMM estimator, derived under the assumption of correctly specified moment conditions in section 1.2.2 of this chapter, is no longer valid and needs to be adjusted to account for the misspecification of the model. The inference in misspecified models is discussed in Chapter 4.

Exercise 1.7. Recall the problem of minimum distance estimation from Exercise 1.4. Develop a test of the hypothesis that there exists ϕ_0 such that $\theta_0 = \varphi(\phi_0)$.

1.6   Bootstrap Inference

The bootstrap is a resampling technique for approximating distributions of estimators and test statistics. While the bootstrap was formally introduced in statistics relatively recently by Efron (1979), the notion of the bootstrap can be traced back to much earlier literature. For example, Cowles (1934) has ingeniously implemented the bootstrap idea for evaluating the statistical significance of trading strategies based on stock market forecasts by randomly reshuffling cards of possible investment decisions. Hall (1992, 1994) and Horowitz (2001), among others, provide excellent surveys of the theoretical foundations of the bootstrap and its applications in statistics and econometrics.

Let $\{w_i\}_{i=1}^{n}$ be an *IID* sample from a population of w with distribution

$$F_0(u) = \Pr\{w \le u\}$$

that belongs to a family of distribution functions $\mathcal{F}$. Using this sample, we estimate the parameter of interest

$$\hat{\theta} = \theta(w_1, w_2, ..., w_n).$$

The sampling (finite sample) distribution of this estimator centered around the true parameter is $G_n(u) = \Pr\{\hat{\theta} - \theta_0 \leq u\}$. If G_n is known, one could conduct exact inference and form exact confidence intervals for θ_0.

Since $\hat{\theta}$ is a function only of the sample, G_n is a function only of F_0, which is generally unknown. The bootstrap method operates conditionally on the realized sample by replacing the unknown distribution function of the data with an estimator. In particular, the bootstrap approximation of G_n replaces F_0 with the empirical distribution function

$$F_n(u) = \frac{1}{n}\sum_{i=1}^{n}\mathbb{I}\{w_i \leq u\}$$

which is the sample analog of $F_0(u) = \Pr\{w \leq u\} = E\left[\mathbb{I}\{w \leq u\}\right]$. The empirical distribution function provides an excellent estimator of the unknown population distribution function since, by the Glivenko–Cantelli lemma,

$$\sup_{u \in \mathbb{R}}|F_n(u) - F_0(u)| \overset{a.s.}{\to} 0.$$

Note again that F_0 is the true (but unknown) distribution that generated the data $(w_1, w_2, ..., w_n)$ which is used to construct the estimator F_n. Conditional on the data, we can apply the analogy principle and pretend that F_n is the true distribution. Then, we can draw by replacement repeated random samples of size n from F_n denoted by $(w_1^*, w_2^*, ..., w_n^*)$.

More formally, using functional notation as in Hall (1994), we define the estimator $\hat{\theta} = \theta(F_n)$ and the true value of the parameter of interest $\theta_0 = \theta(F_0)$. The exact finite sample distribution of the estimator is

$$G_n(u) = \Pr\left\{\theta(F_n) - \theta(F_0) \leq u \,|\, F_0\right\}.$$

Since F_0 is unknown, G_n cannot be calculated directly and requires an approximation. The bootstrap principle replaces the pair (F_n, F_0) with (F_n^*, F_n) and the bootstrap approximation of G_n is given by

$$G_n^*(u) = \Pr\left\{\theta(F_n^*) - \theta(F_n) \leq u \,|\, F_n\right\}.$$

The approximation $G_n^*(u)$ can be computed via simulations by repeatedly drawing bootstrap samples $\{w_i^*\}_{i=1}^{n}$ from F_n and re-estimating the parameter of interest $\theta^* = \theta(w_1^*, w_2^*, ..., w_n^*)$ a large number B of times. Then, the computed approximation is given by

$$\hat{G}_n^*(u) = \frac{1}{B}\sum_{j=1}^{B}\mathbb{I}\{\theta_j^* - \hat{\theta} \leq u\}$$

and $\hat{G}_n^*(u) \overset{p}{\to} G_n^*(u)$ as $B \to \infty$. This bootstrap distribution can be used for bias correction of the original estimate $\hat{\theta}$, confidence interval construction, and hypotheses testing.

For any $\delta > 0$ and $F_0 \in \mathcal{F}$, the bootstrap provides a consistent estimator of the distribution of the statistic of interest if

$$\lim_{n\to\infty} \Pr\left\{\sup_{u\in\mathbb{R}} |G_n^*(u) - G_\infty(u)| > \delta\right\} = 0,$$

where $G_\infty(u)$ denotes the asymptotic distribution of the statistic. For example, if the estimator $\hat{\theta}$ is normally distributed as $n \to \infty$

$$\sqrt{n}(\hat{\theta} - \theta_0) \xrightarrow{d} \mathcal{N}(0, \Omega),$$

the bootstrap estimator should, conditional on the data, have the same asymptotic distribution

$$\sqrt{n}(\theta^* - \hat{\theta}) \xrightarrow{d} \mathcal{N}(0, \Omega).$$

Two basic conditions are believed to be needed for consistency of the bootstrap. First, for any $\delta > 0$, $\lim_{n\to\infty} \Pr\{\sup_{u\in\mathbb{R}} |F_n(u) - F_0(u)| > \delta\} = 0$, i.e., the sampling distribution of the data $F_n(u)$ is a consistent estimator of the true distribution F_0. Second, the asymptotic distribution of the statistic $G_\infty(u, F)$ is continuous in u for any $F \in \mathcal{F}$. This condition requires continuity of the mapping from the sampling distribution of the data to the limiting distribution of the test statistic. In general, the bootstrap would fail to be consistent (first-order accurate) if discontinuity is present in the asymptotic distribution as, for instance, in unit root models. However, Inoue and Kilian (2003) establish that the continuity of the limiting distribution is not a necessary condition for the consistency of the bootstrap and demonstrate that, in some cases, the bootstrap can remain valid even in the presence of discontinuities.

The accuracy of the bootstrap approximation is based on higher-order (Edgeworth) expansions of $G_n(u)$ and $G_n^*(u)$ and is discussed in Chapter 5. The main result is that the bootstrap for asymptotically pivotal statistics, if carried out judiciously, is generally more accurate than the first-order asymptotic theory. By contrast, in the case of non-pivotal statistics (the estimator $\hat{\theta}$, for example), the order of the error from the bootstrap approximation is the same as the order of accuracy of the asymptotic approximation.

Given these theoretical results, one of the most popular methods for bootstrap inference is based on studentized statistics such as the t-statistic

$$t_n = \frac{\hat{\theta} - \theta}{\mathrm{se}(\hat{\theta})},$$

where $\mathrm{se}(\hat{\theta})$ denotes the standard error of the estimator $\hat{\theta}$. This bootstrap method is known in the literature as the *percentile-t method*. To illustrate the implementation of this method, suppose that we are concerned with the construction of $100(1 - \alpha)\%$ confidence intervals, where α is the significance level (for example, 0.05 or 0.1). Let $\tau_t^*(1-\alpha)$ be the $(1-\alpha)$-quantile of the distribution of

$$t_n^* = \frac{\theta^* - \hat{\theta}}{\operatorname{se}(\theta^*)}.$$

Then, the $100(1-\alpha)\%$ *equal-tailed confidence interval* for the parameter of interest θ_0 is given by

$$C_t^{ET}(\theta_0) = \left[\hat{\theta} - \operatorname{se}(\hat{\theta})\,\tau_t^* \left(1 - \frac{\alpha}{2}\right),\ \hat{\theta} - \operatorname{se}(\hat{\theta})\,\tau_t^* \left(\frac{\alpha}{2}\right) \right].$$

This method can also be used for constructing median unbiased estimates of θ_0.

Alternatively, one could construct the $100(1-\alpha)\%$ *symmetric confidence interval* for θ_0 as

$$C_t^{SYM}(\theta_0) = \left[\hat{\theta} - \operatorname{se}(\hat{\theta})\,\tau_t^{**} \left(1 - \alpha\right),\ \hat{\theta} + \operatorname{se}(\hat{\theta})\,\tau_t^{**} \left(1 - \alpha\right) \right],$$

where $\tau_t^{**}(1-\alpha)$ denotes the $(1-\alpha)$-quantile of the distribution of

$$t_n^{**} = \frac{|\theta^* - \hat{\theta}|}{\operatorname{se}(\theta^*)}.$$

Confidence intervals (sets) for θ_0 can be constructed similarly using other asymptotically pivotal statistics such as the distance metric (likelihood ratio), Lagrange multiplier or Wald statistics, although the endpoints of these confidence intervals are typically calculated numerically for a sequence of null hypotheses and, hence, are computationally more demanding. The bootstrap $100(1-\alpha)\%$ confidence interval based on the $\mathcal{T}$ ($\mathcal{W}$, $\mathcal{LM}$ or $\mathcal{DM}$) statistic is given by

$$C_{\mathcal{T}}(\theta) = \{\theta \in \Theta : \mathcal{T} \le \tau_{\mathcal{T}}^*(1-\alpha)\},$$

where $\tau_{\mathcal{T}}^*(1-\alpha)$ is the $(1-\alpha)$ quantile of the distribution of $\mathcal{T}^*$.

The bootstrap of regression models with IID data is typically performed using residual-based resampling which imposes the structure of the model in generating bootstrap data. One drawback of this method is that it does not mimic correctly the properties of the data in the presence of heteroskedasticity. An alternative bootstrap method is based on resampling data pairs. This resampling scheme is model-free and is robust to model misspecification and heteroskedasticity. In models with dependent data, one could also resort to either a residual-based resampling from a correctly specified dynamic model or a block bootstrap resampling that captures the dependence structure of the data.

We will illustrate residual-based resampling in the context of a nonparametric regression discussed in section 1.4. Consider the model

$$y = g(x) + \sigma(x)e,$$

where $g(x)$ and $\sigma(x)$ are the conditional mean and conditional standard deviation functions, and e is assumed to have zero mean and unit variance and be mean independent of x. Let $\hat{g}(x)$ and $\hat{\sigma}(x)$ denote nonparametric estimates of $g(x)$ and $\sigma(x)$, and let

$$\hat{e}_i = \frac{y_i - \hat{g}(x_i)}{\hat{\sigma}(x_i)} - \frac{1}{n} \sum_{j=1}^{n} \frac{y_j - \hat{g}(x_j)}{\hat{\sigma}(x_j)}$$

for $i = 1, ..., n$, be the recentered, standardized nonparametric regression residuals. The recentering and standardization ensure that the residuals have mean zero and variance one as in the original sample.

The interest lies in conducting inference (confidence band construction, for example) on the nonparametric regression functions $g(x)$ and $\sigma(x)$. As we demonstrated in section 1.4.2, this requires explicit estimation of unknown functions of the data that enter the asymptotic distributions. The bootstrap provides a more practical approach for approximating the finite sample distributions of the statistics of interest. The bootstrap samples are obtained as $y_i^* = \hat{g}(x_i) + \hat{\sigma}(x_i)e_i^*$, $i = 1, ..., n$, where $\{e_i^*\}_{i=1}^{n}$ are drawn with replacement from the empirical distribution of the recentered and standardized residuals $\hat{e}_i$. Next, each bootstrap sample is used to re-estimate $g(x_i)$ and $\sigma(x_i)$ at the same design points. Let $g^*(x)$ and $\sigma^*(x)$ denote the corresponding estimated bootstrap analogs. Repeating this procedure many times provides an approximation to the distributions of $(g^*(x) - \hat{g}(x))$ and $(\sigma^*(x) - \hat{\sigma}(x))$ at each design point. Then, $100(1 - \alpha)\%$ pointwise confidence bands, based on the *percentile* bootstrap method, can be constructed as

$$C^{ET}(g(x)) = \left[\hat{g}(x) - \tau_g^* \left(1 - \frac{\alpha}{2} \right), \ \hat{g}(x) - \tau_g^* \left(\frac{\alpha}{2} \right) \right]$$

and

$$C^{ET}(\sigma(x)) = \left[\hat{\sigma}(x) - \tau_\sigma^* \left(1 - \frac{\alpha}{2} \right), \ \hat{\sigma}(x) - \tau_\sigma^* \left(\frac{\alpha}{2} \right) \right],$$

where $\tau_g^*(1 - \alpha)$ and $\tau_\sigma^*(1 - \alpha)$ denote the $(1 - \alpha)$-quantiles of the distributions of $g^*(x) - \hat{g}(x)$ and $\sigma^*(x) - \hat{\sigma}(x)$. This bootstrap procedure is also valid for times series data when x is a lagged dependent variable.

Finally, we turn our attention to the implementation of the bootstrap in moment condition models. Many empirical studies have reported that the finite sample properties of GMM estimators are rather poor. For example, the two-step GMM estimator appears to be biased in finite samples and the magnitude of the bias increases as the number of instruments gets large (see Chapter 5). Also, the $\mathcal{J}$ test for overidentifying restrictions tends to over-reject when the asymptotic critical values are used. Given the popularity of the GMM in econometrics, the bootstrap methods proved to be a useful tool for improved approximation of the finite sample distributions of GMM estimators and test statistics. Recall that even if the model is correctly specified, $m_n(\hat{\theta}) \neq 0$ when the number of moment conditions exceeds the number of parameters. Therefore, the data generated from F_n would not satisfy the moment restrictions that hold in the population, and the bootstrap moment conditions would inherit a bias. To correct for the bias, the bootstrap moment conditions need to be recentered as

$$m^*(w_i^*, \theta) = m(w_i^*, \theta) - \frac{1}{n} \sum_{j=1}^n m(w_j, \hat{\theta}),$$

where $\{w_i^*\}_{i=1}^n$ denotes the bootstrap sample. These recentered moment conditions can then be used to construct the GMM objective function and obtain the GMM bootstrap estimator $\theta^* = \arg\min_{\theta \in \Theta} Q_n^*(\theta)$, where

$$Q_n^*(\theta) = m_n^*(\theta)' \left(\frac{1}{n} \sum_{i=1}^n m^*(w_i^*, \bar{\theta}^*) m^*(w_i^*, \bar{\theta}^*)' \right)^{-1} m_n^*(\theta),$$

$\bar{\theta}^*$ is the first-step estimator based on the bootstrap data, and $m_n^*(\theta) = n^{-1} \sum_{i=1}^n m^*(w_i^*, \theta)$.

The bootstrap GMM estimator can then be used to compute the statistic of interest; for example, $\mathcal{J}^* = nQ_n^*(\theta^*)$. After repeating this procedure B times, we can compute bootstrap critical values $\tau_{\mathcal{J}}^*(1 - \alpha)$ or bootstrap p-values as $B^{-1} \sum_{j=1}^B \mathbb{I}\{\mathcal{J} < \mathcal{J}_j^*\}$. For more details, see Hall and Horowitz (1996) and Hall (2005).

Exercise 1.8. Write out formulas for the bootstrap analogs of the $\mathcal{W}$, $\mathcal{LM}$ and $\mathcal{DM}$ test statistics in the contexts of ML and GMM estimation.

References

Anatolyev, S. (2006) Kernel estimation under linear-exponential loss. *Economics Letters*, 91, 39–43.

Andrews, D.W.K. (1991) Heteroskedasticity and autocorrelation consistent covariance matrix estimation. *Econometrica*, 59, 817–858.

Andrews, D.W.K. (1994) Empirical process methods in econometrics. In: R.F. Engle and D. McFadden (eds.),*Handbook of Econometrics*, Vol. 4, Elsevier: Amsterdam, Chapter 37, 2247–2294.

Chen, X. (2007) Large sample sieve estimation of semi-nonparametric models. In: J.J. Heckman and E.E. Leamer (eds.), *Handbook of Econometrics*, Vol. 6/2, Elsevier: Amsterdam, Chapter 76, 5549–5632.

Cowles, A. (1934) Can stock market forecasters forecast? *Econometrica*, 1, 309–324.

den Haan, W.J., and A. Levin (1997) A practitioner's guide to robust covariance matrix estimation. In: *Handbook of Statistics*, Vol. 15, Elsevier: Amsterdam, Chapter 12, 291–341.

Donald, S.G., and W.K. Newey (2000) A jackknife interpretation of the continuous updating estimator. *Economics Letters*, 67, 239–243.

Duffie, D., and K.J. Singleton (1993) Simulated moments estimation of Markov models of asset prices. *Econometrica*, 61, 929–952.

Efron, B. (1979) Bootstrap methods: Another look at the jackknife. *Annals of Statistics*, 7, 1–26.

Fan, J., N.E. Heckman and M.P. Wand (1995) Local polynomial kernel regression for generalized linear models and quasi-likelihood functions. *Journal of the American Statistical Association*, 90, 141–150.

Franses, P., and D. van Dijk (2000) *Nonlinear Time Series Models in Empirical Finance*. Cambridge University Press: Cambridge.

Gospodinov, N., R. Kan and C. Robotti (2010) Further results on the limiting distribution of GMM sample moment conditions. Working Paper 2010-11, Federal Reserve Bank of Atlanta.

Gourieroux, C., A. Monfort and E. Renault (1993) Indirect inference. *Journal of Applied Econometrics*, 8, S85–S118.

Gregory, A.W., and M.R. Veal (1985) Formulating Wald tests of nonlinear restrictions. *Econometrica*, 53, 1465–1468.

Hall, A.R. (2005) *Generalized Method of Moments*. Oxford University Press: Oxford.

Hall, P. (1992) *The Bootstrap and Edgeworth Expansion*. Springer-Verlag: New York.

Hall, P. (1994) Methodology and theory for the bootstrap. In: R.F. Engle and D. McFadden (eds.), *Handbook of Econometrics*, Vol. 4, Elsevier: Amsterdam, Chapter 39, 2341–2381.

Hall, P., and J.L. Horowitz (1996) Bootstrap critical values for tests based on generalized-method-of-moments estimators. *Econometrica*, 64, 891–916.

Hansen, L.P. (1982) Large sample properties of generalized method of moments estimators. *Econometrica*, 50, 1029–1054.

Hansen, L.P., J. Heaton and A. Yaron (1996) Finite-sample properties of some alternative GMM estimators. *Journal of Business and Economic Statistics*, 14, 262–280.

Hansen, L.P., and R.J. Hodrick (1980) Forward exchange rates as optimal predictors of future spot rates. *Journal of Political Economy*, 88, 829–853.

Härdle, W. (1990) *Applied Nonparametric Regression*. Cambridge University Press: New York.

Härdle, W., and O. Linton (1994) Applied nonparametric methods. In: R.F. Engle and D. McFadden (eds.), *Handbook of Econometrics*, Vol. 4, Elsevier: Amsterdam, Chapter 38, 2295–2339.

Horowitz, J.L. (2001) The bootstrap. In: J.J. Heckman and. E.E. Leamer (eds.), *Handbook of Econometrics*, Vol. 5, Chapter 52, 3159–3228.

Imbens, G. (1997) One-step estimators for over-identified generalized method of moments models. *Review of Economic Studies*, 64, 359–383.

Inoue, A., and L. Kilian (2003) The continuity of the limit distribution in the parameter of interest is not essential for the validity of the bootstrap. *Econometric Theory*, 19, 944–961.

Kiefer, N.M., T.J. Vogelsang and H. Bunzel (2000) Simple robust testing of regression hypotheses. *Econometrica*, 68, 695–714.

Koenker, R., and G. Bassett (1978) Regression quantiles. *Econometrica*, 46, 33–50.

Koenker, R., and G. Bassett (1982) Robust tests for heteroskedasticity based on regression quantiles. *Econometrica*, 50, 43–61.

Li, Q., and J.S. Racine (2007) *Nonparametric Econometrics: Theory and Practice*. Princeton University Press: Princeton.

Manski, C.F. (1991) Regression. *Journal of Economic Literature*, 29, 34–50.

Nadaraya, E.A. (1965) On nonparametric estimates of density functions and regression curves. *Theory of Applied Probability*, 10, 186–190.

Newey, W.K., and D. McFadden (1994) Large sample estimation and hypothesis testing. In: R.F. Engle and D. McFadden (eds.), *Handbook of Econometrics*, Vol. 4, Elsevier: Amsterdam, Chapter 36, 2111–2245.

Newey, W.K., and K.D. West (1987) A simple, positive semi-definite, heteroskedasticity and autocorrelation consistent covariance matrix. *Econometrica*, 55, 703–708.

Pagan, A., and A. Ullah (1999) *Nonparametric Econometrics*. Cambridge University Press: Cambridge.

Racine, J.S. (2008) Nonparametric econometrics: A primer. *Foundations and Trends in Econometrics*, 3, 1–88.

Smith, R.J. (2005) Automatic positive semi-definite HAC covariance matrix and GMM estimation. *Econometric Theory*, 21, 158–170.

Sowell, F.B. (1996) Optimal tests for parameter instability in the generalized method of moments framework. *Econometrica*, 64, 1085–1107.

Wahba, G. (1990) *Spline Models for Observational Data.* SIAM: Philadelphia.

Watson, G.S. (1964) Smooth regression analysis. *Sankhya*, 26, 359–372.

Part II

Estimation of Moment Condition Models

Chapter 2

Generalized Empirical Likelihood Estimators

2.1 Introduction

Until recently, nonparametric and parametric maximum likelihood, instrumental variables and robust estimation have been treated as different frameworks, with their own advantages and drawbacks, for estimating unknown model parameters. The generalized method of moments (GMM) provided the first unified estimation framework by demonstrating that most of the existing estimators can be expressed as solutions to an estimating equation derived from particular moment restrictions. Even after the invention of the GMM, however, the distinction between likelihood-based and moment-based estimation still remained. Since the beginning of the 1990s, a class of nonparametric likelihood estimators such as the empirical likelihood, seemingly unrelated to GMM, has been established to possess appealing asymptotic and finite sample properties in a wide range of applications. More recently, Newey and Smith (2004) have shown that this class of nonparametric likelihood-based estimators for moment condition models, called generalized empirical likelihood (GEL) estimators, is much more general than it was initially thought, and that it can be used as a convenient analytical, estimation and inference framework. The development and analysis of the class of GEL estimators is arguably one of the most influential recent contributions to the econometric literature. This class of efficient estimators includes the celebrated empirical likelihood, exponential tilting and continuously updated GMM estimators. The GEL framework leads to a better understanding of the properties of the moment-based estimators and allows for more powerful test procedures, more efficient estimation of density and distribution functions and improved bootstrap methods.

In this chapter, we review the construction of nonparametric likelihood and discuss its relation to efficient estimation of density and distribution functions. Then, we extend this method to models defined by moment restrictions and develop the generalized empirical likelihood framework. The first- and higher-order asymptotic properties of the GEL estimators are illustrated. We also discuss extensions to models with dependent data, GEL-based tests and confidence intervals as well as the relation of GEL to power divergence and

Kullback–Leibler information criteria. The results in this chapter are developed for unconditional moment restriction models. The extension of GEL estimators to models defined by conditional moment restrictions is discussed in the next chapter. Other reviews of some of the topics discussed below include Owen (2001), Kitamura (2007) and Mittelhammer, Judge and Miller (2000).

2.2 Empirical Likelihood and Generalized Empirical Likelihood

2.2.1 Nonparametric Likelihood

Consider a random sample $\{x_i\}_{i=1}^n$ from population distribution $F(x)$ with probability density function $f(x)$. Recall that for IID data, the joint likelihood function is given by the product of individual densities:

$$\prod_{i=1}^n f(x_i).$$

The standard parametric approach assumes a particular parametric form of the unknown density $f(x|\eta)$, where η denotes a parameter vector that characterizes $f(x)$. The likelihood function is then maximized with respect to η, which yields the parametric maximum likelihood estimator and allows us to recover estimates of $f(x)$ and $F(x)$ from the observed sample. For example, if it is assumed that the sample is generated from $\mathcal{N}(\varphi, \sigma^2)$, then $f\left(x \mid \varphi, \sigma^2\right) = \left(2\pi\sigma^2\right)^{-1/2} \exp\left(-(x-\varphi)^2/2\sigma^2\right)$, and the unknown parameters $\eta = \left(\varphi, \sigma^2\right)'$ that characterize the population distribution can be estimated by parametric ML.

By contrast, the nonparametric approach does not parameterize the unknown density $f(x)$ and sets η to the n-dimensional vector $\mathbf{p} = (p_1, p_2, ..., p_n)$, where $p_i = f(x_i)$, $i = 1, 2, ..., n$, denotes a sequence of discrete probability weights assigned to each sample observation. This is equivalent to specifying the sample density function as $f_n(u) = \sum_{i=1}^n p_i \mathbb{I}\{x_i = u\}$ and the sample distribution function as $F_n(u) = \sum_{i=1}^n p_i \mathbb{I}\{x_i \le u\}$. Alternatively, this may be viewed as a sampling experiment from the multinomial population concentrated at the sample points. The *nonparametric maximum likelihood* estimate of $\mathbf{p}$ solves the maximization problem

$$\max_{\mathbf{p}} \frac{1}{n} \sum_{i=1}^n \log(p_i)$$

subject to the constraint

$$\sum_{i=1}^{n} p_i = 1.$$

As in the ML problem, the use of the logarithmic transformation and the scaling factor $\frac{1}{n}$ does not affect the optimal solution for p_i. Note also that the logarithmic form of the objective function ensures the (strict) positivity of the probability weights p_i.

The Lagrangian for this constrained maximization problem is given by

$$\mathcal{L}(p_1, p_2, ..., p_n, \mu) = \frac{1}{n} \sum_{i=1}^{n} \log(p_i) - \mu \left(\sum_{i=1}^{n} p_i - 1 \right),$$

where μ denotes the Lagrange multiplier. The first-order condition with respect to p_i is given by

$$\frac{\partial \mathcal{L}(p_1, p_2, ..., p_n, \mu)}{\partial p_i} = \frac{1}{np_i} - \mu = 0,$$

or $\mu p_i = \frac{1}{n}$. Summing both sides over all i yields $\mu \sum_{i=1}^{n} p_i = 1$, or $\mu = 1$ using that $\sum_{i=1}^{n} p_i = 1$. Thus, the *implied probabilities* are

$$\hat{p}_i = \frac{1}{n}, \quad i = 1, ..., n,$$

and the nonparametric estimates of the probability density and cumulative distribution functions are

$$\hat{f}(u) = \frac{1}{n} \sum_{i=1}^{n} \mathbb{I}\{x_i = u\}$$

and

$$\hat{F}(u) = \frac{1}{n} \sum_{i=1}^{n} \mathbb{I}\{x_i \le u\}.$$

The former is the empirical probability mass function, and the latter is the familiar empirical distribution function (EDF) which implies that the EDF is a nonparametric maximum likelihood estimate of the population distribution.

2.2.2 Empirical Likelihood

Suppose now that we have a model in the form of a system of unconditional moment restrictions

$$E[m(w, \theta_0)] = 0,$$

where $\theta_0 \in \Theta$ is a $k \times 1$ vector of true parameters, w is a vector of observables with $w = x$, $w = (y, x)$ or $w = (y, x, z)$, $\{w_i\}_{i=1}^{n}$ is a random sample, and $m(w, \theta)$ is an $\ell \times 1$ vector of moment conditions. As before, let $\mathbf{p} = (p_1, p_2, ..., p_n)$ be a collection of probability weights assigned to each sample observation, and consider the *empirical likelihood* problem

$$\max_{\mathbf{p}, \theta} \frac{1}{n} \sum_{i=1}^{n} \log(p_i) \tag{2.1}$$

subject to

$$\sum_{i=1}^{n} p_i m(w_i, \theta) = 0$$

and

$$\sum_{i=1}^{n} p_i = 1.$$

Compared to the nonparametric likelihood problem, the new element in this setup is the first constraint which represents the moment restrictions with respect to the distribution $\mathbf{p}$.

Note that if the moment restrictions are exactly identifying, $\ell = k$ and the first constraint is non-binding. Consequently, the solution for $\mathbf{p}$ is the same as without restrictions, i.e., $p_i = \frac{1}{n}$ for all i, while the solution for θ is

$$\hat{\theta} = \arg_{\theta} \left[\frac{1}{n} \sum_{i=1}^{n} m(w_i, \theta) = 0 \right],$$

which coincides with the classical method of moments estimator.

In the case when the moment restrictions are overidentifying, $\ell > k$ and the first constraint is generally binding. If we denote by λ the $\ell \times 1$ vector of Lagrange multipliers associated with the first constraint, the Lagrangian is

$$\mathcal{L}(p_1, p_2, ..., p_n, \lambda, \mu) = \frac{1}{n} \sum_{i=1}^{n} \log(p_i) - \lambda' \sum_{i=1}^{n} p_i m(w_i, \theta) - \mu \left(\sum_{i=1}^{n} p_i - 1 \right).$$

The first-order condition of the Lagrangian with respect to p_i is

$$\frac{1}{np_i} - \lambda' m(w_i, \theta) - \mu = 0. \tag{2.2}$$

After multiplying (2.2) by p_i and summing over all i, we obtain again that $\mu = 1$. Then, plugging $\mu = 1$ into (2.2) yields

$$p_i = \frac{1}{n} \frac{1}{1 + \lambda' m(w_i, \theta)}.$$

Next, substituting the expression for p_i into the first constraint gives rise to the nonlinear equation

$$\frac{1}{n} \sum_{i=1}^{n} \frac{m(w_i, \theta)}{1 + \lambda' m(w_i, \theta)} = 0,$$

which defines an implicit solution for λ in terms of θ. The first-order condition of the Lagrangian with respect to θ is

$$-\lambda' \sum_{i=1}^{n} p_i \frac{\partial m(w_i, \theta)}{\partial \theta'} = 0.$$

Combining the results, we can define the $(k + \ell) \times 1$ vector $(\hat{\theta}', \hat{\lambda}')'$ as the solution to the following (just-identified) system of equations:

$$\frac{1}{n} \sum_{i=1}^{n} \frac{m(w_i, \hat{\theta})}{1 + \hat{\lambda}' m(w_i, \hat{\theta})} = 0, \tag{2.3}$$

$$\frac{1}{n} \sum_{i=1}^{n} \frac{\partial m(w_i, \hat{\theta})'/\partial \theta}{1 + \hat{\lambda}' m(w_i, \hat{\theta})} \hat{\lambda} = 0. \tag{2.4}$$

The solution $\hat{\theta}$ is called the *empirical likelihood (EL) estimator* of θ, and $\hat{\lambda}$ is a vector of estimated *EL multipliers*. The *EL implied probabilities* are determined as

$$\hat{p}_i = \frac{1}{n} \frac{1}{1 + \hat{\lambda}' m(w_i, \hat{\theta})}, \quad i = 1, ..., n.$$

Note that all EL probabilities are positive due to the structure of the original maximization problem, and fluctuate around the concentration level $\frac{1}{n}$, which they would be equal to in the absence of information embedded in the moment restrictions.

Alternatively, substituting the expression for p_i into the Lagrangian and recalling the properties of a Lagrangian, we obtain that the EL estimator $\hat{\theta}$ and EL multipliers $\hat{\lambda}$ solve the *EL saddlepoint problem*

$$\max_{\theta \in \Theta} \min_{\lambda} \frac{1}{n} \sum_{i=1}^{n} - \log \left(1 + \lambda' m(w_i, \theta) \right). \tag{2.5}$$

The empirical likelihood estimates of probability density and cumulative distribution functions use the EL implied probabilities and are given by

$$\hat{f}(u) = \frac{1}{n} \sum_{i=1}^{n} \frac{\mathbb{I}\{w_i = u\}}{1 + \hat{\lambda}' m(w_i, \hat{\theta})} \tag{2.6}$$

and

$$\hat{F}(u) = \frac{1}{n} \sum_{i=1}^{n} \frac{\mathbb{I}\{w_i \leq u\}}{1 + \hat{\lambda}' m(w_i, \hat{\theta})}. \tag{2.7}$$

The estimator in (2.7) is expected to be more efficient than the EDF because it embeds additional information.

2.2.3   Generalized Empirical Likelihood

A useful generalization of the empirical likelihood estimator results in the class of *generalized empirical likelihood (GEL) estimators* (Smith, 1997). Unfortunately, except for the EL estimator, the other members of the GEL class do not have a likelihood interpretation. However, as we demonstrate below, there are various interesting relations between the GEL class of estimators and other concepts and estimation approaches which make the GEL framework particularly insightful and appealing.

The GEL class can be conveniently introduced by replacing the log function in the saddlepoint problem (2.5) with an arbitrary criterion that is subject to certain shape restrictions. Let $\rho(v)$ denote a smooth scalar function that satisfies $\rho(0) = 0$, $\partial\rho(0)/\partial v = \partial^2\rho(0)/\partial v^2 = -1$ (which are just convenient normalizations) and indexes members of the GEL class. The *GEL estimator* $\hat{\theta}$ and the *GEL multipliers* $\hat{\lambda}$ solve the saddlepoint problem

$$\min_{\theta\in\Theta} \sup_{\lambda\in\Lambda_n} \sum_{i=1}^{n} \rho\left(\lambda' m\left(w_i,\theta\right)\right), \qquad (2.8)$$

where $\Lambda_n = \{\lambda : \lambda' m\left(w_i,\theta\right) \in \Upsilon,\ i = 1,...,n\}$ and Υ is some open set containing zero (Newey and Smith, 2004).

When $\rho(v) = \log(1-v)$ and $\Upsilon = (-\infty, 1)$, the GEL problem reduces (up to a change of signs) to the basic EL estimation setup (Imbens, 1997). Another special case is the celebrated continuously updated (CU) GMM proposed by Hansen, Heaton and Yaron (1996); see section 1.2.2 of Chapter 1. The CU estimation corresponds to the case $\rho(v) = -\frac{1}{2}v^2 - v$ (see Newey and Smith, 2004). The choice $\rho(v) = 1 - \exp(v)$ leads to the exponential tilting (ET) estimator that was developed in Kitamura and Stutzer (1997) from different principles.

The first-order conditions for $(\hat{\theta}, \hat{\lambda})$ are

$$\frac{1}{n}\sum_{i=1}^{n} \frac{\partial\rho\left(\hat{\lambda}'m(w_i,\hat{\theta})\right)}{\partial\theta} = \frac{1}{n}\sum_{i=1}^{n} \frac{\partial\rho\left(\hat{\lambda}'m(w_i,\hat{\theta})\right)}{\partial v}\frac{\partial m(w_i,\hat{\theta})'}{\partial\theta}\hat{\lambda} = 0, \quad (2.9)$$

$$\frac{1}{n}\sum_{i=1}^{n} \frac{\partial\rho\left(\hat{\lambda}'m(w_i,\hat{\theta})\right)}{\partial\lambda} = \frac{1}{n}\sum_{i=1}^{n} \frac{\partial\rho\left(\hat{\lambda}'m(w_i,\hat{\theta})\right)}{\partial v}m(w_i,\hat{\theta}) = 0. \quad (2.10)$$

Note that while the true value of θ is θ_0, the true value of λ is $\lambda_0 = 0$. Indeed, the sample moment conditions (2.9)–(2.10) become in the limit the population moment restrictions

$$E\left[\frac{\partial\rho\left(\lambda_0'm(w,\theta_0)\right)}{\partial v}\frac{\partial m(w,\theta_0)'}{\partial\theta}\lambda_0\right] = 0,$$

$$E\left[\frac{\partial\rho\left(\lambda_0'm(w,\theta_0)\right)}{\partial v}m(w,\theta_0)\right] = 0.$$

It is easy to see that setting $\lambda_0 = 0$ makes the first restriction vacuous and transforms the second restriction into the original system comprising the model.

From the first-order conditions one can derive the *GEL implied probabilities*:

$$\hat{p}_i = \left(\sum_{j=1}^{n} \frac{\partial \rho \left(\hat{\lambda}' m(w_j, \hat{\theta}) \right)}{\partial v} \right)^{-1} \frac{\partial \rho \left(\hat{\lambda}' m(w_i, \hat{\theta}) \right)}{\partial v}, \quad i = 1, ..., n.$$

The normalization is done to ensure that the GEL probabilities sum to one. Unfortunately, not all GEL estimators give rise to positive implied probabilities by construction. While the EL and ET probabilities are positive by construction, the CU probabilities may not be. Antoine, Bonnal and Renault (2007) show that the CU implied probabilities have a closed form and propose a shrinkage-type correction to the CU probabilities to restore their non-negativity in finite samples.

The GEL estimates of the probability density and cumulative distribution functions use the GEL implied probabilities and are constructed as

$$\hat{f}(u) = \left(\sum_{i=1}^{n} \frac{\partial \rho \left(\hat{\lambda}' m(w_i, \hat{\theta}) \right)}{\partial v} \right)^{-1} \sum_{i=1}^{n} \frac{\partial \rho \left(\hat{\lambda}' m(w_i, \hat{\theta}) \right)}{\partial v} \mathbb{I}\{w_i = u\}$$

and

$$\hat{F}(u) = \left(\sum_{i=1}^{n} \frac{\partial \rho \left(\hat{\lambda}' m(w_i, \hat{\theta}) \right)}{\partial v} \right)^{-1} \sum_{i=1}^{n} \frac{\partial \rho \left(\hat{\lambda}' m(w_i, \hat{\theta}) \right)}{\partial v} \mathbb{I}\{w_i \leq u\}.$$

The probability weights implied by the classical GMM estimation are provided in Back and Brown (1993). Brown and Newey (2002) argue that using the implied probabilities in bootstrapping may increase its efficiency. The usual resampling scheme is modified so that the original observation w_i is drawn with probability $\hat{p}_i$ rather than the conventional uniform weight $\frac{1}{n}$ implied by sampling from the empirical distribution. Of course, when some of the implied probabilities are negative, implementation of efficient bootstrapping is problematic.

2.2.4   Asymptotic Properties of GEL Estimators

Establishing the consistency and the rate of convergence of the GEL estimators $\hat{\theta}$ and $\hat{\lambda}$ involves some technical arguments and we refer the reader to Newey and Smith (2004) for details. Surprisingly, it is easier to derive the asymptotic distribution for the generalized EL estimator than for the basic EL estimator. Recall that

$$M = E \left[\frac{\partial m(w, \theta_0)}{\partial \theta'} \right]$$

denotes the "expected score" which is assumed to be of full rank k, and

$$V = E\left[m\left(w,\theta_0\right)m\left(w,\theta_0\right)'\right]$$

is the variance of the moment function which is assumed to be non-singular.

The usual tool for deriving the asymptotic distribution is a Taylor series expansion of the first-order conditions for the estimator under consideration. The first-order Taylor series expansion of (2.9) about (θ_0, λ_0), scaled by $\sqrt{n}$, is given by

$$\frac{1}{\sqrt{n}}\sum_{i=1}^{n}\frac{\partial\rho\left(\lambda_0'm\left(w_i,\theta_0\right)\right)}{\partial\theta} + \frac{1}{n}\sum_{i=1}^{n}\frac{\partial^2\rho\left(\lambda_0'm\left(w_i,\theta_0\right)\right)}{\partial\theta\partial\theta'}\sqrt{n}\left(\hat{\theta}-\theta_0\right)$$

$$+\frac{1}{n}\sum_{i=1}^{n}\frac{\partial\rho^2\left(\lambda_0'm\left(w_i,\theta_0\right)\right)}{\partial\theta\partial\lambda'}\sqrt{n}\left(\hat{\lambda}-\lambda_0\right) = o_P\left(1\right).$$

Because $\lambda_0 = 0$, the above expression simplifies to

$$\frac{1}{n}\sum_{i=1}^{n}\frac{\partial m\left(w_i,\theta_0\right)'}{\partial\theta}\sqrt{n}\,\hat{\lambda} = o_P\left(1\right)$$

using the property $\partial^2\rho(0)/\partial v^2 = -1$. Then, replacing $\frac{1}{n}\sum_{i=1}^{n}\partial m\left(w_i,\theta_0\right)'/\partial\theta$ by its population analog yields

$$M'\sqrt{n}\,\hat{\lambda} = o_P\left(1\right). \tag{2.11}$$

Similarly, the first-order Taylor series expansion of (2.10), scaled by $\sqrt{n}$, is given by

$$\frac{1}{\sqrt{n}}\sum_{i=1}^{n}\frac{\partial\rho\left(\lambda_0'm\left(w_i,\theta_0\right)\right)}{\partial\lambda} + \frac{1}{n}\sum_{i=1}^{n}\frac{\partial^2\rho\left(\lambda_0'm\left(w_i,\theta_0\right)\right)}{\partial\lambda\partial\theta'}\sqrt{n}\left(\hat{\theta}-\theta_0\right)$$

$$+\frac{1}{n}\sum_{i=1}^{n}\frac{\partial\rho^2\left(\lambda_0'm\left(w_i,\theta_0\right)\right)}{\partial\lambda\partial\lambda'}\sqrt{n}\left(\hat{\lambda}-\lambda_0\right) = o_P\left(1\right),$$

or

$$\frac{1}{\sqrt{n}}\sum_{i=1}^{n}m\left(w_i,\theta_0\right) + \frac{1}{n}\sum_{i=1}^{n}\frac{\partial m\left(w_i,\theta_0\right)}{\partial\theta'}\sqrt{n}\left(\hat{\theta}-\theta_0\right)$$

$$+\frac{1}{n}\sum_{i=1}^{n}m\left(w_i,\theta_0\right)m\left(w_i,\theta_0\right)'\sqrt{n}\,\hat{\lambda} = o_P\left(1\right)$$

using the properties $\partial\rho(0)/\partial v = \partial^2\rho(0)/\partial v^2 = -1$. Hence,

$$\frac{1}{\sqrt{n}}\sum_{i=1}^{n}m\left(w_i,\theta_0\right) + M\sqrt{n}\left(\hat{\theta}-\theta_0\right) + V\sqrt{n}\,\hat{\lambda} = o_P\left(1\right). \tag{2.12}$$

Finally, by premultiplying (2.12) by $M'V^{-1}$ and subtracting (2.11), we obtain

$$M'V^{-1}\frac{1}{\sqrt{n}}\sum_{i=1}^{n} m\left(w_i,\theta_0\right) + M'V^{-1}M\sqrt{n}\left(\hat{\theta}-\theta_0\right) = o_P\left(1\right),$$

or, by rearranging,

$$\sqrt{n}\left(\hat{\theta}-\theta_0\right) = -\left(M'V^{-1}M\right)^{-1} M'V^{-1}\frac{1}{\sqrt{n}}\sum_{i=1}^{n} m\left(w_i,\theta_0\right) + o_P\left(1\right). \quad (2.13)$$

Two remarkable facts about expression (2.13) are worth emphasizing. The first is the independence of this expansion of any objects related to the shape of $\rho\left(v\right)$. This means that all GEL estimators are asymptotically equivalent. The second notable feature is the asymptotic equivalence to the efficient GMM estimator which follows from the observation that the expansion in (2.13) is exactly the same as that for the GMM.

Invoking the CLT for $n^{-1/2}\sum_{i=1}^{n} m\left(w_i,\theta_0\right)$ in (2.13) yields the asymptotic normality of the GEL estimator of θ:

$$\sqrt{n}\left(\hat{\theta}-\theta_0\right) \overset{d}{\to} \mathcal{N}\left(0,\Omega_\theta\right),$$

where

$$\Omega_\theta = \left(M'V^{-1}M\right)^{-1}.$$

The asymptotic normality of the GEL estimator of λ can be obtained similarly. Premultiplying (2.12) by V^{-1}, plugging in the expansion (2.13) and rearranging, we have

$$\sqrt{n}\,\hat{\lambda} = -\left(V^{-1}-V^{-1}M\Omega_\theta M'V^{-1}\right)\frac{1}{\sqrt{n}}\sum_{i=1}^{n} m\left(w_i,\theta_0\right) + o_P\left(1\right). \quad (2.14)$$

Thus,

$$\sqrt{n}\,\hat{\lambda} \overset{d}{\to} \mathcal{N}\left(0,\Omega_\lambda\right),$$

where

$$\Omega_\lambda = V^{-1} - V^{-1}M\Omega_\theta M'V^{-1}.$$

Under exact identification, $\hat{\lambda}=0$ and Ω_λ is a null matrix. Under overidentification, the matrix Ω_λ has reduced rank $\ell-k$ even though it has dimensionality ℓ. This means that the elements of $\hat{\lambda}$ are asymptotically linearly dependent. Indeed, there are only $\ell - k$ pieces of information in the moment restrictions beyond the k identifying restrictions that are used in the estimation of θ.

Note also that premultiplying both sides of (2.14) by M' shows that $\sqrt{n}M'\hat{\lambda}$ has a degenerate asymptotic distribution. This implies that for a nonzero vector α which is in the span of the column space of M, the linear combination

$\alpha' \hat{\lambda}$ has a non-standard asymptotic distribution and rate of convergence. See Gospodinov, Kan and Robotti (2010) for deriving the appropriate limiting theory in a similar context.

Moreover, (2.13) and (2.14) imply

$$\text{cov}\left(\sqrt{n}(\hat{\theta} - \theta_0), \sqrt{n}\,\hat{\lambda}\right) = \left(M'V^{-1}M\right)^{-1} M'V^{-1}\text{var}\left(m\left(w, \theta_0\right)\right)$$
$$\times \left(V^{-1} - V^{-1}M\Omega_\theta M'V^{-1}\right) + o\left(1\right)$$
$$= o\left(1\right).$$

This means that the GEL estimators of θ_0 and λ_0 are asymptotically independent.

The asymptotic equivalence of EL estimation to GMM may seem somewhat surprising given the dimensionality of the original EL problem (2.1) where, in addition to θ and λ, the decision variables are n probability weights p_i. In cases when the number of parameters increases at the same rate as the sample size, the parametric estimators are typically inconsistent. Here, however, the equivalence of the original EL problem to the corresponding saddlepoint representation (2.5) allows consistent estimation of the parameters by reducing the original infinite-dimensional problem to a sequence of finite-dimensional problems. Moreover, the asymptotic independence between $\sqrt{n}(\hat{\theta} - \theta_0)$ and $\sqrt{n}\,\hat{\lambda}$ implies that the presence of the multipliers as auxiliary parameters in the optimization does not affect the efficiency of the parameter estimates.

Exercise 2.1. Derive the asymptotic distribution of the CDF estimator, defined in (2.7), that uses EL implied probabilities. Show that this estimator is asymptotically at least as efficient as the EDF.

2.2.5   GEL Asymptotic Tests

The standard asymptotics for the GEL estimators suggests that the usual tools for asymptotic inference about parameter restrictions (t- and Wald tests) and model specification ($\mathcal{J}$-test) should also be applicable in the GEL framework. However, the nonparametric likelihood interpretation of EL estimation provides alternative tests which are asymptotically equivalent to the conventional ones.

Tests of parameter restrictions can be developed inside the GEL framework by augmenting the GEL optimization problem with the (possibly nonlinear) parameter restriction $d(\theta) = 0$ for some continuous function $d(\cdot) : \mathbb{R}^k \rightarrow \mathbb{R}^q$, and solving the constrained GEL saddlepoint problem for the restricted estimators $\tilde{\theta}$ and $\tilde{\lambda}$ under the null hypothesis. Then, the distance metric (an analog of the likelihood ratio for MLE or the GMM distance metric) statistic is given by

$$\mathcal{DM} = 2\sum_{i=1}^{n}\left[\rho\left(\tilde{\lambda}' m(w_i, \tilde{\theta})\right) - \rho\left(\hat{\lambda}' m(w_i, \hat{\theta})\right)\right]$$

and is asymptotically distributed as χ_q^2. For a more detailed discussion on the asymptotic and finite sample properties of the $\mathcal{DM}$ statistic based on various members of the GEL class of estimators, see Gospodinov (2002, 2005).

For testing the null hypothesis $H_0 : E[m(w, \theta_0)] = 0$ of correct model specification, the likelihood ratio-type $\mathcal{GELR}$ test and the score-type $\mathcal{GELM}$ test are also available and provide an alternative to the Wald-type $\mathcal{J}$-test. For example, in the original EL problem, the maximized values of the nonparametric likelihood function with and without the moment restriction $\sum_{i=1}^{n} p_i m(w_i, \theta) = 0$ are given by

$$-n \log(n) - \sum_{i=1}^{n} \log\left(1 + \hat{\lambda}' m(w_i, \hat{\theta})\right)$$

and $-n \log(n)$, respectively. Hence, the empirical likelihood ratio is given by

$$\mathcal{ELR} = 2 \sum_{i=1}^{n} \log\left(1 + \hat{\lambda}' m(w_i, \hat{\theta})\right).$$

Generalizing the function $\log(1 - v)$ to a general $\rho(v)$, we obtain the generalized empirical likelihood ratio statistic

$$\mathcal{GELR} = 2 \sum_{i=1}^{n} \rho\left(\hat{\lambda}' m(w_i, \hat{\theta})\right).$$

It is straightforward to verify that under the null hypothesis of correct model specification, $\mathcal{GELR} \xrightarrow{d} \chi_{\ell-k}^2$. Moreover, $\mathcal{GELR}$ is asymptotically equivalent to the $\mathcal{J}$-type statistic

$$\mathcal{GELJ} = \sum_{i=1}^{n} m(w_i, \hat{\theta})' \left(\sum_{i=1}^{n} m(w_i, \hat{\theta}) m(w_i, \hat{\theta})'\right)^{-1} \sum_{i=1}^{n} m(w_i, \hat{\theta}).$$

In finite samples, it may prove beneficial if the weighting matrix in the middle is estimated using the GEL implied probabilities.

Finally, the GEL score test is constructed as

$$\mathcal{GELM} = n \hat{\lambda}' \hat{\Omega}_{\lambda}^{-} \hat{\lambda},$$

where $\hat{\Omega}_{\lambda}^{-}$ is the generalized inverse of a consistent estimate of Ω_{λ}. Under the null hypothesis of correct model specification, $\mathcal{GELM} \xrightarrow{d} \chi_{\ell-k}^2$ and is asymptotically equivalent to the $\mathcal{GELJ}$ statistic. An alternative to the use of the generalized inverse $\hat{\Omega}_{\lambda}^{-}$ is $\hat{V}$, which consistently estimates V. For details, see Smith (1997) and Imbens, Spady and Johnson (1998).

Exercise 2.2. Suppose that we want to test the joint hypothesis $\theta = \theta_0$ *and* the validity of the moment restrictions, i.e., $H_0 : E[m(w, \theta_0)] = 0$, using the EL estimator. Demonstrate that the criterion-based test of this joint hypothesis can be decomposed into the distance metric test of $\theta = \theta_0$ and the empirical likelihood ratio test of correct model specification. Then, show that the test statistic for this joint null hypothesis can be expressed as

$$\sum_{i=1}^{n} m(w_i, \theta_0)' \left(\sum_{i=1}^{n} m(w_i, \theta_0) m(w_i, \theta_0)' \right)^{-1} \sum_{i=1}^{n} m(w_i, \theta_0) + o_P(1).$$

Exercise 2.3. Show that under the null hypothesis of correct model specification, $\mathcal{GELR} \overset{d}{\to} \chi^2_{\ell-k}$ and $\mathcal{GELM} \overset{d}{\to} \chi^2_{\ell-k}$. Furthermore, show that under the null hypothesis of correct model specification, $\mathcal{GELR}$, $\mathcal{GELM}$, $\mathcal{GELJ}$ and their mentioned modifications are asymptotically equivalent.

2.2.6 Computational Issues

As we mentioned above, the estimation of k parameters θ, n probability weights p_i $(i = 1, ..., n)$ and ℓ Lagrange multipliers λ for the GEL problem may appear at first to be a daunting task. By contrast, the conventional two-step GMM estimator requires two optimizations over the k dimensional space of the parameter vector θ. The computational requirements of the GEL estimators can be one of the major obstacles for widespread use of these methods in empirical applications.

However, the computational implementation of the GEL may not be that difficult. For example, we already demonstrated that by concentrating out the probability weights p_i, the optimization problem is reduced, for a given function $\rho(\cdot)$, to the saddlepoint problem

$$\min_{\theta \in \Theta} \max_{\lambda \in \Lambda_n} \sum_{i=1}^{n} \rho\left(\lambda' m(w_i, \theta)\right)$$

which is of dimension $k + \ell$. This saddlepoint optimization can be conveniently separated into "inner maximization" and "outer minimization" problems, where the former is nested into the latter. In the inner loop, for a given θ, the maximization with respect to λ

$$\max_{\lambda} \sum_{i=1}^{n} \rho\left(\lambda' m(w_i, \theta)\right)$$

is globally concave and can be executed using derivative-based optimization procedures such as the Newton–Raphson algorithm. One difficulty that may arise, however, is the failure of the condition $\lambda' m(w_i, \theta) \in \Upsilon$ to be satisfied for all i, in which case the optimization problem has no feasible solution. One possibility is to impose this constraint directly in the above optimization, although several other recipes that deal with this problem are also available in the literature (see, for instance, Kitamura, 2007). An interesting feature of one member of the GEL class, the continuously updated GMM estimator, is that the above maximization renders a closed form expression for $\hat{\lambda}$ in terms of $m(w_i, \theta)$. This facilitates the computational problem considerably but it comes at the cost that the implicit probability weights can take negative values.

The outer minimization problem

$$\min_{\theta} \sum_{i=1}^{n} \rho\left(\hat{\lambda}(\theta)' m(w_i, \theta)\right),$$

where $\hat{\lambda}(\theta)$ denotes the maximizer from the inner loop, is more challenging due to the existence of multiple local minima. Some convergence and numerical problems may also arise due to possible singularities and the fact that the Hessian is not guaranteed to be positive definite. This instability of the GEL estimators is particularly worrisome in Monte Carlo studies when the parameter vector has to be estimated repeatedly for a large number of simulated samples. Despite these concerns, some recently developed algorithms and procedures would likely contribute to making the GEL a standard estimation approach in major econometric software toolboxes.

While the EL enjoys some appealing theoretical properties (see section 2.5 below), the structure of its objective function and first-order conditions raises some causes for concern. For example, as we showed in (2.3), the first-order conditions of the inner problem have the form

$$\frac{1}{n} \sum_{i=1}^{n} \frac{m(w_i, \hat{\theta})}{1 + \hat{\lambda}' m(w_i, \hat{\theta})} = 0,$$

and the denominator can approach zero with a nontrivial probability. This could be a particular problem in misspecified models as a small amount of misspecification makes the EL estimator numerically ill-behaved and leads to a breakdown in its asymptotic theory (Imbens, Spady and Johnson, 1998; Schennach, 2007). By contrast, the first-order conditions of the ET inner problem are given by

$$\frac{1}{n} \sum_{i=1}^{n} m(w_i, \hat{\theta}) \exp(\hat{\lambda}' m(w_i, \hat{\theta})) = 0,$$

and are expected to be better behaved due to the strict convexity of the function $\exp(\lambda' m(w_i, \theta))$ in λ and the nonsingularity of the ET influence function. For more details regarding the computational properties of the empirical likelihood and exponential tilting estimators, see Hansen (2009, Chapter 8), Imbens (2002) and Kitamura (2007).

2.3   Relation of GEL to Other Methods and Notions

2.3.1   GMM

It is important to stress that the first-order conditions for GEL and GMM estimators have the same form

$$\hat{M}'\hat{V}^{-1} \sum_{i=1}^{n} m(w_i, \hat{\theta}) = 0,$$

where $\hat{M}$ and $\hat{V}$ are consistent estimators of M and V. This leads, in particular, to the first-order asymptotic equivalence of the GMM and any GEL estimators derived above. The differences within the class of GEL estimators only arise in their higher-order asymptotic behavior, which we discuss in section 2.5 below and section 5.2.4 in Chapter 5. The higher-order asymptotic advantages of GEL estimators are usually attributed to their one-step nature as opposed to the multi-step nature of GMM.

2.3.2   Power Divergence

The GMM estimator may be viewed as minimizing the distance of the sample counterparts of the moment conditions $E[m(w, \theta)]$ from zero using a quadratic form in $E[m(w, \theta)|F_n] = \int m(w, \theta) dF_n(w)$, where $F_n(w)$ denotes the empirical measure of the sample that places a probability mass of $\frac{1}{n}$ on each data point.

Let P_n be another probability measure that assigns multinomial weights $\mathbf{p} = (p_1, p_2, ..., p_n)$ to each of the observations such that it satisfies exactly the moment conditions $E[m(w, \theta)|P_n] = \int m(w, \theta) dP_n = 0$. An alternative approach to estimation is to select from the set of distributions Φ that satisfy exactly the moment conditions, a probability measure P_n closest to the empirical measure F_n in the sense of the Cressie and Read (1984) *power divergence criterion*

$$D_\delta(F_n, P_n) = \frac{2}{\delta(1+\delta)} \sum_{i=1}^{n} p_i \left((np_i)^\delta - 1\right),$$

where δ is a fixed scalar parameter that determines the shape of the criterion function. Thus, the estimator is defined as the solution to

$$\min_{P_n \in \Phi, \theta \in \Theta} D_\delta(F_n, P_n) \qquad (2.15)$$

subject to

$$E[m(w, \theta)|P_n] = \int m(w, \theta) dP_n(w) = 0. \qquad (2.16)$$

This form of the analogy principle maps the empirical distribution function onto the space of feasible distribution functions and chooses the probability measure that is most likely to have generated the observed data subject to the moment conditions (Manski, 1988).

The solution to the constrained optimization problem (2.15)–(2.16) is a straightforward application of the Lagrange multiplier principle. In particular, if we let δ approach 0, the solution to the problem

$$\min_{\mathbf{p},\theta} -\frac{2}{n}\sum_{i=1}^{n}\log\left(np_i\right) \tag{2.17}$$

subject to

$$\sum_{i=1}^{n}p_im\left(w_i,\theta\right)=0 \text{ and } \sum_{i=1}^{n}p_i=1 \tag{2.18}$$

is the empirical likelihood estimator. Similarly, the case of $\delta \to -1$ gives rise to the exponential tilting estimator .

Another estimator from this class, known as the Euclidean likelihood estimator, can be obtained for $\delta \to -2$ and is given by the argument that solves

$$\min_{\mathbf{p},\theta} \frac{1}{n}\sum_{i=1}^{n}(n^2p_i^2-1) \tag{2.19}$$

subject to (2.18). The Lagrangian for this problem, divided by 2 for convenience, is given by

$$\frac{1}{2n}\sum_{i=1}^{n}(n^2p_i^2-1)-\lambda'\sum_{i=1}^{n}p_im\left(w_i,\theta\right)-\mu\left(\sum_{i=1}^{n}p_i-1\right),$$

and the first-order condition with respect to p_i has the form

$$np_i-\lambda'm\left(w_i,\theta\right)-\mu=0. \tag{2.20}$$

Taking averages of both sides yields $\mu=1-\lambda'm_n(\theta)$, where $m_n(\theta)=n^{-1}\sum_{i=1}^{n}m\left(w_i,\theta\right)$. Substituting for μ into (2.20) and solving for p_i gives

$$p_i=\frac{1+\lambda'\left(m\left(w_i,\theta\right)-m_n(\theta)\right)}{n}. \tag{2.21}$$

Next, after plugging the expression for p_i into (2.19), the first-order conditions of the resulting criterion function with respect to λ and θ are given by

$$\sum_{t=1}^{n}\frac{1+\lambda'\left(m\left(w_i,\theta\right)-m_n(\theta)\right)}{n}\left(\begin{array}{c}m(w_i,\theta)\\\frac{\partial m\left(w_i,\theta\right)'}{\partial\theta}\lambda\end{array}\right)=0. \tag{2.22}$$

From the first ℓ equations in (2.22) it follows that

$$\lambda=-\left(\sum_{i=1}^{n}\left(m\left(w_i,\theta\right)-m_n(\theta)\right)\left(m\left(w_i,\theta\right)-m_n(\theta)\right)'\right)^{-1} \tag{2.23}$$

$$\times\sum_{i=1}^{n}m\left(w_i,\theta\right).$$

Finally, substituting expression (2.23) into the bottom k equations of (2.22) delivers the first-order conditions for the Euclidean likelihood estimator of θ

$$\sum_{i=1}^{n} p_i \frac{\partial m\left(w_i, \theta\right)'}{\partial \theta} \left(\sum_{i=1}^{n} \left(m\left(w_i, \theta\right) - m_n(\theta)\right)\left(m\left(w_i, \theta\right) - m_n(\theta)\right)'\right)^{-1} \quad (2.24)$$

$$\times \sum_{i=1}^{n} m\left(w_i, \theta\right) = 0,$$

where p_i is given in (2.21). Similarly, substituting (2.23) for λ in expression (2.21) for p_i and then plugging back into the objective function (2.19) yields

$$m_n(\theta)' V_n^{-1}(\theta) m_n(\theta), \quad (2.25)$$

where

$$V_n(\theta) = \frac{1}{n} \sum_{i=1}^{n} \left(m\left(w_i, \theta\right) - m_n(\theta)\right)\left(m\left(w_i, \theta\right) - m_n(\theta)\right)'.$$

Hence, (2.25) and (2.24) are the objective function and the first-order conditions of the CU estimator, discussed in section 1.2.2 of Chapter 1, with the only difference that the weighting matrix is computed from the demeaned moment conditions.

2.3.3   Kullback–Leibler Information Criterion

The *Kullback–Leibler Information Criterion (KLIC)* measures the distance between two distributions, say $f_1(w)$ and $f_2(w)$:

$$\mathcal{KLIC}(f_1 : f_2) = E_{f_1}\left[\log \frac{f_1(w)}{f_2(w)}\right],$$

where $E_{f_1}[\cdot]$ denotes the mathematical expectation with respect to $f_1(w)$. For more discussion on KLIC, see Chapter 4.

Let $\mathbf{e}$ denote the empirical distribution function and $\mathbf{p}$ be the usual discrete distribution that assigns probability p_i to the sample point w_i, $i = 1, \ldots, n$. It is straightforward to check that the minimization of $\mathcal{KLIC}(\mathbf{e} : \mathbf{p})$ subject to $\sum_{i=1}^{n} p_i m(w_i, \theta) = 0$ and $\sum_{i=1}^{n} p_i = 1$ yields the empirical likelihood estimator of θ and the corresponding EL implied probabilities. Indeed, minimizing

$$\mathcal{KLIC}(\mathbf{e} : \mathbf{p}) = E_{\mathbf{e}}\left[\log \frac{\mathbf{e}}{\mathbf{p}}\right] = \sum_{i=1}^{n} \frac{1}{n} \log \frac{1}{n p_i}$$

is equivalent to the maximization of $\sum_{i=1}^{n} \log p_i$ which gives the EL estimator.

If we now switch the roles of $\mathbf{e}$ and $\mathbf{p}$ and consider the minimization of $\mathcal{KLIC}(\mathbf{p} : \mathbf{e})$ subject to the same constraints, this will deliver the exponential tilting estimator of θ and the corresponding implied probabilities. One can verify that minimizing

$$\mathcal{KLIC}(\mathbf{p}:\mathbf{e}) = E_{\mathbf{p}} \left[\log \frac{\mathbf{p}}{\mathbf{e}} \right] = \sum_{i=1}^{n} p_i \log \frac{p_i}{1/n}$$

yields the ET estimator (Kitamura and Stutzer, 1997).

2.4   GEL for Time Series Data

Suppose now that $\{w_t\}_{t=1}^{n}$ is an observable segment of a strictly stationary and ergodic time series. When $m(w_t, \theta_0)$ is serially uncorrelated, it is easy to see, using similar asymptotic arguments as before, that the basic GEL still works and is asymptotically equivalent to the efficient GMM. The downside is that the GEL probabilities $\hat{p}_t$ lose the property of being a full characterization of the joint distribution of the data as they do not reflect the time dependence structure. For example, they can no longer be used for efficient bootstrapping, although they still can be employed to construct an improved estimate of the marginal (unconditional) distribution of one observation.

When $m(w_t, \theta_0)$ is serially correlated, the derivation of the asymptotics and hence the asymptotic equivalence to the efficient GMM break down. Indeed, the last term on the left-hand side in (2.12) is $E\left[m(w_t, \theta_0) m(w_t, \theta_0)'\right] \sqrt{n}\,\hat{\lambda}$ while in the case of serially correlated $m(w_t, \theta_0)$ it should be $V\sqrt{n}\,\hat{\lambda}$, where $V = \sum_{j=-\infty}^{+\infty} E\left[m(w_t, \theta_0) m(w_{t-j}, \theta_0)'\right]$ is now the long-run variance. This mismatch leads to a "big sandwich" form of the asymptotic variance, to asymptotic correlatedness between the GEL estimator and GEL multipliers, and hence to asymptotic inefficiency of the former.

The literature has several suggestions how to modify the GEL estimator. Imbens (1997) proposed adjusting for the asymptotic correlation between $\hat{\theta}$ and $\hat{\lambda}$ to attain asymptotic efficiency:

$$\tilde{\theta} = \hat{\theta} - \widehat{\text{cov}}(\hat{\theta}, \hat{\lambda})\widehat{\text{var}}(\hat{\lambda})^{-1}\hat{\lambda},$$

where $\widehat{\text{var}}(\hat{\lambda})$ and $\widehat{\text{cov}}(\hat{\theta}, \hat{\lambda})$ are consistent estimates of the blocks of the asymptotic variance matrix of $(\hat{\theta}', \hat{\lambda}')'$. The implementation of this approach is straightforward but it results in a multi-step estimator, losing the attractiveness of the GEL approach.

Another approach also proposed in Imbens (1997) is applicable when the order of serial correlation is finite and known, say p. The first-order conditions

(2.9)–(2.10) are modified as follows:

$$\frac{1}{n}\sum_{t=1}^{n}\frac{\partial\rho\left(\hat{\lambda}'m^{\sigma}(w_t,\hat{\theta})\right)}{\partial v}\frac{\partial m(w_t,\hat{\theta})'}{\partial\theta}\hat{\lambda}=0,$$

$$\frac{1}{n}\sum_{t=1}^{n}\frac{\partial\rho\left(\hat{\lambda}'m^{\sigma}(w_t,\hat{\theta})\right)}{\partial v}m(w_t,\hat{\theta})=0,$$

where

$$m^{\sigma}\left(w_t,\theta\right)=\sum_{j=-p}^{p}m\left(w_{t-j},\theta\right)$$

is the moment function summed over the neighboring $2p$ periods.[1] This correction is distantly reminiscent of the Hansen–Hodrick (1980) HAC variance estimation (see also section 1.3 in Chapter 1). A serious drawback of this modification is that the modified system does not correspond to an optimization problem like (2.8).

A more elegant and universal solution suggested in Kitamura (1997), Kitamura and Stutzer (1997) and Smith (1997, 2000) is in the spirit of the Andrews (1991) HAC variance estimation (see section 1.3 in Chapter 1). The moment function is smoothed from the outset:

$$m_t^{\omega}\left(\theta\right)=\sum_{j=t-n}^{t-1}\omega\left(j\right)m\left(w_{t-j},\theta\right),$$

where the system of weights is such that

$$\sum_{j=-\infty}^{\infty}\omega\left(j\right)=1,\quad\omega\left(j\right)=\frac{1}{b}K\left(\frac{j}{b}\right),$$

$K\left(u\right)$ is a symmetric, continuously differentiable kernel function from $(-\infty, +\infty)$ to $\mathbb{R}$ with $K(0)\neq 0$ and $\int K\left(u\right)du=1$, and b is a bandwidth such that $b\to\infty$ as $n\to\infty$ with a suitable rate. Then, $m_t^{\omega}\left(\theta\right)$ is used in place of $m\left(w_t,\theta\right)$ in the saddle point problem for the *smoothed generalized empirical likelihood (SGEL) estimator* $\hat{\theta}_{SGEL}$ and the associated $\ell\times 1$ vector of *SGEL multipliers* $\hat{\lambda}_{SGEL}$

$$\min_{\theta\in\Theta}\quad\sup_{\lambda:\,\lambda'm_t^{\omega}\in\Upsilon}\sum_{t=1}^{n}\rho\left(\lambda'm_t^{\omega}\left(\theta\right)\right).$$

It turns out that the sample moments have the following asymptotic limits:

$$\frac{b}{\int K\left(u\right)^2 du}\frac{1}{n}\sum_{t=1}^{n}m_t^{\omega}\left(\theta_0\right)m_t^{\omega}\left(\theta_0\right)'\xrightarrow{p}V$$

---

[1] If an index of some component of a summand is beyond the sample limits, the entire summand is dropped.

and

$$\frac{1}{n} \sum_{t=1}^{n} \frac{\partial m_t^{\omega}(\theta_0)}{\partial \theta'} \xrightarrow{p} M.$$

Due to the match (up to a multiplicative constant) between the sample variance of the smoothed moment function and the long-run variance of the original moment function, the SGEL estimator is asymptotically equivalent to
efficient GMM. The asymptotics for the SGEL multipliers is now given by

$$\left(\int K(u)^2 \, du \right) \frac{\sqrt{n}}{b} \hat{\lambda} \xrightarrow{d} \mathcal{N}(0, \Omega_\lambda),$$

i.e., $\hat{\lambda}$ has a lower rate of convergence than under random sampling. The
specification tests $\mathcal{GELR}$ and $\mathcal{GELM}$ that use the asymptotics for $\hat{\lambda}$ should,
of course, be modified; see Smith (1997). For example,

$$\mathcal{GELM} = \left(\int K(u)^2 \, du \right)^2 \frac{n}{b^2} \hat{\lambda}' \hat{\Omega}_\lambda^- \hat{\lambda}.$$

As in HAC variance estimation, in the smoothed GEL approach one cannot
take advantage of the serial correlation structure of the moment function
(such as finite order serial correlation), and instead has to act as if the serial
correlation structure was of unknown form. Another unappealing feature of
SGEL is the need to choose a value for the bandwidth. However, it exhibits a
serious advantage in its higher-order asymptotic properties (see section 2.5.2
below).

2.5   Bias Properties of Method of Moments Estimators

As we have already noted, all members of the GEL class and various versions of the GMM estimator have identical asymptotic properties. However,
in finite samples, they are expected to exhibit different behavior arising, for
instance, from the one-step and multi-step nature of different methods. Newey
and Smith (2004) suggest assessing the biasedness of the estimators by looking
at how many terms compose the analytical expressions of their second-order
asymptotic biases (see Chapter 5 for the tools of higher-order asymptotic
analysis), and even more importantly, the precise manner in which their magnitude is related to the number of moment restrictions in the model. However,
as Anatolyev (2008) shows in the context of a stylized consumption-based
capital asset pricing model, the overall bias of different estimators may also
depend crucially on the signs and numerical values of separate bias components. Nevertheless, this approach allows us to provide useful insights as the
number of terms is a good, albeit imperfect, indication of some general ten-
dencies prevailing in the biasedness properties of estimators. Ramalho (2005)

presents a Monte Carlo study of small sample biases of various GMM and GEL estimators for models of covariance structures.

2.5.1   *IID* Case

Under random sampling, Newey and Smith (2004) derive higher-order asymptotic biases of GMM and GEL estimators which have interesting practical implications. Newey and Smith (2004) show that the second-order asymptotic bias has the following components:

$$B_{GMM} = B_0 + B_V + B_M,$$

$$B_{GEL} = B_0 + \left(1 + \frac{1}{2}\frac{\partial^3 \rho(0)}{\partial v^3}\right) B_V,$$

where

$$B_0 = \Omega_\theta M' V^{-1} \left(E\left[\frac{\partial m(w,\theta_0)}{\partial \theta'}\Omega_\theta M' V^{-1} m(w,\theta_0)\right] \right.$$

$$\left. - \sum_{j=1}^{k} E\left[\frac{\partial^2 m(w,\theta_0)}{\partial \theta' \partial \theta_j}\frac{\Omega_\theta}{2}\iota_j\right]\right),$$

$$B_V = \Omega_\theta M' V^{-1} E\left[m(w,\theta_0)m(w,\theta_0)'\Omega_\lambda m(w,\theta_0)\right],$$

$$B_M = -\Omega_\theta E\left[\frac{\partial m(w,\theta_0)'}{\partial \theta}\Omega_\lambda m(w,\theta_0)\right].$$

Here, it is assumed that the GMM estimator is iterated or is run through at least three iterations, and ι_j is the jth unit vector.

The sources of these bias components are the following (hence the notation): B_0 arises from estimation of θ from the optimal exactly identifying moment restrictions $E\left[M'V^{-1}m(w,\theta_0)\right] = 0$ and cannot be dispensed with, B_M arises from estimation of M, and B_V arises from estimation of V. Newey and Smith (2004) establish that in a linear instrumental variables model, the term B_M is proportional to the number of moment restrictions ℓ (see the results of section 5.2.3.2 in Chapter 5). One practical implication is that when instruments are in abundant supply (e.g., in problems formulated as conditional moment restrictions), a researcher should not select too many of them in GMM estimation in order to prevent inflating the bias. Another implication is that the class of GEL estimators is preferable to GMM because the component B_M is absent in the second-order asymptotic bias of GEL.

Note also that the basic EL estimator corresponding to $\rho(v) = \log(1-v)$ has no bias component associated with B_V. As we mentioned above, the number of terms in the expression for the second-order asymptotic bias may serve as a (rough) measure of the biasedness of various estimators. According to this criterion, the EL estimator appears to be the best and the GMM estimator to be the worst, with the other GEL estimators (including CU) falling in the middle.

Newey and Smith (2004) give the following interpretation of the sources of these biases. The first-order conditions for GEL estimators can be expressed in the following form:

$$\sum_{i=1}^{n} \hat{p}_i \frac{\partial m(w_i, \hat{\theta})'}{\partial \theta} \left(\sum_{i=1}^{n} \hat{\pi}_i m(w_i, \hat{\theta}) m(w_i, \hat{\theta})' \right)^{-1} \sum_{i=1}^{n} m(w_i, \hat{\theta}) = 0.$$

The use of the GEL probabilities $\hat{p}_i$ in the first term renders the estimate of the Jacobian M efficient, which results in the absence of B_M-type biases for GEL. The second term is an estimate of the variance V using the weights $\hat{\pi}_i$ which are equal to $\hat{p}_i$ in the case of EL and are generally different for other GEL members. As a consequence, the B_V-type biases are absent in EL but present in most of the other GEL estimators. In contrast, the first-order conditions for the GMM estimators (see section 1.2.2 of Chapter 1) are similar in form but use EDF probabilities $\frac{1}{n}$ in both terms; hence, the presence of both B_M and B_V type biases for GMM. Donald and Newey (2000) suggest a similar explanation based on the orthogonality between the moments and the residuals in certain auxiliary regressions.

2.5.2 Time Series Case

For time series models, Anatolyev (2005) derives the second-order asymptotic biases for the GEL and GMM classes of estimators. It turns out that they have a similar, although more complex, structure, but with some important specifics. In particular,

$$B_{SGEL} = B_0^{\omega} + \left(1 + \frac{1}{2} \frac{\partial^3 \rho(0)}{\partial v^3} \frac{\int K(x)^3 \, dx}{\left(\int K(r)^2 \, dr \right)^2} \right) B_V^{\omega},$$

where B_0^{ω} and B_V^{ω} now contain long-run covariances instead of regular ones. Hence, even for the smoothed EL, the bias expression contains the component associated with B_V^{ω} unless the kernel is rectangular. Anatolyev (2005) gives an interpretation of the sources of various bias components in the spirit of Donald and Newey (2000).

Another important observation is that even when there is no serial correlation and no smoothing is done in GEL (including CU), the term B_M^{ω}, which is the time series analog of B_M, appears in B_{GEL}. Hence, it is preferable to run smoothed GEL even when there is no serial correlation in the moment function and hence there is no need to smooth. In the case of GMM though, smoothing does not eliminate B_M^{ω}.

Let us consider an illustrative instrumental variables model

$$y_t = \theta_0 x_t + \varepsilon_t,$$

where ε_t is $IID(0,1)$, and the scalar parameter θ_0 is identified by a strictly exogenous $\ell \times 1$ vector of zero-mean instruments z_t following a restricted VAR(1) $z_t = \alpha z_{t-1} + \xi_t$ with IID innovations that are serially independent of ε_t. Let x_t be represented as $x_t = \gamma' z_t + \sum_{i=-\infty}^{+\infty} \phi^{|i|} \varepsilon_{t-i}$. Then, following Anatolyev (2005), it can be shown that

$$(B_M^\omega)_{GMM} = \frac{\ell - 1}{\gamma' V \gamma} \frac{1 + \alpha\phi}{1 - \alpha\phi},$$

$$(B_M^\omega)_{EL} = \frac{\ell - 1}{\gamma' V \gamma} \frac{2\alpha\phi}{1 - \alpha\phi}$$

and

$$(B_M^\omega)_{SEL} = 0.$$

These expressions suggest that the bias component for the GMM and non-smoothed EL estimators is proportional to the number of instruments ℓ and can become sizable when ℓ is large. To gain some further insight, assume that $\gamma' V \gamma$ remains unchanged as ℓ varies. In this case, it is possible that the numerical value of $(B_M^\omega)_{GMM}$ can exceed substantially $(B_M^\omega)_{EL}$ in absolute value: for instance, when $\alpha = \phi = \frac{1}{3}$, the difference is fivefold. However, if both α and ϕ are close to one in absolute value but have different signs (which is somewhat unlikely to happen with economic data), the magnitude of the GMM bias can be numerically tiny because the different components offset each other almost completely, while that expression for the non-smoothed EL can be quite large.

2.5.3   Hybrid Estimators

By combining the EL objective function and ET probability weights, Schennach (2007) proposes a modification called *exponentially tilted empirical likelihood* (ETEL). This estimator preserves the superior higher-order properties of the EL estimator, including its minimal bias and third-order asymptotic efficiency. At the same time, due to the positivity of the ET implied probabilities, the estimator enjoys the computational advantages of ET and proves helpful whenever positive probability weights are important (e.g., in efficient bootstrapping). Furthermore, in contrast to the EL estimator, the asymptotic properties of the ETEL estimator are shown not to degrade and the implied probabilities remain positive when the system of moment restrictions is misspecified.

In an IID environment, Antoine, Bonnal and Renault (2007) suggest using the CU implied probabilities to correct the GMM first-order conditions so that the asymptotic expansion of the resulting estimator coincides with that for the EL problem. In a somewhat similar vein, Guay and Pelgrin (2007) construct a new estimator in time series context that replaces the GMM implied probabilities (Back and Brown, 1993) with EL implied probabilities for the sake of improving the higher-order asymptotic properties of the CU and other GMM estimators. The estimators proposed in these articles are three-step estimators.

2.6 Appendix: Solutions to Selected Exercises

Exercise 2.1. For the EL, the efficient CDF estimate is

$$\hat{F}(u) = \frac{1}{n} \sum_{i=1}^{n} \hat{p}_i \mathbb{I} \{w_i \leq u\},$$

where $\hat{p}_i = p_i(\hat{\theta}, \hat{\lambda})$, and

$$p_i(\theta, \lambda) = \frac{1}{n} \frac{1}{1 - \lambda' m(w_i, \theta)}.$$

To derive the asymptotics, let us take a first-order Taylor expansion of the estimate $\hat{F}(\cdot)$ about $(\theta_0, 0)$

$$\hat{F}(u) = \sum_{i=1}^{n} p_i(\theta_0, 0) \mathbb{I} \{w_i \leq u\} + \left(\sum_{i=1}^{n} \frac{\partial p_i(\theta_0, 0)}{\partial \theta'} \mathbb{I} \{w_i \leq u\} \right) \left(\hat{\theta} - \theta_0 \right)$$

$$+ \left(\sum_{i=1}^{n} \frac{\partial p_i(\theta_0, 0)}{\partial \lambda'} \mathbb{I} \{w_i \leq u\} \right) \hat{\lambda} + o_P \left(\frac{1}{n^{1/2}} \right).$$

The first term is simply the EDF. The derivatives of $p_i(\theta, \lambda)$, evaluated at the true parameter values, are

$$\frac{\partial p_i(\theta_0, 0)}{\partial \theta'} = \frac{1}{n} \frac{1}{(1 - \lambda' m(w_i, \theta))^2} \lambda' \frac{\partial m(w_i, \theta)}{\partial \theta'} \bigg|_{\theta = \theta_0, \lambda = 0} = 0,$$

$$\frac{\partial p_i(\theta_0, 0)}{\partial \lambda'} = \frac{1}{n} \frac{1}{(1 - \lambda' m(w_i, \theta))^2} m(w_i, \theta)' \bigg|_{\theta = \theta_0, \lambda = 0} = \frac{1}{n} m(w_i, \theta_0)'.$$

Hence, plugging these expressions into the expansion for $\hat{F}(u)$, we obtain

$$\sqrt{n} \left(\hat{F}(u) - F(u) \right) = \frac{1}{\sqrt{n}} \sum_{i=1}^{n} (\mathbb{I} \{w_i \leq u\} - F(u))$$

$$+ \left(\frac{1}{n} \sum_{i=1}^{n} m(w_i, \theta_0) \mathbb{I} \{w_i \leq u\} \right)' \sqrt{n} \hat{\lambda} + o_P(1).$$

We already know that

$$\sqrt{n}\,\hat{\lambda} = -\Omega_\lambda \frac{1}{\sqrt{n}} \sum_{i=1}^{n} m\,(w_i, \theta_0) + o_P(1).$$

In order to proceed, we need the joint asymptotics for the averages of $\mathbb{I}\,\{w_i \le u\}$ $- F(u)$ and $m\,(w_i, \theta_0)$ which is given by

$$\frac{1}{\sqrt{n}} \sum_{i=1}^{n} \begin{pmatrix} \mathbb{I}\,\{w_i \le u\} - F(u) \\ m\,(w_i, \theta_0) \end{pmatrix} \xrightarrow{d} \mathcal{N} \left(0, \begin{bmatrix} F(u)\,(1 - F(u)) & \mu(u)' \\ \mu(u) & V \end{bmatrix} \right),$$

where $\mu(u) = \mathbb{E}\,[m\,(w, \theta_0)\,\mathbb{I}\,\{w \le u\}]$. Summarizing,

$$\sqrt{n}\left(\hat{F}(u) - F(u)\right) = \frac{1}{\sqrt{n}} \sum_{i=1}^{n} (\mathbb{I}\,\{w_i \le u\} - F(u))$$

$$-\mu(u)'\Omega_\lambda \frac{1}{\sqrt{n}} \sum_{i=1}^{n} m\,(w_i, \theta_0) + o_P(1)$$

$$\xrightarrow{d} \mathcal{N}\,(0, F(u)\,(1 - F(u)) - \mu(u)'\Omega_\lambda \mu(u)),$$

using that $\Omega_\lambda V \Omega_\lambda = \Omega_\lambda$. The estimator is indeed at least as efficient as the empirical distribution function because $\mu(u)'\Omega_\lambda \mu(u)$ is non-negative.

References

Anatolyev, S. (2005) GMM, GEL, serial correlation and asymptotic bias. *Econometrica*, 73, 983–1002.

Anatolyev, S. (2008) Method-of-moments estimation and choice of instruments: numerical computations. *Economics Letters*, 100, 217–220.

Andrews, D.W.K. (1991) Heteroskedasticity and autocorrelation consistent covariance matrix estimation. *Econometrica*, 59, 817–858.

Antoine, B., H. Bonnal and E. Renault (2007) On the efficient use of the informational content of estimating equations: Implied probabilities and Euclidean empirical likelihood. *Journal of Econometrics*, 138, 461–487.

Back, K., and D.P. Brown (1993) Implied probabilities in GMM estimators. *Econometrica*, 61, 971–975.

Brown, B.W., and W.K. Newey (2002) Generalized method of moments, efficient bootstrapping, and improved inference. *Journal of Business and Economic Statistics*, 20, 507–517.

Cressie, N., and T. Read (1984) Multinomial goodness-of-fit test. *Journal of the Royal Statistical Society, Series B*, 46, 440–464.

Donald, S., and W. K. Newey (2000) A jackknife interpretation of the continuous updating estimator. *Economics Letters*, 67, 239–243.

Gospodinov, N. (2002) Improved finite-sample inference in overidentified models with weak instruments. In: Y.P. Chaubey (ed.), *Recent Advances in Statistical Methods*, Imperial College Press: London, 132–146.

Gospodinov, N. (2005) Robust asymptotic inference in autoregressive models with martingale difference errors. *Econometric Reviews*, 24, 59–81.

Gospodinov, N., R. Kan and C. Robotti (2010) Further results on the limiting distribution of GMM sample moment conditions. Working Paper 2010-11, Federal Reserve Bank of Atlanta.

Guay, A., and F. Pelgrin (2007) Using implied probabilities to improve estimation with unconditional moment restrictions. Manuscript, Université du Québec à Montréal.

Hansen, B.E. (2009) *Econometrics*. Manuscript, University of Wisconsin, Madison.

Hansen, L.P., J. Heaton and A. Yaron (1996) Finite-sample properties of some alternative GMM estimators. *Journal of Business and Economic Statistics*, 14, 262–280.

Hansen, L.P., and R.J. Hodrick (1980) Forward exchange rates as optimal predictors of future spot rates: An econometric analysis. *Journal of Political Economy*, 88, 829–853.

Imbens, G.W. (1997) One-step estimators for over-identified generalized method of moments models. *Review of Economic Studies*, 64, 359–383.

Imbens, G.W. (2002) Generalized method of moments and empirical likelihood. *Journal of Business and Economic Statistics*, 20, 493–506.

Imbens, G.W., R.H. Spady and P. Johnson (1998) Information theoretic approaches to inference in moment condition models. *Econometrica*, 66, 333–357.

Kitamura, Y. (1997) Empirical likelihood methods with weakly dependent processes. *Annals of Statistics*, 25, 2084–2102.

Kitamura, Y. (2007) Empirical likelihood methods in econometrics: Theory and practice. In: R.W. Blundell, W.K. Newey and T. Persson (eds.), *Advances in Economics and Econometrics: Theory and Applications*, Ninth World Congress, Vol. 3, Econometric Society Monograph Series, ESM 43, Cambrdige University Press: Cambrdige, 174–237.

Kitamura, Y., and M. Stutzer (1997) An information-theoretic alternative to generalized method of moments estimation. *Econometrica*, 65, 861–874.

Manski, C.F. (1988) *Analog Estimation Methods in Econometrics*. Chapman and Hall: New York.

Mittelhammer, R.C., G.G. Judge and D.J. Miller (2000) *Econometric Foundations*. Cambridge University Press: Cambridge.

Newey, W.K., and R.J. Smith (2004) Higher order properties of GMM and generalized empirical likelihood estimators. *Econometrica*, 72, 219–255.

Owen, A. (2001) *Empirical Likelihood*. Chapman and Hall/CRC: New York.

Qin, J., and J. Lawless (1994) Empirical likelihood and general estimating equations. *Annals of Statistics*, 22, 300–325.

Ramalho, J.J.S. (2005) Small sample bias of alternative estimation methods for moment condition models: Monte Carlo evidence for covariance structures. *Studies in Nonlinear Dynamics & Econometrics*, 9:1, article 3.

Schennach, S.M. (2007) Point estimation with exponentially tilted empirical likelihood. *Annals of Statistics*, 35, 634–672.

Smith, R.J. (1997) Alternative semi-parametric likelihood approaches to generalized method of moments estimation. *Economic Journal*, 107, 503–519.

Smith, R.J. (2000) Empirical likelihood estimation and inference. In: P. Marriott and M. Salmon (eds.), *Applications of Differential Geometry to Econometrics*, Cambridge University Press: Cambridge, 119–150.

Chapter 3

Estimation of Models Defined by Conditional Moment Restrictions

3.1 Introduction

As we argued in Chapter 1, most of the dynamic economic models based on optimizing behavior are defined in terms of a set of conditional moment restrictions of the form $E[h(y, x, \theta_0)|z] = 0$. However, the law of iterated expectations is often applied to the population conditional moment restrictions to obtain an unconditional moment restriction of the form $E[\Psi(z) h(y, x, \theta_0)] = 0$, where $\Psi(z)$ is usually chosen in an arbitrary manner or is restricted by data availability, and this unconditional moment restriction is subsequently used for GMM estimation. If $\Psi(z)$ is not selected using optimality considerations, such as attaining the lower asymptotic variance bound, this approach will result in efficiency losses. As a consequence, a substantial research effort has been directed towards finding and operationalizing the matrix of optimal instruments $\Xi(z)$ so that the asymptotic variance of the method of moments estimator attains the semiparametric efficiency bound. The first part of this chapter is devoted to derivation of optimal instruments and their operationalization for both linear and nonlinear models.

In addition to efficiency considerations, exploiting fully the information in conditional moment restrictions may also have important implications for the consistency of the estimator. This observation has spurred a new interest in developing parameter estimators in models defined by conditional moment restrictions that are consistent and asymptotically efficient. Some of the estimators are based on feasible procedures for estimating explicitly the matrix of optimal instruments for a finite number or a continuum of moment conditions. Other methods operate directly on the conditional moment restriction and achieve efficiency by implicit estimation of the optimal instruments. While most of these approaches are asymptotically equivalent, they vary substantially in terms of their initial motivation, finite sample properties and the degree of numerical complexity and computation. These recent approaches are discussed in the second part of this chapter.

3.2 Optimal Instruments

It is often the case that an econometric model implies a large set of instruments which can be bigger than what is sufficient for identifying the parameters of interest. In this situation, it seems natural to try to combine all information into an *optimal instrument* in order to get the highest possible precision of estimation. This section reviews the approach of optimal instrumentation. More complete surveys of the literature on optimal instruments and related methods can be found in Hall (2005) and Anatolyev (2006).

3.2.1 Instruments and Optimality Condition

Consider the linear instrumental variables (IV) model:

$$y_t = x_t'\theta_0 + e_t, \quad E\left[e_t|\Im_t\right] = 0, \tag{3.1}$$

where x_t is a $k \times 1$ vector of explanatory variables and $\Im_t$ denotes the information set that contains information embedded in an $\ell \times 1$ vector of instruments z_t. When the data are IID, $\Im_t$ contains simply z_t. When the variables are stationary time series, $\Im_t$ contains information in z_t and all of its history $z_{t-1}, z_{t-2}, \ldots$. Typically z_t includes x_t and lags of y_t of certain order q. If the lag order is $q = 1$, the problem (3.1) is called *single-period*; otherwise (when $q > 1$), it is called *multiperiod*.

The instruments z_t are called *basic*, as opposed to those that can be generated by taking functions of z_t and its lags. If the data are IID, the maximal set of *allowable instruments* is $\mathcal{Z}_t = \{\varsigma_t : \varsigma_t = f(z_t)$ for some measurable $f\}$. In time series context, any stationary $\Im_t$-measurable $k \times 1$ vector ς_t with a finite fourth moment is a valid instrument, so the maximal set of allowable instruments is $\mathcal{Z}_t = \{\varsigma_t : \varsigma_t = f(z_t, z_{t-1}, \ldots)$ for some measurable $f\}$. Note that, without loss of generality, we consider only exactly identifying instruments. The IV estimator corresponding to $\varsigma_t \in \mathcal{Z}_t$ is given by

$$\hat{\theta}_\varsigma = \left(\sum_{t=1}^{n} \hat{\varsigma}_t x_t'\right)^{-1} \sum_{t=1}^{n} \hat{\varsigma}_t y_t,$$

where $\hat{\varsigma}_t$ is some feasible version of ς_t that yields the same level of asymptotic efficiency. The instrument $\varsigma_t \in \mathcal{Z}_t$ that attains, in matrix sense, the smallest asymptotic variance among all members of $\mathcal{Z}_t$ is the *optimal instrument* relative to $\mathcal{Z}_t$. Note that, because premultiplication of an instrument by an arbitrary non-singular conformable constant matrix does not change the estimator, the optimal instrument is defined up to such premultiplication.

Hansen (1985) derived the *optimality condition* for the instrument ς_t relative to $\mathcal{Z}_t$. When the data are stationary time series, the optimality condition is written as

$$E\left[x_t \varsigma_t'\right] = \sum_{j=-\infty}^{+\infty} \text{cov}\left(\varsigma_t e_t, \varsigma_{t-j} e_{t-j}\right) \quad \text{for all } \varsigma_t \in \mathcal{Z}_t. \tag{3.2}$$

For *IID* data or single-period problems, the long-run covariance on the right-hand side of (3.2) reduces to the simple covariance $\text{cov}\left(\varsigma_t e_t, \varsigma_t e_t\right)$. The optimality condition is general in that it allows for narrower sets $\mathcal{Z}_t$ provided that $\mathcal{Z}_t$ forms a linear space. It is this optimality condition that is usually used for derivation of the optimal instrument, provided that the data is serially uncorrelated or the serial correlation is of finite order.

Optimal instrumentation can be viewed as a procedure that involves three successive steps: (1) finding the *form* of the optimal instrument ς_t, (2) constructing a *feasible* optimal instrument $\hat{\varsigma}_t$, (3) *using* the constructed instrument to estimate β and the associated asymptotic variance. This asymptotic variance, say Ω_ς, is called *the efficiency bound* relative to $\mathcal{Z}_t$.

3.2.2 Maximal Set of Allowable Instruments

For *IID* data or single-period problems with stationary time series, the optimality condition implies the following form of the optimal instrument:

$$\varsigma_t = \frac{E\left[x_t | \Im_t\right]}{E\left[e_t^2 | \Im_t\right]}. \tag{3.3}$$

If the data are *IID*, this is equivalent to the form of the optimal instrument derived by Chamberlain (1987). In the case when x_t coincides with z_t, this instrument implies generalized least squares (GLS) estimation. When the data are stationary time series, the conditional expectations that enter the optimal instrument may depend on the entire history of z_t.

Operationalizing the instrument in (3.3) boils down to estimation of the conditional expectations in its numerator and denominator. In a cross-sectional environment, there is a variety of methods for their estimation: kernels (Carroll, 1982), nearest neighbors (Robinson, 1987), series (Newey, 1990) and splines (Donald, Imbens and Newey, 2003). In a time series context, these conditional expectations may be functions of the whole history of z_t, and their estimation remains an open question. If such an object has low persistence, one may approximate it with an expectation conditional on a few last lags (e.g., Tschernig and Yang, 2000); if its persistence is high, one can employ some of the ideas underlying the semiparametric GARCH (Linton and Mammen, 2005).

When the problem is multiperiod with finite q, the optimal instrument no longer takes the simple static form in (3.3). To illustrate the main ideas for the multiperiod problem, assume first that there is conditional homoskedasticity, i.e., the conditional variance and all conditional autocovariances are constant.

Hansen (1985) showed that the optimal instrument in this case follows the recursive process

$$\Gamma(L)\zeta_t \propto E\left[\Gamma(L^{-1})^{-1}x_t|\Im_t\right],\tag{3.4}$$

where $\Gamma(L) = \gamma_0 + \gamma_1 L + \ldots + \gamma_{q-1}L^{q-1}$ is a $(q-1)^{\text{th}}$ order polynomial in the Wold representation of e_t given by $e_t = \Gamma(L)\varepsilon_t$ with ε_t being a unit variance white noise. West and Wilcox (1996) showed how to implement the optimal instrument in (3.4) for the first-order condition from a dynamic inventory model, and investigated the small sample properties of the feasible estimator. Hansen and Singleton (1996) discussed an application of the instrument (3.4) in the context of a capital asset pricing model.

Under conditional heteroskedasticity, the structure of the optimal instrument is even more complex than (3.4). Anatolyev (2003) derived its form building on the work of Hansen (1985) and Hansen, Heaton and Ogaki (1988) on efficiency bounds. He showed that the form of the process followed by the optimal instrument is

$$\Phi_t(L)\zeta_t = E\left[\Pi_t(L^{-1})x_t|\Im_t\right],$$

where, in contrast to (3.4), the filters $\Phi_t(L)$ and $\Pi_t(L)$ are time varying and tied to the heteroskedasticity and serial correlation characteristics of the errors via an implicit system of nonlinear stochastic equations. The system of equations that determines $\Phi_t(L)$ and $\Pi_t(L)$ generally does not admit an analytical solution. The construction of the optimal instrument may be implemented along two different directions. One approach involves the estimation of the implicitly defined processes directly by designing a converging iterative scheme. The second possibility is approximating the system of equations and obtaining an explicit, although approximate, solution. For details, see Anatolyev (2006) and the references therein.

Exercise 3.1. Consider the following MA(p) data generating mechanism:

$$y_t = \alpha + \Gamma(L)\varepsilon_t,$$

where ε_t is a mean zero IID sequence, and $\Gamma(L)$ is a lag polynomial of finite order p. Derive the optimal instrument for estimation of α based on the conditional moment restriction

$$E\left[y_t|y_{t-p-1}, y_{t-p-2}, \ldots\right] = \alpha.$$

3.2.3   Linear Set of Instruments

As we argued above, in multiperiod time series problems, the form of the optimal instrument and its practical implementation can be quite involved. An alternative approach is based on the idea of shrinking the maximal set of allowable instruments to one that would make the theory and implementation more tractable. The *linear set of instruments* consists of only linear functions of lags of the basic instruments:

$$\mathcal{Z}_t = \left\{ \varsigma_t : \varsigma_t = \sum_{i=0}^{\infty} \kappa_i z_{t-i} \text{ for some } k \times \ell \text{ weights } \kappa_i \right\}.$$

Of course, even though the efficiency gains obtained from the use of lags may be big, the linear set is significantly narrower than the entire class of allowable instruments. For example, in the regression context (when $x_t = z_t$) with martingale difference errors, the optimal instrument relative to the maximal set implies GLS estimation, while the optimal instrument relative to the linear set implies OLS estimation.

The optimal instrumentation relative to the linear set is developed in West (2001) and West, Wong and Anatolyev (2009). Again, the optimality condition (3.2) facilitates the derivation of the optimal instrument. For example, in a zero mean AR(1) model

$$y_t = \rho y_{t-1} + \varepsilon_t$$

with symmetrically distributed martingale difference innovations ε_t, the linear set of instruments is

$$\mathcal{Z}_t = \left\{ \varsigma_t : \varsigma_t = \sum_{i=1}^{\infty} \kappa_i y_{t-i} \text{ for some scalar weights } \kappa_i \right\}.$$

Then, it is easy to show (see West, 2001) that the optimal instrument is given by

$$\varsigma_t = \sum_{i=1}^{\infty} \rho^{i-1} \frac{E\left[\varepsilon_t^2\right]^2}{E\left[\varepsilon_t^2 \varepsilon_{t-i}^2\right]} \varepsilon_{t-i}.$$

West, Wong and Anatolyev (2009) consider more general, not necessarily autoregressive, models. In the q-period conditional model (3.1) with $k = 1$ for simplicity, the optimality condition in a matrix form can be written as

$$\Pi = S\Phi,$$

where

$$S \equiv \sum_{j=-q+1}^{q-1} E\left[\mathbf{e}_t \mathbf{e}'_{t-j} e_t e_{t-j}\right],$$

$\Pi = E\left[\mathbf{e}_t x_t\right]$ and $\mathbf{e}_t = (\varepsilon_t, \varepsilon_{t-1}, ..., \varepsilon_{t-n+1})'$. The matrix Φ contains the optimal weights ϕ_i in the representation of the optimal instrument $\varsigma_t = \sum_{i=0}^{n-1} \phi_i \varepsilon_{t-i}$, where ε_t is the Wold innovation in the basic instrument z_t. The vector of optimal weights is determined by $\Phi = S^{-1}\Pi$. West, Wong and Anatolyev (2009) show how to operationalize this instrument and construct a feasible estimator.

Exercise 3.2. Consider an AR(1) model $x_t = \rho x_{t-1} + \varepsilon_t$, where the disturbance ε_t is generated as $\varepsilon_t = \eta_t \eta_{t-1}$ and η_t is an *IID* sequence with mean zero and variance one. Find the optimal instrument relative to the linear set of instruments with the basic instrument x_{t-1}. How many lags of x_t does the optimal instrument employ? Outline how to construct its feasible version.

3.2.4   Extension to Nonlinear Models

Many of the ideas presented above generalize to nonlinear models written in the form of conditional moment restrictions. Suppose the model is

$$E\left[h\left(w_t, \theta_0\right) | \Im_t\right] = 0, \tag{3.5}$$

where $h\left(w, \theta\right)$ is an $\ell \times 1$, possibly nonlinear in θ, moment function, and $\Im_t$ is information in the basic instrument z_t and possibly its history. Suppose also that the data are *IID* or the problem is single-period. The maximal set of allowable instruments is $\mathcal{Z}_t = \{ \Psi_t : \Psi_t = f\left(\Im_t\right)$ for some measurable $f \}$. Indeed, for any conformable matrix function Ψ_t of $\Im_t$, the conditional moment restriction implies $E\left[\Psi_t h\left(w_t, \theta_0\right)\right] = 0$. The optimal instrument Ξ_t leads to the just-identified method of moments estimator based on the system of moment restrictions

$$E\left[\Xi_t h\left(w_t, \theta_0\right)\right] = 0,$$

which is asymptotically most efficient among all estimators based on instruments from $\mathcal{Z}_t$. The optimal choice (Chamberlain, 1987), which is an analog of (3.3), is

$$\Xi_t = D_t' \Sigma_t^{-1},$$

where

$$D_t = E\left[\left.\frac{\partial h\left(w_t, \theta_0\right)}{\partial \theta'}\right| \Im_t\right]$$

and

$$\Sigma_t = E\left[h\left(w_t, \theta_0\right) h\left(w_t, \theta_0\right)' | \Im_t\right].$$

The efficiency bound relative to $\mathcal{Z}_t$ is given by

$$\Omega_{\Xi} = E\left[D_t' \Sigma_t^{-1} D_t\right]^{-1},$$

which is also the *semiparametric efficiency bound* (Chamberlain, 1987), i.e., a lower bound for any consistent and asymptotically normal estimator of θ_0 based on the conditional moment restriction (3.5).

The optimality of the instrument Ξ_t can be shown using similar arguments as in demonstrating the efficiency of the optimal GMM in Chapter 1. The GMM estimator based on $E\left[\Psi_t h\left(w_t, \theta_0\right)\right] = 0$, for any function Ψ_t of $\Im_t$ with row dimension $\ell \geq k$, is asymptotically distributed as $\mathcal{N}(0, \Omega_\Psi)$, where $V_\Psi = \left(M'WM\right)^{-1} M'WVWM\left(M'WM\right)^{-1}$, $M = E\left[\Psi_t \partial h\left(w_t, \theta_0\right) / \partial \theta'\right]$, $V = E\left[\Psi_t h\left(w_t, \theta_0\right) h\left(w_t, \theta_0\right)' \Psi_t'\right]$, and W is an $\ell \times \ell$ weighting matrix.

Let $u_1 = M'W\Psi_t h(w_t, \theta_0)$ and $u_2 = \Xi_t h(w_t, \theta_0)$. By the law of iterated expectations we have (see Newey, 1993)

$$
\begin{aligned}
\Omega_\Psi - \Omega_\Xi &= E[u_1 u_2']^{-1} E[u_1 u_1'] E[u_2 u_1']^{-1} - E[u_2 u_2']^{-1} \\
&= E[u_1 u_2']^{-1} \left(E[u_1 u_1'] - E[u_1 u_2'] \left(E[u_2 u_2'] \right)^{-1} E[u_2 u_1'] \right) E[u_2 u_1']^{-1} \\
&= E[UU'] \geq 0,
\end{aligned}
$$

where $U = E[u_1 u_2']^{-1}(u_1 - E[u_1 u_2'] E[u_2 u_2']^{-1} u_2)$. Hence, Ω_Ξ is a lower asymptotic variance bound, and Ξ_t is optimal relative to $\mathcal{Z}_t$. Note once again that the optimal GMM estimator in Chapter 1 exploits the optimal choice of a weighting matrix given the instrument Ψ_t. In this chapter, "optimal" is meant in the sense of an optimal choice Ξ_t for the instruments Ψ_t. In both cases, optimality is understood from the perspective of minimization of the asymptotic variance of the estimator of θ_0.

Typically, the optimal instrument matrix Ξ_t depends on unknown parameters and functions. A feasible approach is to replace the unknown Ξ_t with its consistent estimate $\hat{\Xi}_t$, which can be obtained by estimating D_t and Σ_t using various nonparametric methods (see section 1.4 of Chapter 1). After the estimates $\hat{\Xi}_t$ for all t in the sample are available, the parameter estimate can be obtained from the estimating equations

$$
\frac{1}{n} \sum_{t=1}^n \hat{\Xi}_t h(w_t, \theta) = 0.
$$

See Newey (1993) for a discussion on other possibilities of obtaining the estimator numerically.

To illustrate the main idea behind the feasible implementation of the optimal instrument, let $w_t = (y_t, x_t)$, $z_t = x_t$, and consider the nonlinear regression model

$$
y_t = g(x_t, \theta_0) + e_t, \tag{3.6}
$$

where $E[e_t | x_t] = 0$, and $g(\cdot)$ is a known function. In this case, $h(w_t, \theta) = y_t - g(x_t, \theta)$, $D_t = -\partial g(x_t, \theta_0)/\partial \theta'$, $\Sigma_t = E[e_t^2 | x_t]$, and

$$
\Xi_t = -\frac{1}{E[e_t^2 | x_t]} \frac{\partial g(x_t, \theta_0)}{\partial \theta}.
$$

Since $g(\cdot)$ is known, $\hat{D}(x_t) = -\partial g(x_t, \bar{\theta})/\partial \theta'$, where $\bar{\theta}$ is some preliminary consistent estimator (e.g., nonlinear least squares estimator) of θ_0. The conditional variance Σ_t is an unknown function that needs to be estimated nonparametrically (see Newey, 1993, for a comprehensive treatment of the nonparametric estimation of optimal instruments). For example, the estimate of Σ_t can be obtained as

$$
\hat{\Sigma}_t = \sum_{j=1}^N w_{tj} \left(y_t - g(x_t, \bar{\theta}) \right)^2,
$$

where ω_{tj} are nearest neighbor weights. Alternatively, $\hat{\Sigma}_t$ can be estimated using a series estimator as

$$\hat{\Sigma}_t = \hat{\Upsilon}\Psi_{J,t},$$

where $\Psi_{J,t} = (\psi_{1,t}, ..., \psi_{J,t})'$ is a $J \times 1$ vector of realizations of basis functions, and $\hat{\Upsilon}$ is the matrix of coefficients in a linear regression of $(y_t - g(x_t, \bar{\theta}))^2$ on $\Psi_{J,t}$. The smoothing parameters N and J can be determined using a cross validation criterion (see section 1.4.3 in Chapter 1).

Finally, the unknown conditional expectations can be estimated by weighted kernel regressions (see Cai, 2001). Let the conditional expectation of interest be

$$\mu_t = E[\phi(w_t)| z_t],$$

where $\phi(\cdot)$ is a known measurable function with $E|\phi(w_t)| < \infty$ and z_t is a scalar. For example, in the model considered in the previous paragraph, $w_t = (y_t, x_t)$, $z_t = x_t$ and $\phi(w_t) = (y_t - g(x_t, \theta))^2$. The idea of the weighted kernel regression is based on the nonparametric likelihood estimation discussed in Chapter 2. Let $\{p_t(z)\}_{t=1}^n$ be non-negative weight functions for the kernel estimator at the design point z that satisfy

$$\sum_{t=1}^{n} (z_t - z)\, p_t(z)\, K_b(z_t - z) = 0 \quad \text{and} \quad \sum_{t=1}^{n} p_t(z) = 1, \qquad (3.7)$$

where $K_b(\cdot)$ is a kernel function with a smoothing parameter b. The weights $\{p_t(z)\}_{t=1}^n$ are determined as parameters that maximize the empirical likelihood $\sum_{t=1}^{n} \log p_t(z)$ subject to the constraints (3.7). This maximization yields

$$p_t(z) = \frac{1}{n} \frac{1}{1 + \lambda(z_t - z) K_b(z_t - z)},$$

where λ is the Lagrange multiplier associated with the first constraint in (3.7) that can be obtained by maximizing the profile empirical likelihood

$$\sum_{t=1}^{n} \log\left(1 + \lambda(z_t - z) K_b(z_t - z)\right).$$

Then, the weighted Nadaraya–Watson estimator of $\mu(z) = E[\phi(w_t)| z]$ is given by

$$\hat{\mu}(z) = \frac{\sum_{t=1}^{n} \phi(w_t)\, p_t(z)\, K_b(z_t - z)}{\sum_{t=1}^{n} p_t(z)\, K_b(z_t - z)}.$$

The values $\{\mu_t\}_{t=1}^n$ are computed using this estimator evaluated at the sample $\{z_t\}_{t=1}^n$ as design points.

In practice, the full implementation of the idea of optimal instrumentation, especially in a time series environment, proves to be a complicated exercise. Nevertheless, the optimal instrument theory can still be put to use for a more efficient estimation of model parameters. For example, consider the consumption function

$$y_t = \alpha + \delta x_t^\gamma + e_t,$$

where y_t denotes consumption at time t, x_t is (endogenous) income at time t, and all variables are jointly stationary. The lagged values of income are predetermined so that e_t is mean independent of the past history of x_t and y_t: $E[e_t|x_{t-1}, y_{t-1}, x_{t-2}, y_{t-2}, \ldots] = 0$. Because the error has a martingale difference structure, the optimal instrument can be expressed as

$$\zeta_t = \frac{1}{E[e_t^2|x_{t-1}, y_{t-1}, \ldots]} \left(\begin{array}{c} 1 \\ E[x_t^\gamma|x_{t-1}, y_{t-1}, \ldots] \\ E[x_t^\gamma \log x_t|x_{t-1}, y_{t-1}, \ldots] \end{array} \right).$$

Preliminary estimates of the parameters α, δ and γ can be obtained using, for instance, the instrument vector $(1, x_{t-1}, x_{t-2})'$. Based on these estimates, one can construct feasible versions of e_t^2 and x_t^γ and then fit parametrically e_t^2, x_t^γ and $x_t^\gamma \log x_t$ to recent lagged variables from $\{x_{t-1}, y_{t-1}, x_{t-2}, y_{t-2}, \ldots\}$ employing, for example, a GARCH-type model for e_t^2 and simple linear regressions for the other two. The fitted values can be used further to form feasible ζ_t's that are eventually employed to estimate the parameters. Naturally, because of the use of auxiliary parameterizations, such an instrument will be only "nearly optimal."

Exercise 3.3. Consider the nonlinear regression model

$$y_t = g(x_t, \theta_0) + e_t,$$

where $E[e_t|x_t] = 0$, $E[e_t^2|x_t] = \sigma^2(x_t, \theta_0, \eta_0)$ and $g(\cdot)$ and $\sigma^2(\cdot)$ are known functions. Consider two estimators of θ_0: one based only on the restriction $E[h_1(y_t, x_t, \theta_0)|x_t] = 0$ with

$$h_1(y_t, x_t, \theta_0) = y_t - g(x_t, \theta_0)$$

and another based on the restrictions $E[h_2(y_t, x_t, \theta_0, \eta_0)|x_t] = 0$ with

$$h_2(y_t, x_t, \theta_0, \eta_0) = \left(\begin{array}{c} y_t - g(x_t, \theta_0) \\ (y_t - g(x_t, \theta_0))^2 - \sigma^2(x_t, \theta_0, \eta_0) \end{array} \right).$$

Assume that $E[e_t^3|x_t] = 0$. Find the matrix of optimal instruments for the second estimator. Derive the asymptotic variances of both estimators of θ_0 and show under what conditions they are equal.

3.3 Alternative Approaches

In this section, we discuss alternative approaches that attain the semiparametric efficiency bound without explicitly estimating the optimal instruments.

In addition to efficiency and computational consideration, these new methods have also been motivated by the observation that an estimation procedure based on unconditional moments, when the model is defined by conditional moment restrictions, may result in inconsistency of the estimator (Dominguez and Lobato, 2004). To illustrate the main idea, we adapt an example from Dominguez and Lobato (2010) in which the economic theory implies the conditional moment restriction $E[y_t^{-\theta_0} - 1|\Im_t] = 0$ but the estimation of the unknown parameter θ_0 is based on the unconditional moment $E[y_t^{-\theta_0}] = 1$. Suppose for concreteness that y_t takes three values, 0.75, 1 and 1.25, with probabilities 0.3, 0.4 and 0.3, respectively. It is easy to verify that there are two values of θ_0 (namely, -1 and 0) that satisfy the unconditional moment restriction. Therefore, the estimator is not uniquely identified by the unconditional moments and, hence, inconsistent.

In the subsequent discussion, we consider only the case when $\Im_t$ is generated by the s-dimensional (for a finite s) vector of conditioning variables (basic instruments) z_t. This setup covers IID data as well as single-period problems with time series data.

3.3.1   Local GMM and GEL Estimation

We first introduce a method that operates directly on the conditional moment restriction $E[h(w_t, \theta_0)|z_t] = 0$ implied by theory and can be considered a localized version of the GMM and GEL estimators. Define the weights

$$\omega_{tj} = \frac{K_b(z_j - z_t)}{\sum_{i=1}^{n} K_b(z_i - z_t)},$$

where $K_b(\cdot)$ is a symmetric positive kernel function and b is a bandwidth. The local GMM estimator minimizes a quadratic form in the sample counterparts of the conditional moment restrictions $E[h(w_t, \theta_0)|z_t] = 0$. In particular, by replacing the empirical distribution weights n^{-1} with the data-determined kernel weights ω_{tj}, we have $h_t^\omega(\theta) = \sum_{j=1}^{n} \omega_{tj} h_j(\theta)$ and $V_t^\omega(\theta) = \sum_{j=1}^{n} \omega_{tj}(h_j(\theta) - h_t^\omega(\theta))(h_j(\theta) - h_t^\omega(\theta))'$, where $h_j(\theta) \equiv h(w_j, \theta)$. Then, the *local continuously updated (LCU) GMM* estimator is defined as

$$\hat{\theta}_{LCU} = \arg\min_{\theta \in \Theta} \sum_{t=1}^{n} \mathbf{I}_{tn} h_t^\omega(\theta)' V_t^\omega(\theta)^{-1} h_t^\omega(\theta), \qquad (3.8)$$

where $\mathbf{I}_{tn}$ is a trimming term that bounds the denominator of the kernel weights ω_{tj} away from zero. The trimming term is typically defined as

$$\mathbf{I}_{tn} = \mathbb{I}\left\{ n^{-1} \sum_{j=1}^{n} K_b(z_j - z_t) \geq c_n \right\}$$

with some sequence $c_n \to 0$ (Kitamura, Tripathi and Ahn, 2004), or

$$\mathbf{I}_{tn} = \mathbb{I}\{z_t \in \mathbb{S}\}$$

with the set $\mathbb{S}$ being a compact subset in the support of the conditioning variable z (Tripathi and Kitamura, 2003).

The *local two-step GMM (LGMM)* version of the estimator in (3.8) can be constructed as

$$\hat{\theta}_{LGMM} = \arg\min_{\theta \in \Theta} \sum_{t=1}^{n} \mathbf{I}_{tn} h_t^{\omega}(\theta)' V_t^{\omega}(\bar{\theta})^{-1} h_t^{\omega}(\theta), \qquad (3.9)$$

where $\bar{\theta}$ is a preliminary consistent estimator of θ_0. The first-order conditions of the local GMM estimator in (3.9) are given by

$$\sum_{t=1}^{n} \mathbf{I}_{tn} \sum_{j=1}^{n} \omega_{tj} \frac{\partial h_j(\hat{\theta}_{LGMM})'}{\partial \theta} V_t^{\omega}(\bar{\theta})^{-1} h_t^{\omega}(\hat{\theta}_{LGMM}) = 0. \qquad (3.10)$$

A closer inspection of these equations reveals that the local GMM estimator implicitly uses the optimal instruments as $\sum_{j=1}^{n} \omega_{tj} \, \partial h_j(\hat{\theta}_{LGMM})'/\partial\theta$ and $V_t^{\omega}(\bar{\theta})$ provide consistent estimators of D_t' and Σ_t defined in the previous section (Smith, 2007). The conditions for consistency, asymptotic normality and semiparametric efficiency of the local GMM estimator are presented in Kitamura, Tripathi and Ahn (2004) for *IID* data and Gospodinov and Otsu (2010) for time series data.

Smith (2007) shows that the local continuously updated GMM estimator (3.8) belongs to the class of local Cressie–Read minimum distance estimators which also includes the local (or smoothed) empirical likelihood estimator proposed by Kitamura, Tripathi and Ahn (2004). More specifically, adapting the nonparametric likelihood estimators that we discussed before to $E[h(w_t, \theta_0)|z_t] = 0$ involves minimizing the localized version of the Cressie–Read criterion

$$\frac{2}{\delta(1+\delta)} \sum_{t=1}^{n} \mathbf{I}_{tn} \sum_{j=1}^{n} \omega_{tj} \left[\left(\frac{\omega_{tj}}{p_{tj}} \right)^{\delta} - 1 \right],$$

subject to

$$\sum_{j=1}^{n} p_{tj} h_j(\theta) = 0$$

and

$$\sum_{j=1}^{n} p_{tj} = 1$$

for all $t = 1, ..., n$, where ω_{tj} are empirical (nonparametrically estimated) weights defined above and p_{tj} are implied conditional probabilities corresponding to the distribution function of the data conditional on z_t. As in the case with unconditional moment restrictions (see section 2.3.2 in Chapter 2), if $\delta \to 0$, we obtain the *local empirical likelihood (LEL)* estimator

$$\hat{\theta}_{LEL} = \arg\min_{\theta \in \Theta} \sum_{t=1}^{n} \mathbf{I}_{tn} \sum_{j=1}^{n} \omega_{tj} \log(1 + \lambda_t' h_j(\theta)), \qquad (3.11)$$

where $\lambda = (\lambda'_1, ..., \lambda'_n)'$ is an $n\ell$-vector of Lagrange multipliers associated with ℓ moment conditions for each $t = 1, ..., n$.

One drawback of the LEL estimator is that it requires the computation of $n\ell$ (sample size × dimension of h) Lagrange multipliers that are solutions to the nonlinear equation $\max_{\lambda_t} \sum_{j=1}^n \omega_{tj} \log(1 + \lambda'_t h_j(\theta))$ for a given θ. As a result, the computational costs are substantial and grow with the sample size. Alternatively, if $\delta \to -2$, we obtain the objective function of the local continuously updated GMM estimator (3.8) for which the Lagrange multipliers have a closed form solution given by $\lambda_t = -V_t^\omega(\theta)^{-1} h_t^\omega(\theta)$, $t = 1, ..., n$. For more details, see Antoine, Bonnal and Renault (2007), Kitamura, Tripathi and Ahn (2004) and Smith (2007).

More generally, define the *local generalized empirical likelihood (LGEL)* estimator as (Smith, 2007)

$$\hat{\theta}_{LGEL} = \arg\min_{\theta \in \Theta} \max_{\lambda_t \in \Lambda_n} \sum_{t=1}^n \mathbf{I}_{tn} \sum_{j=1}^n \omega_{tj} \rho\left(\lambda'_t h_j(\theta)\right),$$

where $\rho(\varsigma)$ denotes a smooth scalar function that indexes different members of the GEL class and is normalized to satisfy $\rho(0) = 0$, $\partial\rho(0)/\partial v = \partial^2\rho(0)/\partial v^2 = -1$, and $\Lambda_n = \{\lambda : \|\lambda\| \le Cn^{-1/\epsilon}\}$ for some ϵ (typically $\epsilon > 8$) and $C > 0$ (Smith, 2007). As in the unconditional case, different choices of $\rho(\cdot)$ give rise to the estimators introduced above. For example, the local GMM estimator in (3.8) is obtained for $\rho(v) = -(1+v)^2/2$ and the LEL estimator in (3.11) is obtained for $\rho(v) = \log(1 - v)$.

The local GEL estimator is characterized by the following implied conditional probabilities

$$p_{tj} = \frac{\omega_{tj}\dfrac{\partial\rho(\hat{v}_{tj})}{\partial v}}{\sum_{i=1}^n \omega_{ti}\dfrac{\partial\rho(\hat{v}_{ti})}{\partial v}},$$

where $v_{tj} = \lambda'_t h_j(\theta)$ and $\hat{v}_{tj} = \hat{\lambda}'_t h_j(\hat{\theta}_{LGEL})$, and solves the first-order conditions

$$\sum_{t=1}^n \mathbf{I}_{tn} \sum_{j=1}^n \omega_{tj} \frac{\partial\rho(\hat{v}_{tj})}{\partial v} \frac{\partial h_j(\hat{\theta}_{LGEL})'}{\partial\theta}$$

$$\times \left(\sum_{j=1}^n \omega_{tj}\rho_*(\hat{v}_{tj}) h_j(\hat{\theta}_{LGEL}) h_j(\hat{\theta}_{LGEL})'\right)^{-1} h_t^\omega(\hat{\theta}_{LGEL}) = 0,$$

where $\rho_*(v) = (\partial\rho(v)/\partial v + 1)/v$ for $v \ne 0$ and $\rho_*(0) = -1$.

For example, for the LEL estimator, $\partial\rho(v)/\partial v = 1/(1 - v) = -\rho_*(v)$ and $\hat{p}_{tj} = \omega_{tj}(1 - \hat{\lambda}'_t h_j(\hat{\theta}_{LEL}))^{-1} = \omega_{tj}\partial\rho(\hat{v}_{tj})/\partial v = -\rho_*(\hat{v}_{tj})$. Hence, for the local empirical likelihood estimator

$$\sum_{t=1}^{n} \mathbf{I}_{tn} \sum_{j=1}^{n} \hat{p}_{tj} \frac{\partial h_j(\hat{\theta}_{LEL})'}{\partial \theta} \left(\sum_{j=1}^{n} \hat{p}_{tj} h_j(\hat{\theta}_{LEL}) h_j(\hat{\theta}_{LEL})' \right)^{-1} h_t^\omega(\hat{\theta}_{LEL}) = 0,$$

and the conditional probabilities $\hat{p}_{tj}$ are used for estimating both the conditional Jacobian D_t and the conditional variance matrix Σ_t. Similarly, for the LCU estimator, $\partial \rho(v)/\partial v = -(1+v)$, $\rho_*(v) = -1$ and

$$\tilde{p}_{tj} = \omega_{tj}(1 + \tilde{\lambda}_t' h_j(\hat{\theta}_{LCU})) \left(\sum_{i=1}^{n} \omega_{ti}(1 + \tilde{\lambda}_t' h_i(\hat{\theta}_{LCU})) \right)^{-1}.$$

As a result, the LCU estimator uses the conditional probabilities $\tilde{p}_{tj}$ for estimating the conditional Jacobian matrix D_t but the kernel weights ω_{tj} for estimating the conditional variance matrix Σ_t. In contrast, as indicated below equation (3.10), the local GMM estimator uses the kernel weights ω_{tj} for estimating both the conditional Jacobian and conditional variance matrices. This will have similar implications for higher-order properties of different estimators as in the case of the unconditional GEL estimators discussed in section 2.5 of Chapter 2.

This approach can be readily adapted for testing hypotheses on the parameters of the form $d(\theta) = 0$, where $d(\cdot) : \mathbb{R}^k \rightarrow \mathbb{R}^q$ is continuous and twice differentiable in a region about θ_0. Let

$$\tilde{\theta}_{LGEL} = \arg \min_{\theta \in \Theta} \max_{\lambda_t \in \Lambda_n} \sum_{t=1}^{n} \mathbf{I}_{tn} \sum_{j=1}^{n} \omega_{tj} \rho \left(\lambda_t' h_j(\theta) \right) \text{ subject to } d(\theta) = 0$$

denote the constrained estimate under the null hypothesis $H_0 : d(\theta) = 0$. Then, the testing procedure can be based on the local GEL ratio statistic

$$\mathcal{LGELR} = 2 \sum_{t=1}^{n} \mathbf{I}_{tn} \sum_{j=1}^{n} \omega_{tj} \left[\rho \left(\hat{\lambda}_t' h_j(\hat{\theta}_{LGEL}) \right) - \rho \left(\tilde{\lambda}_t' h_j(\tilde{\theta}_{LGEL}) \right) \right], \quad (3.12)$$

which is asymptotically distributed as a χ_q^2 random variable.

A similar approach can be used for testing the correct specification of the conditional moment restriction or the hypothesis (see Tripathi and Kitamura, 2003)

$$H_0 : \Pr\{E[h(w_t, \theta)|z_t] = 0\} = 1 \text{ for some } \theta \in \Theta. \quad (3.13)$$

From (3.12) it follows that under the null hypothesis in (3.13), the local empirical likelihood ratio statistic becomes

$$\mathcal{LELR}_0 = 2 \sum_{t=1}^{n} \mathbb{I}\{z_t \in \mathbb{S}\} \sum_{j=1}^{n} \omega_{tj} \log(1 + \hat{\lambda}_t' h_j(\hat{\theta}_{LEL}))$$

for the compact set $\mathbb{S}$ given by $[0, 1]^s$. As we mentioned above, the estimation of the LEL Lagrange multipliers can be computationally intensive and they can be replaced by the asymptotically equivalent LCU-type Lagrange multipliers $\hat{\lambda}_t = \left(\sum_{j=1}^{n} \omega_{tj} h_j(\hat{\theta}_{LEL}) h_j(\hat{\theta}_{LEL})' \right)^{-1} \sum_{j=1}^{n} \omega_{tj} h_j(\hat{\theta}_{LEL})$. One difficulty in this setup arises from the fact that $\mathcal{LELR}_0$ needs to be properly recentered and standardized in order to obtain a valid asymptotic distribution. For this purpose, let $c_1 = \int K_b(u)^2 du$ and $c_2 = \int \left(\int K_b(v) K_b(u - v) dv \right)^2 du$. Then, Tripathi and Kitamura (2003) show that under the null hypothesis in (3.13) and $s \leq 3$, the studentized statistic

$$\frac{\mathcal{LELR}_0 - b^{-s} \ell c_1}{c_2 \sqrt{2 b^{-s} \ell}}$$

is asymptotically distributed as a standard normal random variable.

3.3.2   Estimation Based on a Continuum of Moment Conditions

The methods discussed in the previous two subsections employ nonparametric methods for estimating the conditional moment restriction in a local neighborhood of realizations of the conditioning variable, and their feasibility depends crucially on the existence of a finite (and possibly small) set of conditioning variables that ensure parameter identifiability. In general, parameter identifiability requires spanning of the whole set of functions in $\Im_t$ and gives rise to estimators based on a continuum of unconditional moment restrictions.

Consider again the conditional moment restriction $E\left[h\left(w_t, \theta_0\right) | z_t\right] = 0$, where z_t is an s-dimensional vector with a distribution function $F_z(\tau), \tau \in \mathbb{R}^s$. As we argued above, an arbitrary choice of instrument Ψ_t not only affects the efficiency of the estimator but may compromise the identifiability of the parameter of interest and render the moment-based estimator inconsistent. Dominguez and Lobato (2004) observe that the conditional moment restriction is equivalent to a continuum of unconditional moment restrictions given by

$$E[h(w, \theta) \mathbb{I}\{z \leq \tau\}], \quad \tau \in \mathbb{R}^s,$$

where $\mathbb{I}\{z \leq \tau\} = \prod_{i=1}^{s} \mathbb{I}\left\{z^{(i)} \leq \tau^{(i)}\right\}$. Since the conditional restriction implies that $\Pr\{E[h(w, \theta)|z] = 0\} < 1$ for all $\theta \neq \theta_0$, we have that

$$\int_{\mathbb{R}^s} |E[h(w, \theta_0) \mathbb{I}\{z \leq \tau\}]|^2 dF_z(\tau) = 0$$

and

$$\int_{\mathbb{R}^s} |E[h(w, \theta) \mathbb{I}\{z \leq \tau\}]|^2 dF_z(\tau) > 0$$

for all $\theta \neq \theta_0$, where $|\cdot|$ denotes the Euclidean norm. Hence, θ_0 is the unique value that satisfies

$$\theta_0 = \arg \min_{\theta \in \Theta} \int_{\mathbb{R}^s} |E[h(w, \theta) \mathbb{I}\{z \leq \tau\}]|^2 dF_z(\tau). \qquad (3.14)$$

The estimator of θ_0 can then be defined to minimize the sample analog of (3.14) as

$$\hat{\theta}_{DL} = \arg\min_{\theta \in \Theta} \frac{1}{n} \sum_{t=1}^{n} \left| \frac{1}{n} \sum_{j=1}^{n} h(w_j, \theta) \mathbb{I}\{z_j \leq z_t\} \right|^2 . \qquad (3.15)$$

Note that the estimator in (3.15) can be rewritten as

$$\hat{\theta}_{DL} = \arg\min_{\theta \in \Theta} \frac{1}{n} \sum_{t=1}^{n} \left| \sum_{j=1}^{n} \bar{\omega}_{tj} h(w_j, \theta) \right|^2 ,$$

where $\bar{\omega}_{tj} = n^{-1} \mathbb{I}\{z_j \leq z_t\}$. This estimator has a similar form as the inefficient (based on the identity weighting matrix) LGMM estimator with weights that depend on all observations of the conditioning variable instead of being local around z_t as in the LGMM estimator.

The minimization problem in (3.15) is straightforward since it does not involve weighting matrices and nonparametric estimation. One problem with this estimator, however, is that it may not fully capture all the information in the conditional moment restriction and is, hence, inefficient. For this reason, Dominguez and Lobato (2004) propose a two-step efficient estimator that explores information in the optimal instruments. Let $Q_n(\theta)$ denote the objective function of the efficient estimator $\hat{\theta}_E$ and $\partial Q_n(\theta)/\partial\theta$ and $\partial^2 Q_n(\theta)/\partial\theta\partial\theta'$ be the first two derivatives of this objective function. These derivatives typically involve conditional expectations which can be estimated nonparametrically as described in section 3.2.4 of this chapter. Then, the efficient Dominguez–Lobato estimator can be constructed iteratively as

$$\hat{\theta}_{DLE} = \hat{\theta}_{DL} - \left(\frac{\partial^2 Q_n(\hat{\theta}_{DL})}{\partial\theta\partial\theta'} \right)^{-1} \frac{\partial Q_n(\hat{\theta}_{DL})}{\partial\theta}$$

which satisfies $\theta_{DLE} - \ddot{\theta}_E = o_P(n^{-1/2})$. The finite sample behavior of this estimator is investigated in Dominguez and Lobato (2004).

Testing the correct specification of the conditional moment restriction, $H_0 : E[h(w_t, \theta_0)|z_t] = 0$ almost surely, can be based on the statistic (Dominguez and Lobato, 2010)

$$\mathcal{J}_{DL} = \sum_{t=1}^{n} \left| \frac{1}{n} \sum_{j=1}^{n} h(w_j, \hat{\theta}_{DL}) \mathbb{I}\{z_j \leq z_t\} \right|^2 .$$

Since the asymptotic distribution of this test statistic depends on the data, Dominguez and Lobato (2010) propose a bootstrap approximation for implementing the specification test.

More generally, let $\mathbb{G}(z, \tau)$ be a real analytic function that is not a polynomial and $H(\theta, \tau) = E[h(w, \theta)\mathbb{G}(z, \tau)]$ for $\tau \in \mathbb{R}^s$. Then, the function $\mathbb{G}(.)$ is said to be a *generically comprehensive revealing function* (Stinchcombe and White, 1998) if the unconditional moment restriction induced by this function satisfies

$$E\left[h(w,\theta_0)\mathbb{G}(z,\tau)\right]=0 \text{ for almost all } \tau \in \mathbb{T} \subset \mathbb{R}^s,$$

where $\mathbb{T}$ is an arbitrarily small subset of $\mathbb{R}^s$ with a nonempty interior (see also Hsu and Kuan, 2008). Then,

$$E\left[h(w,\theta_0)|z\right]=0 \iff H(\theta_0,\tau)=0, \text{ for almost all } \tau \in \mathbb{T} \subset \mathbb{R}^s.$$

Choices of $\mathbb{G}(.)$ include the exponential function $\exp(i\tau'z)$ (Carrasco and Florens, 2000), the logistic function, etc. Next, we will discuss the efficient estimator proposed by Carrasco and Florens (2000) which is based on a continuum of moment conditions induced by the revealing function $\mathbb{G}(z,\tau)=\exp(i\tau'z)$, where $i=\sqrt{-1}$.

Let $Z(\tau,z_t)=\exp(i\tau'z_t)$, $m_n(\tau,\theta)=n^{-1}\sum_{t=1}^n h(w_t,\theta)Z(\tau,z_t)$, π be a positive probability measure, $\mathbb{L}^2(\pi)$ denote the Hilbert space of square integrable functions with respect to π, $\langle\cdot,\cdot\rangle$ and $|\cdot|$ signify the inner product and the norm in $\mathbb{L}^2(\pi)$, and $\mathcal{K}_n$ $\{\mathcal{K}_n:\mathbb{L}^2(\pi)\to\mathbb{L}^2(\pi)\}$ be the sample covariance operator of the instruments defined as

$$(\mathcal{K}_n m)(\tau_1)=\int \frac{1}{n}\sum_{t=1}^n Z(\tau_1,z_t)\overline{Z(\tau_2,z_t)}m(\tau_2)\pi(\tau_2)d\tau_2,$$

where $\overline{Z(\tau_2,z_t)}$ denotes the complex conjugate of $Z(\tau_2,z_t)$. Due to an infinite number of moment conditions, $\mathcal{K}_n$ is nearly singular and needs to be regularized.

Let $(\mathcal{K}_n^\alpha)^{-1}$ be the regularized inverse of $\mathcal{K}_n$ with a regularization parameter α. A number of regularization schemes are reviewed in Carrasco, Florens and Renault (2007). One popular regularization scheme is the Tikhonov regularization defined as

$$(\mathcal{K}_n^\alpha)^{-1}=(\mathcal{K}_n^2+\alpha I_n)^{-1}\mathcal{K}_n,$$

where $\alpha>0$, so that

$$(\mathcal{K}_n^\alpha)^{-1}r=\sum_{j=1}^n \frac{\hat\lambda_j}{\hat\lambda_j^2+\alpha}\left\langle\hat\phi_j,r\right\rangle\hat\phi_j,$$

where $\hat\lambda_1\geq\hat\lambda_2\geq...\geq\hat\lambda_n>0$ are the nonzero eigenvalues of $\mathcal{K}_n$, and $\hat\phi_j$, $j=1,...,n$, are their corresponding orthonormalized eigenfunctions. Then, the Carrasco–Florens estimator is given by

$$\hat\theta_{CF}=\arg\min_{\theta\in\Theta}\left|(\mathcal{K}_n^\alpha)^{-1/2}m_n(\cdot,\theta)\right|^2,$$

where $(\mathcal{K}_n^\alpha)^{-1/2}=[(\mathcal{K}_n^\alpha)^{-1}]^{1/2}$. The efficiency properties of this estimator are discussed in Carrasco and Florens (2000). For more details, see Carrasco and Florens (2000) and Carrasco (2009). Below we provide more specifics on the practical implementation of the estimator and choices of π and α in the context of a linear regression model.

This framework based on a continuum of moment conditions can also be used for specification testing. Since the number of moment conditions grows with the sample size, the conventional test for overidentifying restrictions diverges. However, after appropriate recentering and standardization (see also our discussion on specification testing with many instruments in Chapter 6), the test statistic based on the criterion function can have a standard normal limit. More specifically, under some regularity conditions (see Carrasco and Florens, 2000),

$$\frac{n\left|(K_n^{\alpha})^{-1/2}m_n(\cdot,\hat{\theta}_{CF})\right|^2 - \sum_{j=1}^{n}\frac{\hat{\lambda}_j^2}{\hat{\lambda}_j^2 + \alpha}}{\left(2\sum_{j=1}^{n}\frac{\hat{\lambda}_j^4}{(\hat{\lambda}_j^2 + \alpha)^2}\right)^{1/2}} \xrightarrow{d} \mathcal{N}(0,1).$$

Rejection of the null hypothesis implies that

$$\Pr\{E\left[h\left(w_t,\theta\right)|z_t\right] = 0\} < 1$$

for any $\theta \in \Theta$.

3.3.3   A Simple Illustrative Example

The above methods can be relatively difficult to implement and computationally intensive in high-dimensional, nonlinear models. Despite their theoretical appeal, this hampers the widespread application of these methods in empirical work. In simple linear models, however, their implementation can be straightforward by reducing the computational burden to projections of transformed variables.

Consider, for example, a simple linear regression model

$$y_t = \theta_0 x_t + e_t, \qquad (3.16)$$

where $E\left[e_t|x_t\right] = 0$ and $t = 1,\ldots,n$.

Let

$$\omega_{tj} = \frac{K_b\left(x_j - x_t\right)}{\sum_{i=1}^{n} K_b\left(x_i - x_t\right)}$$

for some kernel function K_b (Gaussian kernel, for example) and some bandwidth parameter b. Ignoring, for simplicity, the trimming function $\mathbf{I}_{tn}$, the LCU estimator is given by

$$\hat{\theta}_{LCU} = \arg\min_{\theta \in \Theta} \sum_{t=1}^{n}\left(\sum_{j=1}^{n}\omega_{tj}\left(y_j - \theta x_j\right)^2\right)^{-1}\left(\sum_{j=1}^{n}\omega_{tj}\left(y_j - \theta x_j\right)\right)^2.$$

It is instructive to inspect the form of the LGMM estimator with a unit weighting matrix which is efficient under conditional homoskedasticity. In this case, the minimization of the LGMM objective function has a closed-form solution

$$\hat{\theta}_{LGMM} = \arg\min_{\theta \in \Theta} \sum_{t=1}^{n} \left(\sum_{j=1}^{n} \omega_{tj} \left(y_j - \theta x_j \right) \right)^2$$

$$= \frac{\sum_{t=1}^{n} \tilde{x}_t \tilde{y}_t}{\sum_{t=1}^{n} \tilde{x}_t^2},$$

where $\tilde{y}_t = \sum_{j=1}^{n} \omega_{tj} y_j$ and $\tilde{x}_t = \sum_{j=1}^{n} \omega_{tj} x_j$. It is interesting to note that the LGMM estimator assumes the form of an OLS estimator not in the original variables (y_t, x_t) but in their smoothed analogs $(\tilde{y}_t, \tilde{x}_t)$. Gospodinov and Otsu (2010) undertake a higher-order asymptotic analysis of the LGMM estimator and demonstrate that the LGMM estimator possesses some appealing bias reduction properties for positively autocorrelated processes.

Interestingly, the Dominguez and Lobato (2004) estimator has a similar structure as the LGMM estimator with a unit weighting matrix:

$$\hat{\theta}_{DL} = \arg\min_{\theta \in \Theta} \sum_{t=1}^{n} \left(\sum_{j=1}^{n} (y_j - \theta x_j) \mathbb{I}\left\{ x_j \leq x_t \right\} \right)^2$$

$$= \frac{\sum_{t=1}^{n} \bar{x}_t \bar{y}_t}{\sum_{t=1}^{n} \bar{x}_t^2},$$

where $\bar{y}_t = \sum_{j=1}^{n} y_j \mathbb{I}\left\{ x_j \leq x_t \right\}$ and $\bar{x}_t = \sum_{j=1}^{n} x_j \mathbb{I}\left\{ x_j \leq x_t \right\}$. In this case, the OLS regression is performed on the "integrated" variables.

The estimator based on a continuum of moment conditions proposed by Carrasco and Florens (2000) can also be simplified considerably for linear models. In the setup of model (3.16), the Carrasco–Florens estimator of θ_0 is based on the orthogonality condition $E[(y_t - \theta_0 x_t) \exp(\tau x_t)] = 0$ with $\tau \in \mathbb{R}$. In particular, the sample moment function has the form $m_n(\tau, \theta) = n^{-1} \sum_{t=1}^{n} (y_t - \theta x_t) Z_t$, where $Z_t = \exp(\tau x_t)$, and $\mathcal{K}_n$ is an $n \times n$ matrix with a typical (i, j) element given by $\langle Z_i, Z_j \rangle / n$. Then, using a standard normal integrating density and the Tikhonov regularization scheme (see Carrasco, 2009), the Carrasco–Florens estimator has the form

$$\hat{\theta}_{CF} = \arg\min_{\theta \in \Theta} \left| (\mathcal{K}_n^{\alpha})^{-1/2} m_n(\cdot, \theta) \right|^2$$

$$= \frac{\sum_{t=1}^{n} \hat{x}_t y_t}{\sum_{t=1}^{n} \hat{x}_t x_t},$$

where $\hat{x} = \sum_{j=1}^{n} (\hat{\lambda}_j^2 + \alpha)^{-1} \hat{\lambda}_j^2 (\hat{\psi}_j' x) \hat{\psi}_j$ with $x = (x_1, x_2, ..., x_n)'$, α is the regularization parameter, $\hat{\lambda}_j$ and $\hat{\psi}_j$ are the estimated eigenvalues and eigenvectors of an $n \times n$ matrix with $(i, j)^{\text{th}}$ element

$$k(x_i, x_j) = -\exp\left(\frac{(x_i - x_j)^2}{2\hat{\sigma}_x^2}\right),$$

and $\hat{\sigma}_x^2$ is the sample variance of x_t. The regularization parameter can be set to a constant (0.02, for example) or can be determined by data-driven methods such as cross validation (Carrasco, 2009).

3.4   Appendix: Solutions to Selected Exercises

Exercise 3.1. From the data generating mechanism it follows that the moment function is conditionally homoskedastic. Therefore, the optimal instrument is

$$\Gamma(L)\zeta_t = E\left[\Gamma(L^{-1})^{-1}1|y_{t-p-1}, y_{t-p-2}, \ldots\right],$$

or

$$\Gamma(L)\zeta_t = \Gamma(1)^{-1}.$$

This is a deterministic recursion. Since the instrument should be stationary, ζ_t has to be a constant. Because the value of the constant does not matter, the optimal instrument may be set to unity.

Exercise 3.2. We look for an optimal combination of $\varepsilon_{t-1}, \varepsilon_{t-2}, \ldots$, say

$$\zeta_t = \sum_{i=1}^{\infty} \phi_i^* \varepsilon_{t-i},$$

when the set of allowable instruments is

$$\mathcal{Z}_t = \left\{\varsigma_t = \sum_{i=1}^{\infty} \phi_i \varepsilon_{t-i}\right\}.$$

The optimality condition for each ε_{t-r}, $r \geq 1$, is

$$\forall r \geq 1 \qquad E\left[\varepsilon_{t-r} x_{t-1}\right] = E\left[\varepsilon_{t-r} \zeta_t \varepsilon_t^2\right],$$

or

$$\forall r \geq 1 \qquad \rho^{r-1} = E\left[\varepsilon_{t-r}\left(\sum_{i=1}^{\infty} \phi_i^* \varepsilon_{t-i}\right)\varepsilon_t^2\right].$$

When $r > 1$, this implies $\rho^{r-1} = \phi_r^*$, while when $r = 1$, we have $1 = \phi_1^* E[\eta_{t-1}^2 \eta_{t-2}^2 \eta_t^2 \eta_{t-1}^2] = \phi_1^* E[\eta^4]$. The optimal instrument is then given by

$$
\zeta_t = E\left[\eta^4\right]^{-1} \varepsilon_{t-1} + \sum_{i=2}^{\infty} \rho^{r-1} \varepsilon_{t-i}
$$

$$
= \left(E\left[\eta^4\right]^{-1} - 1\right) \varepsilon_{t-1} + \sum_{i=1}^{\infty} \rho^{r-1} \varepsilon_{t-i}
$$

$$
= \left(E\left[\eta^4\right]^{-1} - 1\right) (x_{t-1} - \rho x_{t-2}) + x_{t-1}
$$

$$
= E\left[\eta^4\right]^{-1} x_{t-1} + \left(E\left[\eta^4\right]^{-1} - 1\right) \rho x_{t-2},
$$

and employs only two lags of x_t. To construct a feasible version, one needs to first consistently estimate ρ (e.g., by OLS) and $E[\eta^4]$ (e.g., by using the sample analog of $E[\varepsilon_{t-1}^2 \varepsilon_t^2]$).

Exercise 3.3. For the first estimator, the optimal instruments are given by

$$
\frac{g_{\theta t}}{E[e_t^2 | x_t]},
$$

where $g_{\theta t} = \partial g(x_t, \theta_0)/\partial \theta$, and the asymptotic variance is

$$
E\left[\frac{g_{\theta t} g_{\theta t}'}{E[e_t^2 | x_t]}\right]^{-1}.
$$

Let $\gamma = (\theta', \eta')'$. The matrix of optimal instruments for the second estimator is $\Xi_t = D_t' \Sigma_t^{-1}$, where

$$
D_t = E\left[\left.\frac{\partial h_2(y_t, x_t, \theta_0, \eta_0)}{\partial \gamma'}\right| x_t\right] = -\left[\begin{array}{cc} g_{\theta t}' & 0 \\ (\sigma_{\theta t}^2)' & (\sigma_{\eta t}^2)' \end{array}\right]
$$

with $\sigma_{\theta t}^2 = \partial \sigma^2(x_t, \theta_0, \eta_0)/\partial \theta$ and $\sigma_{\eta t}^2 = \partial \sigma^2(x_t, \theta_0, \eta_0)/\partial \eta$, and

$$
\Sigma_t^{-1} = E\left[h_2(y_t, x_t, \theta_0, \eta_0) h_2(y_t, x_t, \theta_0, \eta_0)' | x_t\right]^{-1}
$$

$$
= \left[\begin{array}{cc} E[e_t^2 | x_t] & 0 \\ 0 & \kappa_t \end{array}\right]^{-1} = \left[\begin{array}{cc} E[e_t^2 | x_t]^{-1} & 0 \\ 0 & \kappa_t^{-1} \end{array}\right],
$$

with $\kappa_t = E[e_t^4 | x_t] - \left[\sigma^2(x_t, \theta_0, \eta_0)\right]^2$. It then follows that the asymptotic variance matrix $E\left[D_t' \Sigma_t^{-1} D_t\right]^{-1}$ for the second estimator is

$$
E\left[\begin{array}{cc} \dfrac{g_{\theta t} g_{\theta t}'}{E[e_t^2 | x_t]} + \dfrac{\sigma_{\theta t}^2 (\sigma_{\theta t}^2)'}{\kappa_t} & \dfrac{\sigma_{\theta t}^2 (\sigma_{\eta t}^2)'}{\kappa_t} \\ \dfrac{\sigma_{\eta t}^2 (\sigma_{\theta t}^2)'}{\kappa_t} & \dfrac{\sigma_{\eta t}^2 (\sigma_{\eta t}^2)'}{\kappa_t} \end{array}\right]^{-1}.
$$

Using the formula for the inverse of a partitioned matrix, we obtain that the block of the asymptotic variance matrix corresponding to θ is given by

$$
\left(E\left[\frac{g_{\theta t} g_{\theta t}'}{E[e_t^2|x_t]} + \frac{\sigma_{\theta t}^2 \left(\sigma_{\theta t}^2\right)'}{\kappa_t} \right] \right.
$$
$$
\left. - E\left[\frac{\sigma_{\theta t}^2 \left(\sigma_{\eta t}^2\right)'}{\kappa_t} \right] E\left[\frac{\sigma_{\eta t}^2 \left(\sigma_{\eta t}^2\right)'}{\kappa_t} \right]^{-1} E\left[\frac{\sigma_{\eta t}^2 \left(\sigma_{\theta t}^2\right)'}{\kappa_t} \right] \right)^{-1}.
$$

This clearly is equal to the asymptotic variance of the first estimator when $\sigma_{\theta t}^2 = 0$, i.e., the skedastic function does not depend on the parameter of interest θ. Another condition which makes the two asymptotic variances equal is $\alpha_1' \sigma_{\theta t}^2 + \alpha_2' \sigma_{\eta t}^2 = 0$ with probability 1 for some constant vectors α_1 and α_2 conformable to $\sigma_{\theta t}^2$ and $\sigma_{\eta t}^2$.

References

Anatolyev, S. (2003) The form of the optimal nonlinear instrument for multiperiod conditional moment restrictions. *Econometric Theory*, 19, 602–609.

Anatolyev, S. (2006) Optimal instruments in time series: A survey. *Journal of Economic Surveys*, 21, 143–173.

Antoine, B., H. Bonnal and E. Renault (2007) On the efficient use of the informational content of estimating equations: Implied probabilities and Euclidean empirical likelihood. *Journal of Econometrics*, 138, 461–487.

Cai, Z. (2001) Weighted Nadaraya-Watson regression estimation. *Statistics and Probability Letters*, 51, 307–318.

Carrasco, M. (2009) A regularization approach to the many instruments problem. Working Paper, Université de Montréal.

Carrasco, M., and J.P. Florens (2000) Generalization of GMM to a continuum of moment conditions. *Econometric Theory*, 16, 797–834.

Carrasco, M., J.P. Florens and E. Renault (2007) Linear inverse problems and structural econometrics: Estimation based on spectral decomposition and regularization. In: J. Heckman and E. Leamer (eds.), *Handbook of Econometrics*, Vol. 6/2, Elsevier: Amsterdam, Chapter 77, 5633–5751.

Carroll, R.J. (1982) Adapting for heteroscedasticity in linear models. *Annals of Statistics*, 10, 1224–1233.

Chamberlain, G. (1987) Asymptotic efficiency in estimation with conditional moment restrictions. *Journal of Econometrics*, 34, 305–334.

Dominguez, M., and I. Lobato (2004) Consistent estimation of models defined by conditional moment restrictions. *Econometrica*, 72, 1601–1615.

Dominguez, M., and I. Lobato (2010) Consistent inference in models defined by conditional moment restrictions: An alternative to GMM. Working Paper, ITAM.

Donald, S.G., G.W. Imbens and W.K. Newey (2003) Empirical likelihood estimation and consistent tests with conditional moment restrictions. *Journal of Econometrics*, 117, 55–93.

Gospodinov, N., and T. Otsu (2010) Local GMM estimation of time series models with conditional moment restrictions. *Journal of Econometrics*, forthcoming.

Hall, A.R. (2005) *Generalized Method of Moments*. Oxford University Press: Oxford.

Hansen, L.P. (1985) A method for calculating bounds on the asymptotic variance-covariance matrices of generalized method of moments estimators. *Journal of Econometrics*, 30, 203–228.

Hansen, L.P., J.C. Heaton and M. Ogaki (1988) Efficiency bounds implied by multiperiod conditional moment restrictions. *Journal of the American Statistical Association*, 83, 863–871.

Hansen, L.P., and K.J. Singleton (1996) Efficient estimation of linear asset pricing models with moving-average errors. *Journal of Business and Economic Statistics* 14, 53–68.

Hsu, S.-H., and C.-M. Kuan (2008) Estimation of conditional moment restrictions without assuming parameter identifiability. Working Paper, Academia Sinica.

Kitamura, Y., G. Tripathi and H. Ahn (2004) Empirical likelihood-based inference in conditional moment restriction models. *Econometrica*, 72, 1667–1714.

Linton, O., and E. Mammen (2005) Estimating semiparametric ARCH(∞) models by kernel smoothing methods. *Econometrica*, 73, 771–836.

Newey, W.K. (1990) Efficient instrumental variables estimation of nonlinear models. *Econometrica*, 58, 809–837.

Newey, W.K. (1993) Efficient estimation of models with conditional moment restrictions. In: G.S. Maddala, C.R. Rao and H.D. Vinod (eds.), *Handbook of Statistics*, Vol. 11 (Elsevier, Amsterdam) 419-454.

Robinson, P. (1987) Asymptotically efficient estimation in the presence of heteroskedasticity of unknown form. *Econometrica*, 55, 875–891.

Smith, R.J. (2007) Efficient information theoretic inference for conditional moment restrictions. *Journal of Econometrics*, 138, 430–460.

Stinchcombe, M.B., and H. White (1998) Consistent specification testing with nuisance parameters present only under the alternative. *Econometric Theory*, 14, 295–325.

Tripathi, G., and Y. Kitamura (2003) Testing conditional moment restrictions. *Annals of Statistics*, 31, 2059–2095.

Tschernig, R., and L. Yang (2000) Nonparametric lag selection for time series. *Journal of Time Series Analysis*, 21, 457–487.

West, K.D. (2001) On optimal instrumental variables estimation of stationary time series models. *International Economic Review*, 42, 1043–1050.

West, K.D., and D.W. Wilcox (1996) A comparison of alternative instrumental variables estimators of dynamic linear model. *Journal of Business and Economic Statistics*, 14, 281–293.

West, K.D., K.-f. Wong and S. Anatolyev (2009) Instrumental variables estimation of heteroskedastic linear models using all lags of instruments. *Econometric Reviews*, 28, 441–467.

Chapter 4

Inference in Misspecified Models

4.1 Introduction

Most econometric models can be viewed only as approximations of the underlying data generating process and are likely to be misspecified. It is therefore desirable to conduct inference for misspecified models which would take into account the additional uncertainty that arises from possible misspecification. While the analysis of misspecified models in the maximum likelihood framework was originated by White (1982), the methodology for misspecified models defined by moment conditions is a relatively recent development and is still an active research area. Moreover, the proposed inference procedures in misspecified moment condition models are not readily adopted by applied researchers. For example, while most asset pricing models are statistically rejected by the data, many empirical studies continue to report standard errors and test hypotheses on the parameters under the assumption of correctly specified models. This creates internal inconsistency in the inference procedure and tends to underestimate the true uncertainty surrounding the parameter estimates. The aim of this chapter is to present some of the existing results in the literature on misspecified models in a unifying and comprehensive framework for statistical inference that is robust to possible model misspecification.

Maximum likelihood tends to be a natural estimation framework when the data generation process is fully parameterized. When the economic theory does not provide enough information about the underlying probabilistic law that governs the data, the econometrician is prone to a risk of misspecification. The Kullback–Leibler information criterion measures the distance between the specified and true densities and is a convenient tool for assessing and properly incorporating this misspecification risk into the estimation and inference procedure. An interesting result that emerges from this analysis is that the misspecification of the true density preserves some desirable properties of the estimator and this quasi- (or pseudo-) maximum likelihood estimator is still consistent and asymptotically normally distributed. This framework also allows us to compare different misspecified models in order to determine which model is empirically most useful and provides the best approximation to the underlying true data generating mechanism.

This parametric framework can be further generalized by adopting a fully nonparametric view of the true distribution that generates the data, and our knowledge of some characteristics of the model only enters through a set of (conditional or unconditional) moment restrictions. This nonparametric likelihood can handle overidentified moment condition models and is described in greater detail in Chapters 2 and 3. Our use of this framework here is to extend the parametric likelihood comparison of misspecified models to a nonparametric likelihood setup that incorporates explicitly the moment restrictions implied by economic theory. Finally, we point out some problems that arise in the analysis of misspecified moment condition models estimated by GMM and provide a detailed discussion on the estimation, evaluation and model comparison of asset pricing models. This problem serves as a specialized, yet highly relevant practical example of the analysis of inherently misspecified models estimated by GMM with a common weighting matrix.

4.2   Quasi-Maximum Likelihood

4.2.1   Kullback–Leibler Information Criterion

Consider the distributions $f_0(z)$ and $f(z)$. The *Kullback–Leibler Information Criterion* (Kullback and Leibler, 1951), KLIC for short, measures the distance between f_0 and f as

$$\mathcal{KLIC}(f_0 : f) = E_{f_0(z)} \left[\log \frac{f_0(z)}{f(z)} \right] = \int \log \frac{f_0(z)}{f(z)} f_0(z) dz,$$

where $E_{f_0(z)}[\cdot]$ denotes the mathematical expectation with respect to $f_0(z)$. In the case when $f_0(y|x)$ and $f(y|x)$ are conditional distributions of y given x, the KLIC is defined as

$$\mathcal{KLIC}(f_0 : f) = E_{f_0(x,y)} \left[\log \frac{f_0(y|x)}{f(y|x)} \right],$$

where the expectation is taken with respect to the true joint distribution of (y, x). For notational simplicity, we suppress the explicit indexing of the expectation operator with the true marginal or joint distributions of the data.

The KLIC possesses some, but not all, properties of a distance. The KLIC is non-negative due to the *information inequality*

$$\mathcal{KLIC}(f_0 : f) = -\int \log \frac{f(z)}{f_0(z)} f_0(z) dz$$

$$\geq -\log \int \frac{f(z)}{f_0(z)} f_0(z) dz = -\log 1 = 0.$$

Moreover, by the strict concavity of the log function, $\mathcal{KLIC}(f_0 : f) = 0$ if and only if $f(z) = f_0(z)$ for almost all z. However, the symmetry property (with respect to an exchange of arguments) and the triangular inequality do not hold, so KLIC is not, strictly speaking, a distance measure.

Exercise 4.1. Denote by $\mathbf{e}$ the empirical distribution function. Suppose that we have postulated a family of densities $f(z, \theta)$ for the true distribution of z. Interpret the value of θ that minimizes $\mathcal{KLIC}(\mathbf{e} : f)$.

4.2.2 Quasi-Maximum Likelihood Estimator

Consider a situation when $f_0(y|x)$ is the true conditional density, and $f(y|x, \theta)$ is a family of distributions. Suppose that θ is estimated by the maximum likelihood based on $f(y|x, \theta)$ and random sample $\{(y_i, x_i)\}_{i=1}^n$:

$$\hat{\theta} = \arg\max_{\theta \in \Theta} \frac{1}{n} \sum_{i=1}^{n} \log f(y_i|x_i, \theta). \qquad (4.1)$$

If there exists such θ_0 that $f(y|x, \theta_0) = f_0(y|x)$ almost surely, i.e., the postulated density is correctly specified, this is the maximum likelihood estimator with the familiar asymptotic properties of consistency, asymptotic normality and asymptotic efficiency:

$$\hat{\theta} \xrightarrow{p} \theta_0, \quad \sqrt{n}\left(\hat{\theta} - \theta_0\right) \xrightarrow{d} \mathcal{N}\left(0, H^{-1}\right),$$

where

$$H = -E\left[\frac{\partial^2 \log f(y|x, \theta_0)}{\partial \theta \partial \theta'}\right] = E\left[\frac{\partial \log f(y|x, \theta_0)}{\partial \theta} \frac{\partial \log f(y|x, \theta_0)}{\partial \theta'}\right]$$

is the information matrix.

However, if $f(y|x, \theta) \neq f_0(y|x)$ for all θ, the postulated density is misspecified, and the problem (4.1) no longer defines an ML estimator. However, the estimator $\hat{\theta}$ is still an extremum estimator and, under suitable conditions, is still asymptotically normal:

$$\hat{\theta} \xrightarrow{p} \theta_*, \quad \sqrt{n}\left(\hat{\theta} - \theta_*\right) \xrightarrow{d} \mathcal{N}\left(0, H^{-1}VH^{-1}\right),$$

where

$$H = -E\left[\frac{\partial^2 \log f(y|x, \theta_*)}{\partial \theta \partial \theta'}\right]$$

and

$$V = E\left[\frac{\partial \log f(y|x, \theta_*)}{\partial \theta} \frac{\partial \log f(y|x, \theta_*)}{\partial \theta'}\right].$$

The parameter value

$$\theta_* = \arg \max_{\theta \in \Theta} E\left[\log f\left(y|x, \theta\right)\right]$$

is called the *pseudo-true value*, and its estimator $\hat{\theta}$ is called the *quasi-maximum likelihood (QML) estimator* (White, 1982). The population problem for the pseudo-true value may also be expressed as

$$\theta_* = \arg \min_{\theta \in \Theta} E_{f_0}\left[\frac{\log f_0\left(y|x\right)}{\log f\left(y|x, \theta\right)}\right] = \arg \min_{\theta \in \Theta} \mathcal{KLIC}(f_0 : f\left(\cdot, \theta\right)),$$

i.e., the pseudo-true value makes the postulated conditional density closest, in terms of KLIC, to the true conditional density.

Exercise 4.2. Consider a random sample $\{z_i\}_{i=1}^n$ from a population of scalar random variable z with finite moments. Derive the asymptotics of the QML estimator (a) of $\left(\mu, \sigma^2\right)$ when $f\left(z, \mu, \sigma^2\right)$ is $\mathcal{N}\left(\mu, \sigma^2\right)$; (b) of σ^2 when $f\left(z, \sigma^2\right)$ is $\mathcal{N}\left(0, \sigma^2\right)$.

The fact that one uses the maximum likelihood principle with a misspecified distribution does not necessarily imply that the parameters will be estimated inconsistently. For instance, the nonlinear least squared estimator in a regression model, which can be considered as a QML estimator based on the conditionally homoskedastic normal distribution, is consistent under conditional heteroskedasticity or conditional non-normality. In other words, the pseudo-true parameter may well coincide with the true parameter in favorable circumstances.

4.3   Pseudo Likelihood Methods

Gourieroux, Monfort and Trognon (1984a) considered a number of important questions that arise in a regression model framework. What density functions in QML estimation allow for consistent estimation of the regression parameters? If more than one density renders the estimators consistent, which density gives rise to an asymptotically most efficient estimator? The theory put forth in Gourieroux, Monfort and Trognon (1984a, 1984b) has been named *pseudo likelihood methods*, while the QML estimation procedure in this context is referred to as pseudo maximum likelihood (PML) estimation (see also Gourieroux and Monfort, 1993). This work was developed in an *IID* environment, while White (1994) generalized the results to a time series context.

4.3.1 PML of Order 1

Consider the (possibly) nonlinear regression model

$$E\left[y|x\right] = g\left(x, \theta_0\right),\qquad(4.2)$$

where $g\left(\cdot,\cdot\right)$ is a known function, and $\theta_0 \in \Theta$ is the true parameter. Let $f\left(u,\mu\right)$ denote a probability density, where μ is the mean of the density. Given a random sample $\{(y_i, x_i)\}_{i=1}^n$, define

$$\hat{\theta}_1 = \arg\max_{\theta \in \Theta} \frac{1}{n} \sum_{i=1}^n \log f\left(y_i, g\left(x_i, \theta\right)\right)$$

to be a *PML estimator of order 1*, or a *PML1 estimator*. Note that it is permissible to use densities whose support is narrower than the support of the data on y. For instance, it is possible to use the Poisson density with continuously distributed positive y by omitting the term $-\log y!$ from the log-likelihood, or to use the Bernoulli probability mass function when y is distributed between 0 and 1.

Define a *linear exponential family of densities* to be a set of densities written in the form

$$f\left(u,\mu\right) = \exp\left(\alpha_1\left(\mu\right) + \alpha_2\left(u\right) + \alpha_3\left(\mu\right)u\right),$$

where $\alpha_1(\mu)$, $\alpha_2\left(u\right)$, $\alpha_3\left(\mu\right)$ are scalar functions, and μ is the mean of f. For f to be a density and have mean μ, the functions $\alpha_1(\mu)$, $\alpha_2\left(u\right)$, $\alpha_3\left(\mu\right)$ need to obey certain restrictions, most notable of which is $\partial\alpha_1(\mu)/\partial\mu + \mu\,\partial\alpha_3\left(\mu\right)/\partial\mu = 0$. Examples of members of the linear exponential family include normal with unit variance (having $\alpha_3\left(\mu\right) = \mu$), Poisson (having $\alpha_3\left(\mu\right) = \log\mu$), Gamma with a given parameter α (having $\alpha_3\left(\mu\right) = -\alpha/\mu$) and Bernoulli (having $\alpha_3\left(\mu\right) = \log\mu - \log\left(1 - \mu\right)$). Gourieroux, Monfort and Trognon (1984a) give a more complete table of members of this family that are used extensively in applied statistics.

The key result for PML1 estimators is the following. If (4.2) holds and $f\left(u,\mu\right)$ is from the linear exponential family, then the corresponding PML1 estimator is consistent and asymptotically normal:

$$\hat{\theta}_1 \overset{p}{\to} \theta_0, \quad \sqrt{n}\left(\hat{\theta}_1 - \theta_0\right) \overset{d}{\to} \mathcal{N}\left(0, H_1^{-1} V_1 H_1^{-1}\right),$$

where

$$H_1 = E\left[\left.\frac{\partial\alpha_3\left(\mu\right)}{\partial\mu}\right|_{g(x,\theta_0)} \frac{\partial g\left(x,\theta_0\right)}{\partial\theta} \frac{\partial g\left(x,\theta_0\right)}{\partial\theta'}\right]$$

and

$$V_1 = E\left[\left(\left.\frac{\partial\alpha_3\left(\mu\right)}{\partial\mu}\right|_{g(x,\theta_0)}\right)^2 \mathrm{var}\left[y|x\right] \frac{\partial g\left(x,\theta_0\right)}{\partial\theta} \frac{\partial g\left(x,\theta_0\right)}{\partial\theta'}\right].$$

Moreover, the PML1 estimator is consistent for any value of the true para-meter only if $f(u, \mu)$ is from the linear exponential family. A further result concerns asymptotic efficiency: the asymptotic variance $H_1^{-1} V_1 H_1^{-1}$ is mini-mized at

$$E \left[\frac{1}{\text{var}[y|x]} \frac{\partial g(x, \theta_0)}{\partial \theta} \frac{\partial g(x, \theta_0)}{\partial \theta'} \right]^{-1}$$

(i.e., when the "sandwich" collapses) which is attained when

$$\left. \frac{\partial a_3(\mu)}{\partial \mu} \right|_{g(x, \theta_0)} \propto \frac{1}{\text{var}[y|x]}.$$

Hence, the normal density proves to be most advantageous under condi-tional homoskedasticity, the Poisson density – when $\text{var}[y|x]$ is proportional to $g(x, \theta_0)$, the Bernoulli distribution – when $\text{var}[y|x]$ is proportional to $g(x, \theta_0)(1 - g(x, \theta_0))$, the Gamma density – when $\text{var}[y|x]$ is proportional to $\sqrt{g(x, \theta_0)}$, etc.

Exercise 4.3. Determine if using the negative binomial distribution with density

$$f(u, \mu) = \frac{\Gamma(a + u)}{\Gamma(a) \Gamma(1 + u)} \left(\frac{\mu}{a} \right)^u \left(1 + \frac{\mu}{a} \right)^{-(a+u)},$$

where μ is its mean and a is an arbitrary known constant, leads to consistent estimation of θ_0 in the mean regression $E[y|x] = g(x, \theta_0)$ when the true conditional distribution is heteroskedastic normal with a skedastic function $\text{var}[y|x] = 2g(x, \theta_0)$.

Exercise 4.4. Consider the regression model $E[y|x] = g(x, \theta_0)$. Suppose that this regression is conditionally normal and homoskedastic. A researcher, however, uses the following conditional density to construct a PML1 estimator of θ_0:

$$y|x, \theta \sim \mathcal{N}\left(g(x, \theta), g(x, \theta)^2 \right).$$

Establish if such an estimator is consistent for θ_0.

Exercise 4.5. Consider the regression model $E[y|x] = g(x, \theta_0)$. Suppose that a PML1 estimator, based on the density $f(z, \mu)$ parameterized by the mean μ, consistently estimates the true parameter θ_0. Consider another den-sity $w(z, \mu, \varsigma)$ parameterized by two parameters, the mean μ and some other parameter ς, which nests $f(z, \mu)$ (i.e., f is a special case of w). Use the example of the Weibull distribution with density

$$w(z, \mu, \varsigma) = \varsigma \left(\frac{\Gamma(1 + \varsigma^{-1})}{\mu} \right)^\varsigma z^{\varsigma - 1} \exp\left(-\left(\frac{\Gamma(1 + \varsigma^{-1})}{\mu} z \right)^\varsigma \right) \mathbb{I}\{z \geq 0\},$$

where $\varsigma > 0$, to show that the PML1 estimator based on $w(z, \mu, \varsigma)$ does not necessarily consistently estimate θ_0. What is the econometric explanation of this perhaps counter-intuitive result?

4.3.2 PML of Order 2

Suppose now that the regression model

$$E[y|x] = g(x, \theta_0) \tag{4.3}$$

is augmented with the skedastic function

$$\mathrm{var}[y|x] = \sigma^2(x, \theta_0), \tag{4.4}$$

where $g(\cdot, \cdot)$ and $\sigma^2(\cdot, \cdot)$ are known functions, and $\theta_0 \in \Theta$ is the true parameter. Let $f(u, \mu, \nu)$ denote a probability density, where μ is the mean of the density and ν is its variance. Given a random sample $\{(y_i, x_i)\}_{i=1}^{n}$, let

$$\hat{\theta}_2 = \arg \max_{\theta \in \Theta} \frac{1}{n} \sum_{i=1}^{n} \log f\left(y_i, g(x_i, \theta), \sigma^2(x_i, \theta)\right)$$

be a *PML estimator of order 2*, or a *PML2 estimator*.

Define a *quadratic exponential family of densities* to be a set of densities written in the form

$$f(u, \mu, \nu) = \exp\left(\alpha_1(\mu, \nu) + \alpha_2(u) + \alpha_3(\mu, \nu)u + \alpha_4(\mu, \nu)u^2\right),$$

where $\alpha_1(\mu, \nu), \alpha_2(u), \alpha_3(\mu, \nu), \alpha_4(\mu, \nu)$ are scalar functions that obey certain restrictions, μ is the mean of f, and ν is the variance of f. The leading member of the quadratic exponential family is the normal density $f(u, \mu, \nu) = (2\pi\nu)^{1/2} \exp\left(-(u-\mu)^2/(2\nu)\right)$; more examples are provided in Gourieroux, Monfort and Trognon (1984a). If (4.3)–(4.4) hold and $f(u, \mu, \nu)$ is from the quadratic exponential family, then

$$\hat{\theta}_2 \xrightarrow{p} \theta_0, \quad \sqrt{n}\left(\hat{\theta}_2 - \theta_0\right) \xrightarrow{d} \mathcal{N}\left(0, H_2^{-1} V_2 H_2^{-1}\right),$$

where

$$H_2 = -E\left[\frac{\partial^2 \log f\left(y, g(x, \theta_0), \sigma^2(x, \theta_0)\right)}{\partial\theta\partial\theta'}\right]$$

and

$$V_2 = E\left[\frac{\partial \log f\left(y, g(x, \theta_0), \sigma^2(x, \theta_0)\right)}{\partial\theta} \frac{\partial \log f\left(y, g(x, \theta_0), \sigma^2(x, \theta_0)\right)}{\partial\theta'}\right].$$

Moreover, the PML2 estimator is consistent only if $f(u, \mu, \nu)$ is from the quadratic exponential family.

Exercise 4.6. Consider the model

$$y = \alpha + e,$$

where the unobservable e, conditionally on x, is symmetrically distributed with mean zero and variance $x^2 \sigma^2$ with unknown σ^2. The data $\{(y_i, x_i)\}_{i=1}^n$ are IID. Construct a PML2 estimator of α and σ^2 based on the normal distribution and derive its asymptotic properties.

4.4   Comparison of Misspecified Models

4.4.1   Misspecified Models Estimated by QML

Despite the fact that all competing models can be viewed as misspecified, it is still practically useful to determine if any of these models dominates the others in terms of a particular statistical criterion. This section follows closely Vuong (1989) and develops statistical tests for comparing models estimated by QML but in a general time series setup.

Let (y_t, x_t) be a stationary and ergodic process with true (but unknown) conditional density $f_0(y|x)$ and $\mathcal{M}_1$ and $\mathcal{M}_2$ be two (possibly) misspecified parametric models with quasi-likelihood functions

$$Q_{1,n}(\theta) = \frac{1}{n} \sum_{t=1}^{n} \log f_1(y_t|x_t, \theta)$$

and

$$Q_{2,n}(\gamma) = \frac{1}{n} \sum_{t=1}^{n} \log f_2(y_t|x_t, \gamma).$$

The parameters $\theta \in \Theta \subset \mathcal{R}^{k_1}$ for $\mathcal{M}_1$ and $\gamma \in \Gamma \subset \mathcal{R}^{k_2}$ for $\mathcal{M}_2$ are estimated as

$$\hat{\theta} = \arg \max_{\theta \in \Theta} Q_{1,n}(\theta)$$

$$\hat{\gamma} = \arg \max_{\gamma \in \Gamma} Q_{2,n}(\gamma).$$

Also, let θ_* and γ_* denote the corresponding pseudo-true values defined as $\theta_* = \arg \max_{\theta \in \Theta} E\left[\log f_1(y|x, \theta)\right]$ and $\gamma_* = \arg \max_{\gamma \in \Gamma} E\left[\log f_2(y|x, \gamma)\right]$, respectively, and

$$\mathcal{LR}(\hat{\theta}, \hat{\gamma}) = Q_{1,n}(\hat{\theta}) - Q_{2,n}(\hat{\gamma}) = \frac{1}{n} \sum_{t=1}^{n} \log \frac{f_1(y_t|x_t, \hat{\theta})}{f_2(y_t|x_t, \hat{\gamma})}$$

be the likelihood ratio $(\mathcal{LR})$ statistic for model $\mathcal{M}_1$ against model $\mathcal{M}_2$.

Suppose that $\{f_1(y|x) : f_1 \in \mathcal{F}_1\}$ is a family of densities compatible with model $\mathcal{M}_1$. The model $\mathcal{M}_1$ is misspecified if $f_0 \notin \mathcal{F}_1$. The KLIC from $\{f_1(y|x) : f_1 \in \mathcal{F}_1\}$ to $f_0(y|x)$ is given by

$$KLIC\,(f_0 : f_1) = \inf_{f_1 \in \mathcal{F}_1} E\left[\log\left(\frac{f_0(y|x)}{f_1(y|x)}\right)\right].$$

Similarly, if $\{f_2(y|x) : f_2 \in \mathcal{F}_2\}$ is a family of densities compatible with model $\mathcal{M}_2$, the KLIC from $\{f_2(y|x) : f_2 \in \mathcal{F}_2\}$ to $f_0(y|x)$ is given by

$$KLIC\,(f_0 : f_2) = \inf_{f_2 \in \mathcal{F}_2} E\left[\log\left(\frac{f_0(y|x)}{f_2(y|x)}\right)\right].$$

The misspecified ML can be interpreted as the best approximation to the true distribution in terms of KLIC (Akaike, 1973). For parametric likelihood families $\{f_1(y|x, \theta) : \theta \in \Theta\}$ and $\{f_2(y|x, \gamma) : \gamma \in \Gamma\}$,

$$KLIC\,(f_0 : f_1(\cdot, \theta)) = \min_{\theta \in \Theta} E\left[\log\left(\frac{f_0(y|x)}{f_1(y|x, \theta)}\right)\right],$$

$$KLIC\,(f_0 : f_2(\cdot, \gamma)) = \min_{\gamma \in \Gamma} E\left[\log\left(\frac{f_0(y|x)}{f_2(y|x, \gamma)}\right)\right],$$

and

$$\mathcal{LR}(\hat{\theta}, \hat{\gamma}) \overset{a.s.}{\to} E\left[\log \frac{f_1(y|x, \theta_*)}{f_2(y|x, \gamma_*)}\right].$$

The last result indicates that testing the difference between the sample quasi-likelihood functions of models $\mathcal{M}_1$ and $\mathcal{M}_2$ can be used for model selection or testing the hypothesis

$$H_0 : E\left[\log \frac{f_1(y|x, \theta_*)}{f_2(y|x, \gamma_*)}\right] - 0.$$

The competing models $\mathcal{M}_1$ and $\mathcal{M}_2$ can be nested, strictly non-nested or overlapping, which determines what statistical tests should be used for model comparison. If $\mathcal{M}_1 \cap \mathcal{M}_2 = \varnothing$, we have the case of *strictly non-nested models*. For *nested models*, we have $\mathcal{M}_1 \subset \mathcal{M}_2$ or $\mathcal{M}_2 \subset \mathcal{M}_1$. Finally, if $\mathcal{M}_1 \cap \mathcal{M}_2 \neq \varnothing$, $\mathcal{M}_1 \not\subset \mathcal{M}_2$, and $\mathcal{M}_2 \not\subset \mathcal{M}_1$, we refer to $\mathcal{M}_1$ and $\mathcal{M}_2$ as *overlapping models*.

Define the matrices

$$H_{\theta\theta} = E\left[\frac{\partial^2 \log f_1(y_t|x_t, \theta_*)}{\partial\theta\partial\theta'}\right],$$

$$H_{\gamma\gamma} = E\left[\frac{\partial^2 \log f_2(y_t|x_t, \gamma_*)}{\partial\gamma\partial\gamma'}\right],$$

$$V_{\theta\theta} = \sum_{j=-\infty}^{+\infty} E\left[\frac{\partial \log f_1(y_t|x_t,\theta_*)}{\partial \theta}\frac{\partial \log f_1(y_{t+j}|x_{t+j},\theta_*)}{\partial \theta'}\right],$$

$$V_{\gamma\gamma} = \sum_{j=-\infty}^{+\infty} E\left[\frac{\partial \log f_2(y_t|x_t,\gamma_*)}{\partial \gamma}\frac{\partial \log f_2(y_{t+j}|x_{t+j},\gamma_*)}{\partial \gamma'}\right],$$

and

$$V_{\theta\gamma} = \sum_{j=-\infty}^{+\infty} E\left[\frac{\partial \log f_1(y_t|x_t,\theta_*)}{\partial \theta}\frac{\partial \log f_2(y_{t+j}|x_{t+j},\gamma_*)}{\partial \gamma'}\right].$$

Under some regularity conditions, it follows that the QML estimators of θ_*, γ_* and $(\theta_*',\gamma_*')'$ are consistent and asymptotically normally distributed with asymptotic variance matrices

$$\Omega_\theta = H_{\theta\theta}^{-1}V_{\theta\theta}H_{\theta\theta}^{-1},$$

$$\Omega_\gamma = H_{\gamma\gamma}^{-1}V_{\gamma\gamma}H_{\gamma\gamma}^{-1},$$

and

$$\Omega = \begin{pmatrix} \Omega_\theta & \Omega_{\theta\gamma} \\ \Omega_{\theta\gamma}' & \Omega_\gamma \end{pmatrix},$$

where $\Omega_{\theta\gamma} = H_{\theta\theta}^{-1}V_{\theta\gamma}H_{\gamma\gamma}^{-1}$.

Using these results, Vuong (1989) showed that if $f_1(y|x,\theta_*) = f_2(y|x,\gamma_*)$ for almost all (y,x),

$$n \cdot \mathcal{LR}(\hat{\theta},\hat{\gamma}) \xrightarrow{d} \sum_{i=1}^{k_1+k_2} \xi_i\nu_i, \qquad (4.5)$$

where ν_i's are independent chi-square random variables with one degree of freedom and ξ_i's are the eigenvalues of

$$\frac{1}{2}\begin{pmatrix} -H_{\theta\theta} & 0_{k_1\times k_2} \\ 0_{k_2\times k_1} & H_{\gamma\gamma} \end{pmatrix}\Omega. \qquad (4.6)$$

It should be noted that if the information matrix equality holds for $\mathcal{M}_1$ and $\mathcal{M}_2$, i.e., $-H_{\theta\theta} = V_{\theta\theta}$ and $-H_{\gamma\gamma} = V_{\gamma\gamma}$, and

$$V_{\gamma\gamma} - V_{\gamma\theta}V_{\theta\theta}^{-1}V_{\theta\gamma} = 0,$$

the test $2n\cdot\mathcal{LR}(\hat{\theta},\hat{\gamma})$ converges to a central chi-square distribution with $k_1 - k_2$ degrees of freedom (Vuong, 1989).

On the other hand, if $f_1(y|x,\theta_*) \neq f_2(y|x,\gamma_*)$,

$$\sqrt{n}\left(\mathcal{LR}(\hat{\theta},\hat{\gamma}) - E\left[\log\frac{f_1(y|x,\theta_*)}{f_2(y|x,\gamma_*)}\right]\right) \xrightarrow{d} \mathcal{N}(0,\sigma_Q^2), \qquad (4.7)$$

where $\sigma_Q^2 = \lim_{n\to\infty} \text{var}\left[\sqrt{n}\left(Q_{1,n}(\theta_*) - Q_{2,n}(\gamma_*)\right)\right] > 0$ (see Vuong, 1989).

The results in (4.5) and (4.7) show that the limiting behavior of the statistic $\mathcal{LR}(\hat{\theta}, \hat{\gamma})$ is governed by two different asymptotic frameworks (with different rates of convergence and asymptotic distributions) depending on whether $f_1(y|x, \theta_*) = f_2(y|x, \gamma_*)$ for almost all (y, x) or $f_1(y|x, \theta_*) \neq f_2(y|x, \gamma_*)$. Vuong (1989) argues that $f_1(y|x, \theta_*) = f_2(y|x, \gamma_*)$ ($\mathcal{M}_1$ and $\mathcal{M}_2$ are overlapping models) if and only if $\sigma_Q^2 = 0$. The degeneracy of the asymptotic distribution in (4.7) can also occur in models with dependent data when the spectral density at frequency zero of $\sqrt{n}\left(Q_{1,n}(\hat{\theta}) - Q_{2,n}(\hat{\gamma})\right)$ is zero (for example, in the case of an MA unit root).

In order to determine which asymptotic framework should be used for model selection, one could do a pre-test of $H_0 : \sigma_Q^2 = 0$ as

$$n\hat{\sigma}_Q^2 \xrightarrow{d} \sum_{i=1}^{k_1+k_2} 4\xi_i^2 \nu_i, \tag{4.8}$$

where $\hat{\sigma}_Q^2$ is the (possibly heteroskedasticity and autocorrelation consistent) sample analog of σ_Q^2 and ξ_i and ν_i are defined above.

The model comparison procedure between two competing models can then be described as follows. For strictly non-nested models, the test of the null hypothesis $H_0 : E\left[\log f_1(y|x, \theta_*)\right] = E\left[\log f_2(y|x, \gamma_*)\right]$ follows directly from (4.7) and is given by

$$\frac{\sqrt{n}\mathcal{LR}(\hat{\theta}, \hat{\gamma})}{\hat{\sigma}_Q} \xrightarrow{d} \mathcal{N}(0, 1), \tag{4.9}$$

where $\hat{\sigma}_Q^2$ is a consistent estimator of the (long-run) variance σ_Q^2.

In the case of overlapping models that are both misspecified, one should adopt a sequential test procedure by first verifying if $f_1(y|x, \theta_*) = f_2(y|x, \gamma_*)$ using the test of $H_0 : \sigma_Q^2 = 0$ in (4.8). If the null hypothesis cannot be rejected, it follows that the two models are not statistically different from each other. If the null hypothesis is rejected, one should proceed with the test in (4.9) and the conclusion should be based on the outcome of this second test.

Finally, for nested models, one could directly apply the test in (4.5). However, the fact that the models are nested implies particular parameter restrictions on the larger model and that the eigenvalues of matrix (4.6) should be nonnegative. Suppose that, without loss of generality, $\mathcal{M}_2 \subset \mathcal{M}_1$. It follows that there exists a twice continuously differentiable function $\psi(\cdot)$ such that $f_2(y|x, \gamma) = f_1(y|x, \psi(\gamma))$ for any $\gamma \in \Gamma$ and $\theta_* = \psi(\gamma_*)$ (see Vuong, 1989). Then, under $H_0 : E\left[\log f_1(y|x, \theta_*)\right] = E\left[\log f_2(y|x, \gamma_*)\right]$,

$$n \cdot \mathcal{LR}(\hat{\theta}, \hat{\gamma}) \xrightarrow{d} \sum_{i=1}^{k_1} \omega_i \nu_i,$$

where ω_i's are the k_1 eigenvalues of matrix

$$V_{\theta\theta}\left[\frac{\partial\psi(\gamma_*)}{\partial\gamma'}H_{\gamma\gamma}^{-1}\frac{\partial\psi(\gamma_*)'}{\partial\gamma} - H_{\theta\theta}^{-1}\right]$$

that are all real and nonnegative. In section 4.4.3.2 below, we show how to further reduce the dimension of the matrix so that all computed eigenvalues are guaranteed to be positive.

When the number of competing models is larger than two, a pairwise comparison may not determine the best performing model. Alternatively, the KLIC of all competing models is compared to the KLIC of a benchmark model using the vector $\mathcal{LR}$ statistic (White, 2000)

$$\left(\sqrt{n}\left(Q_{0,n}(\hat{\theta}) - Q_{1,n}(\hat{\gamma}_1)\right), ..., \sqrt{n}\left(Q_{0,n}(\hat{\theta}) - Q_{p,n}(\hat{\gamma}_p)\right)\right)'$$

with a null hypothesis $H_0 : \max_{j=1,...,p}\left\{Q_0(\theta_*) - Q_j(\gamma_{*,j})\right\} \leq 0$, where $Q_0(\theta_*)$ and $Q_j(\gamma_{*,j})$ are population analogs of $Q_{0,n}(\hat{\theta})$ and $Q_{j,n}(\hat{\gamma}_j)$. This is a test of whether the best candidate model outperforms the benchmark model, and its critical values are typically determined by bootstrap methods.

Exercise 4.7. Consider the following regression model:

$$E[y|x] = \theta_0 x,$$

where all variables are positive scalars. Suppose we observe a random sample $\{(y_i, x_i)\}_{i=1}^n$. Construct a likelihood ratio test comparing the exponential model $y|x \sim \mathcal{E}(\theta x)$, where $\mathcal{E}(\mu)$ denotes the exponential distribution with mean μ and density

$$\frac{1}{\mu}\exp\left(-\frac{y}{\mu}\right) \cdot \mathbb{I}\{y \geq 0\},$$

and the model based on $y|x \sim \mathcal{LN}\left(\log(\theta x) - \log\sqrt{2}, \log 2\right)$, where $\mathcal{LN}(a, \omega)$ denotes the lognormal distribution with parameters (a, ω), mean $\exp(a + \omega/2)$, variance $\exp(2a + \omega)(\exp(\omega) - 1)$ and density

$$\frac{1}{y\sqrt{2\pi\omega}}\exp\left(-\frac{(\log y - a)^2}{2\omega}\right).$$

Is there a reason to prefer the exponential model to the lognormal model irrespective of the outcome of the likelihood ratio test?

4.4.2 Misspecified Models Estimated by Nonparametric Likelihood

Many interesting economic models are not fully parametric but are defined only to a set of unconditional moment restrictions. In this section, we will replace the parametric likelihood families above with nonparametric likelihood families that are consistent with the moment conditions implied by economic theory.

To illustrate this approach, suppose that we observe a realization of a stationary and ergodic process x_t with true (but unknown) density $f_0(x)$ and support $\mathcal{X}$. Let $E[m_1(x, \theta_0)] = \int m_1(x, \theta) f_0(x) dx = 0$ be an $\ell_1 \times 1$ vector of population moment conditions, where θ is a $k_1 \times 1$ vector of unknown parameters from $\Theta \subset \mathbb{R}^{k_1}$, and $m_1(\cdot)$ is a given function $\{m_1(x, \theta) : \mathcal{X} \times \Theta \to \mathbb{R}^{\ell_1}\}$ with $\ell_1 \geq k_1$. Similarly, let $E[m_2(x, \gamma_0)] = \int m_2(x, \gamma) f_0(x) dx = 0$ be an $\ell_2 \times 1$ vector of population moment conditions, where γ is a $k_2 \times 1$ vector of unknown parameters from $\Gamma \subset \mathbb{R}^{k_2}$, and $m_2(\cdot)$ is a given function $\{m_2(x, \gamma) : \mathcal{X} \times \Gamma \to \mathbb{R}^{\ell_2}\}$ with $\ell_2 \geq k_2$.

Let $\mathcal{F}_1(\theta) = \{f_1(x) | \int m_1(x, \theta) f_1(x) dx = 0\}$, $\theta \in \Theta$ be a nonparametric likelihood family that is compatible with the moment condition $E[m_1(x_t, \theta)] = 0$ and define model $\mathcal{M}_1$ as $\mathcal{M}_1 = \cup_{\theta \in \Theta} \mathcal{F}_1(\theta)$. The KLIC from $f_1(x)$ to $f_0(x)$, subject to $f_1(x) \in \mathcal{F}_1(\theta)$, is given by (see Exercise 4.8 below and Chapter 2 for more details)

$$\mathcal{KLIC}_{f_1 \in \mathcal{F}_1(\theta)}(f_0 : f_1) = \inf_{f_1 \in \mathcal{F}_1(\theta)} \int \log\left(\frac{f_0(x)}{f_1(x)}\right) f_0(x) dx \qquad (4.10)$$

$$= \min_{\theta \in \Theta} \max_{\lambda \in \Lambda} \int \log\left(1 + \lambda(\theta)' m_1(x, \theta)\right) f_0(x) dx,$$

where the implied density that minimizes KLIC is $f_0(x)/(1 + \lambda(\theta)' m_1(x, \theta))$ and $\lambda = \lambda(\theta)$ is the "dual" parameter (Mykland, 1995). The estimators of θ and λ are obtained as a solution to the sample analog of the saddlepoint optimization problem in (4.10).

Model $\mathcal{M}_1$ is said to be *misspecified* if $f_0(x) \notin \mathcal{M}_1$. In this case, we refer to the values θ_* and λ_* that minimize $\mathcal{KLIC}$ in (4.10) as *pseudo-true values*. Similarly, we define the nonparametric family $\mathcal{F}_2(\gamma) = \{f_2(x) | \int m_2(x, \gamma) f_2(x) dx = 0\}$, $\gamma \in \Gamma$ model $\mathcal{M}_2 = \cup_{\gamma \in \Gamma} \mathcal{F}_2(\gamma)$, $\mathcal{KLIC}_{f_2 \in \mathcal{F}_2(\gamma)}(f_0 : f_2)$ and the pseudo-true values γ_* and μ_*.

Some interesting results concerning properties of the nonparametric likelihood estimators that arise under misspecification (Schennach, 2007) are worth mentioning. In particular, the estimators in the nonparametric likelihood class are no longer asymptotically equivalent and the empirical likelihood estimator, which is the solution to (4.10), is ill-behaved and, under some conditions, loses its root-n consistency (Schennach, 2007). One heuristic argument for the poor behavior of the empirical likelihood estimator under misspecification is based on inspection of its influence function, which measures the asymptotic bias of the estimator caused by data contamination. Note that the influence function of the empirical likelihood estimator is proportional to (Imbens, Spady and Johnson, 1998)

$$\frac{1}{1 + \lambda(\theta)' m_1(x, \theta)} \frac{\partial m_1(x, \theta)}{\partial \theta} \lambda(\theta)' m_1(x, \theta).$$

As a result, the influence function of the empirical likelihood estimator becomes unbounded as the denominator may approach zero when $\lambda(\theta)$ deviates from the true parameter value of zero under correctly specified models. While the Euclidean likelihood (see Chapter 2) has a bounded influence function, it can produce negative probability weights for the implied density even asymptotically (Schennach, 2007). One estimator that appears to possess better properties and be robust to misspecification is the exponential tilting estimator. In what follows, we focus our discussion on estimation, evaluation and comparison of possibly misspecified models using the exponential tilting estimator as in Kitamura (1998).

The exponential tilting estimator is obtained as the solution to

$$\mathcal{KLIC}_{f_1 \in \mathcal{F}_1(\theta)}\,(f_1 : f_0)$$

in which the relative positions of $f_1(\cdot,\theta)$ and $f_0(\cdot)$ are reversed compared to (4.10) (see also section 2.3.3 in Chapter 2). Let

$$Q_{1,n}(\theta,\lambda) = n^{-1}\sum_{t=1}^{n}\exp(\lambda' m_1(x_t,\theta))$$

and

$$Q_{2,n}(\gamma,\mu) = n^{-1}\sum_{t=1}^{n}\exp(\mu' m_2(x_t,\gamma)),$$

and define the exponential tilting estimators of $\phi = (\theta',\lambda')'$ and $\psi = (\gamma',\mu')'$ as

$$\hat{\phi} = \arg\max_{\theta}\min_{\lambda} Q_{1,n}(\theta,\lambda)$$

and

$$\hat{\psi} = \arg\max_{\gamma}\min_{\mu} Q_{2,n}(\gamma,\mu).$$

Denote the corresponding pseudo-true values by $\phi_* = (\theta'_*,\lambda'_*)'$ and $\psi_* = (\gamma'_*,\mu'_*)'$.

Define the matrices

$$H_{\phi\phi} = E\left[\frac{\partial^2 \exp(\lambda'_* m_1(x_t,\theta_*))}{\partial\phi\partial\phi'}\right] = \begin{pmatrix} H_{\theta\theta} & H_{\theta\lambda} \\ H'_{\theta\lambda} & H_{\lambda\lambda} \end{pmatrix},$$

where

$$H_{\theta\theta} = E\left[\left(\frac{\partial m_1(x_t,\theta_*)'}{\partial\theta}\lambda_*\lambda'_*\frac{\partial m_1(x_t,\theta_*)}{\partial\theta'} + \frac{\partial}{\partial\theta'}\left(\frac{\partial m_1(x_t,\theta_*)'}{\partial\theta}\lambda_*\right)\right)\right.$$
$$\left.\times \exp(\lambda'_* m_1(x_t,\theta_*))\right],$$

$$H_{\lambda\lambda} = E\left[m_1(x_t,\theta_*)m_1(x_t,\theta_*)'\exp(\lambda'_* m_1(x_t,\theta_*))\right],$$

and

$$H_{\theta\lambda} = E\left[\left(\frac{\partial m_1(x_t,\theta_*)'}{\partial\theta} + \frac{\partial m_1(x_t,\theta_*)'}{\partial\theta}\lambda_* m_1(x_t,\theta_*)'\right)\exp(\lambda'_* m_1(x_t,\theta_*))\right].$$

Similarly, define

$$H_{\psi\psi} = E\left[\frac{\partial^2\exp(\mu'_* m_2(x_t,\gamma_*))}{\partial\psi\partial\psi'}\right] = \begin{pmatrix} H_{\gamma\gamma} & H_{\gamma\mu} \\ H'_{\gamma\mu} & H_{\mu\mu} \end{pmatrix}.$$

Finally, let

$$V_{\phi\phi} = \sum_{j=-\infty}^{+\infty} E\left[\frac{\partial\exp(\lambda'_* m_1(x_t,\theta_*))}{\partial\phi}\frac{\partial\exp(\lambda'_* m_1(x_{t+j},\theta_*))}{\partial\phi'}\right],$$

$$V_{\psi\psi} = \sum_{j=-\infty}^{+\infty} E\left[\frac{\partial\exp(\mu'_* m_2(x_t,\gamma_*))}{\partial\psi}\frac{\partial\exp(\mu'_* m_2(x_{t+j},\gamma_*))}{\partial\psi'}\right],$$

and

$$V_{\phi\gamma} = \sum_{j=-\infty}^{+\infty} E\left[\frac{\partial\exp(\lambda'_* m_1(x_t,\theta_*))}{\partial\phi}\frac{\partial\exp(\mu'_* m_2(x_{t+j},\gamma_*))}{\partial\psi'}\right].$$

Under some regularity conditions (see Kitamura, 1998),

$$\sqrt{n}\begin{pmatrix}\hat\phi - \phi_* \\ \hat\psi - \psi_*\end{pmatrix} \xrightarrow{d} \mathcal{N}(0,\Omega),$$

where

$$\Omega = \begin{pmatrix}\Omega_\phi & \Omega_{\phi\psi} \\ \Omega'_{\phi\psi} & \Omega_\psi\end{pmatrix},$$

$\Omega_\phi = H_{\phi\phi}^{-1}V_{\phi\phi}H_{\phi\phi}^{-1}$, $\Omega_\psi = H_{\psi\psi}^{-1}V_{\psi\psi}H_{\psi\psi}^{-1}$ and $\Omega_{\phi\psi} = H_{\phi\phi}^{-1}V_{\phi\psi}H_{\psi\psi}^{-1}$.

Analogously to the QML case, one could test $H_0 : E\left[\exp(\lambda'_* m_1(x_t,\theta_*))\right] = E\left[\exp(\mu'_* m_2(x_t,\gamma_*))\right]$. Under this null hypothesis, the nonparametric likelihood analog of Vuong's (1989) quasi-likelihood ratio statistic is asymptotically distributed as

$$\sqrt{n}\left(Q_{1,n}(\hat\theta,\hat\lambda) - Q_{2,n}(\hat\gamma,\hat\mu)\right) \xrightarrow{d} \mathcal{N}(0,\sigma_Q^2), \qquad (4.11)$$

where $\sigma_Q^2 = \lim_{n\to\infty}\text{var}\left[\sqrt{n}\left(Q_{1,n}(\theta_*,\lambda_*) - Q_{2,n}(\gamma_*,\mu_*)\right)\right] > 0$. The degeneracy $\sigma_Q^2 = 0$ occurs if (i) both models $\mathcal{M}_1$ and $\mathcal{M}_2$ are correctly specified, or (ii) $\mathcal{M}_1$ and $\mathcal{M}_2$ are overlapping models, i.e., $\mathcal{M}_1 \cap \mathcal{M}_2 \neq \varnothing$, $\mathcal{M}_1 \not\subset \mathcal{M}_2$, and $\mathcal{M}_2 \not\subset \mathcal{M}_1$, or (iii) the spectral density at frequency zero of $\sqrt{n}(Q_{1,n}(\hat\theta,\hat\lambda)-$

$Q_{2,n}(\hat{\gamma}, \hat{\mu}))$ is zero. As a result, one should first test the null hypothesis $H_0 : \sigma_Q^2 = 0$ using the statistic

$$n\hat{\sigma}_Q^2 \xrightarrow{d} \sum_{i=1}^{k_1+k_2} \varphi_i^2 \nu_i,$$

where ν_i's are independent chi-square random variables with one degree of freedom and φ_i's are the eigenvalues of the matrix

$$\begin{pmatrix} -V_{\phi\phi}H_{\phi\phi}^{-1} & -V_{\phi\psi}H_{\psi\psi}^{-1} \\ V_{\phi\psi}H_{\phi\phi}^{-1} & V_{\psi\psi}H_{\psi\psi}^{-1} \end{pmatrix}.$$

If the null hypothesis $H_0 : \sigma_Q^2 = 0$ of this pre-test cannot be rejected, the two models $\mathcal{M}_1$ and $\mathcal{M}_2$ cannot be statistically discriminated given the data. If the null hypothesis is rejected, the researcher should proceed with the normal test in (4.11) to test the null hypothesis $H_0 : Q_1(\theta_*, \lambda_*) - Q_2(\gamma_*, \mu_*) = 0$. For more details and extensions, see Kitamura (1998) and Chen, Hong and Shum (2007).

Exercise 4.8. Show that the solution to the population KLIC problem

$$\inf_{f_1} \int \log\left(\frac{f_0(x)}{f_1(x)}\right) f_0(x) dx$$

subject to

$$\int m_1(x, \theta) f_1(x, \theta) dx = 0 \text{ and } \int f_1(x, \theta) dx = 1$$

is given by

$$\min_{\theta \in \Theta} \max_{\lambda \in \Lambda} \int \log\left(1 + \lambda(\theta)' m_1(x, \theta)\right) f_0(x) dx$$

as in equation (4.10).

4.4.3 Misspecified Models Estimated by GMM with a Pre-specified Matrix

4.4.3.1 GMM Globally Misspecified Models

While some GMM estimators are members of the class of nonparametric (or generalized empirical) likelihood estimators considered in the previous section (see Chapter 2 for a more detailed discussion), applied researchers still routinely adopt the traditional GMM framework of estimation and testing using a quadratic form of the sample moment conditions implied by the economic model. It is therefore interesting to study the limiting behavior of the GMM estimators in misspecified models.

Until recently, the asymptotic properties of the GMM estimators under local and global misspecification of the moment conditions were largely unknown.

One immediate consequence of the lack of fully developed statistical theory under misspecification is that empirical researchers continue to construct standard errors and conduct inference under the assumption of a correctly specified model even though many moment condition models in economics and finance are convincingly rejected by the data using the specification test for overidentifying restrictions.

Hall and Inoue (2003) were among the first to provide an in-depth analysis of GMM estimators in overidentified globally misspecified models and noted that the GMM inference under misspecification depends critically on the choice of a weighting matrix. In particular, the GMM estimators have different pseudo-true values for different choices of weighting matrix. Furthermore, the limiting behavior, including the rate of convergence, of the GMM estimator in misspecified models depends on the type of weighting matrix used in estimation. As a result, Hall and Inoue (2003) derive the asymptotic distribution of the GMM estimator on a case-by-case basis depending on the form and the structure of the weighting matrix.

When the interest of a researcher lies in comparing different possibly misspecified moment condition based models, the analysis is further complicated by the fact that different weighting matrices apply different criteria across competing models, which prevents an objective ranking of models. One possible solution is to use the same weighting matrix (for example, the identity matrix) across all models, although this approach introduces some arbitrariness. Fortunately, in some cases, economic theory dictates the proper choice of a weighting matrix. For example, Hansen and Jagannathan (1997) propose a measure of model misspecification that is based on the distance between the candidate stochastic discount factor (SDF) and the set of true SDFs. Simple manipulations show that this measure (Hansen–Jagannathan distance) can be represented as a quadratic form of model pricing errors and a weighting matrix given by the inverse of the second moment matrix of the returns on the test assets. The Hansen–Jagannathan distance is now widely used in empirical finance as an objective criterion for parameter estimation and specification testing as well as a model comparison measure. The next section presents the limiting theory for model selection of misspecified asset pricing models based on the Hansen–Jagannathan distance (for more details, see Gospodinov, Kan and Robotti, 2010).

4.4.3.2 Hansen–Jagannathan Distance

Suppose that $y_t(\theta)$ denotes a candidate stochastic discount factor that depends on the data and a k_1-vector of parameters θ, R_t is a vector of gross returns on ℓ test assets at time t, $m(\theta) = E[R_t y_t(\theta)] - 1_\ell$ is an $\ell \times 1$ ($\ell > k_1$) vector of pricing errors and $W = (E[R_t R_t'])^{-1}$. The unknown parameters θ are chosen to minimize a quadratic form in average pricing errors given by

$$\hat{\theta} = \arg\min_{\theta \in \Theta} m_n(\theta)' W_n m_n(\theta), \tag{4.12}$$

where $m_n(\theta) = n^{-1} \sum_{t=1}^{n} R_t y_t(\theta) - 1_\ell$ and $W_n = \left(n^{-1} \sum_{t=1}^{n} R_t R_t'\right)^{-1}$. The objective function in (4.12) is referred to in the asset pricing literature as the squared Hansen–Jagannathan (HJ) distance. Note that all competing models are estimated on the same test asset returns R_t using the same weighting matrix W_n. The pseudo-true value of θ is defined as the argument that minimizes the population squared HJ distance $\delta^2(\theta) = m(\theta)'Wm(\theta)$, i.e., $\theta_* = \arg\min_{\theta \in \Theta} \delta^2(\theta)$. Let

$$H = E\left[u_t(\theta_*) \frac{\partial^2 y_t(\theta_*)}{\partial\theta\partial\theta'}\right]$$

and

$$M = E\left[R_t \frac{\partial y_t(\theta_*)}{\partial\theta'}\right],$$

where $u_t(\theta_*) = m_t(\theta_*)'WR_t$ and $m_t(\theta_*) = R_t y_t(\theta_*) - 1_\ell$. Also, let $\hat{\delta}^2$ denote the sample squared HJ distance evaluated at the parameter estimate $\hat{\theta}$ and δ_*^2 be the population squared HJ distance evaluated at the pseudo-true value θ_*.

In the case of a misspecified model ($\delta_*^2 > 0$) and under some regularity conditions,

$$\sqrt{n}(\hat{\theta} - \theta_*) \xrightarrow{d} \mathcal{N}(0, \Omega_\theta),$$

where $\Omega_\theta = \sum_{j=-\infty}^{\infty} E[l_t l_{t+j}']$ and

$$l_t = (H + M'WM)^{-1}\left[M'Wm_t(\theta_*) + \left(\frac{\partial y_t(\theta_*)}{\partial\theta} - M'WR_t\right)u_t(\theta_*)\right].$$

A consistent estimator of the long-run variance Ω_θ can be obtained using a heteroskedasticity and autocorrelation consistent (HAC) estimator (see section 1.3 in Chapter 1) and replacing the population quantities in l_t with their sample analogs.

In the case of a correctly specified model ($\delta_*^2 = 0$), the asymptotic distribution specializes to

$$\sqrt{n}(\hat{\theta} - \theta_*) \xrightarrow{d} \mathcal{N}(0, \tilde{\Omega}_\theta),$$

where $\tilde{\Omega}_\theta = \sum_{j=-\infty}^{\infty} E[\tilde{l}_t \tilde{l}_{t+j}']$ and

$$\tilde{l}_t = (M'WM)^{-1}M'Wm_t(\theta_*).$$

These results can be used to develop a specification test of $H_0 : \delta_*^2 = 0$ in the spirit of the Sargan–Hansen $\mathcal{J}$-test for overidentifying restrictions. In particular, under similar regularity conditions and $H_0 : \delta_*^2 = 0$,

$$n\hat{\delta}^2 \xrightarrow{d} \sum_{i=1}^{\ell-k_1} \xi_i \nu_i,$$

where ν_i's are independent chi-square random variables with one degree of freedom and ξ_i's are the eigenvalues of the matrix

$$P'W^{1/2}VW^{1/2}P,$$

with $V = \sum_{j=-\infty}^{\infty} E\left[m_t(\theta_*)m_{t+j}(\theta_*)'\right]$ and P being an $\ell \times (\ell - k_1)$ orthonormal matrix whose columns are orthogonal to $W^{1/2}M$. Note that under the alternative hypothesis $\delta_*^2 > 0$, $\hat{\delta}^2$ is root-n consistent and $\sqrt{n}(\hat{\delta}^2 - \delta_*^2)$ is asymptotically normally distributed. As a result, the specification test above is consistent under the alternative as it converges to $+\infty$ as n goes to infinity. It is important to emphasize that the asymptotic weighted chi-square distribution arises from the fact that the HJ distance is constructed using a non-optimal weighting matrix. As we showed in section 1.5 of Chapter 1, when the weighting matrix is $W = V^{-1}$, the resulting $\mathcal{J}$-test for overidentifying restrictions is asymptotically chi-square distributed with $\ell - k_1$ degrees of freedom.

Define the models

$$\mathcal{F} = \{y^{\mathcal{F}}(\theta) ; \theta \in \Theta\}$$

and

$$\mathcal{G} = \{y^{\mathcal{G}}(\gamma) ; \gamma \in \Gamma\},$$

where θ and γ are $k_1 \times 1$ and $k_2 \times 1$ parameter vectors, respectively, and Θ and Γ denote their parameter spaces. The corresponding squared HJ distances for models $\mathcal{F}$ and $\mathcal{G}$ are given by

$$\delta_{\mathcal{F}}^2(\theta) = \min_{\theta} m^{\mathcal{F}}(\theta)' W m^{\mathcal{F}}(\theta)$$

and

$$\delta_{\mathcal{G}}^2(\gamma) = \min_{\gamma} m^{\mathcal{G}}(\gamma)' W m^{\mathcal{G}}(\gamma),$$

with pseudo-true values denoted by θ_* and γ_*, respectively. Both models could be correctly specified or misspecified. As before, if $\mathcal{F} \cap \mathcal{G} = \varnothing$, we have the case of strictly non-nested models; if $\mathcal{F} \subset \mathcal{G}$ or $\mathcal{G} \subset \mathcal{F}$ we have the case of nested models; and if $\mathcal{F} \cap \mathcal{G} \neq \varnothing$, $\mathcal{F} \not\subset \mathcal{G}$, and $\mathcal{G} \not\subset \mathcal{F}$, we refer to $\mathcal{F}$ and $\mathcal{G}$ as overlapping models. Also, let $\hat{\delta}_{\mathcal{F}}^2$ and $\hat{\delta}_{\mathcal{G}}^2$, and $\delta_{*\mathcal{F}}^2$ and $\delta_{*\mathcal{G}}^2$ denote the squared HJ distances for the two models evaluated at their parameter estimates and pseudo-true values, respectively.

Under the null hypothesis $H_0 : \delta_{*\mathcal{F}}^2 = \delta_{*\mathcal{G}}^2$, we have

$$\sqrt{n}(\hat{\delta}_{\mathcal{F}}^2 - \hat{\delta}_{\mathcal{G}}^2) \xrightarrow{d} N(0, \sigma_d^2), \tag{4.13}$$

where $\sigma_d^2 = \sum_{j=-\infty}^{\infty} E[d_t d_{t+j}] \neq 0$ and $d_t = \left(2u_t^{\mathcal{F}}(\theta_*)y_t^{\mathcal{F}}(\theta_*) - [u_t^{\mathcal{F}}(\theta_*)]^2\right) - \left(2u_t^{\mathcal{G}}(\gamma_*)y_t^{\mathcal{G}}(\gamma_*) - [u_t^{\mathcal{G}}(\gamma_*)]^2\right)$. This result no longer holds if (i) the two SDFs are equal (nested and overlapping models only), i.e., $y_t^{\mathcal{F}}(\theta_*) = y_t^{\mathcal{G}}(\gamma_*)$, or (ii) the two SDFs are different and are both correctly specified, so that $m^{\mathcal{F}}(\theta_*) = 0$ and $m^{\mathcal{G}}(\gamma_*) = 0$, which implies $\delta^2_{*\mathcal{F}} = \delta^2_{*\mathcal{G}} = 0$.

For strictly non-nested models, $\sigma^2_d = 0$ if and only if $\delta^2_{\mathcal{F}} = \delta^2_{\mathcal{G}} = 0$, i.e., the models are correctly specified. In this case, under the null hypothesis $H_0 : \delta^2_{*\mathcal{F}} = \delta^2_{*\mathcal{G}} = 0$,

$$n(\hat{\delta}^2_{\mathcal{F}} - \hat{\delta}^2_{\mathcal{G}}) \xrightarrow{d} \sum_{i=1}^{2\ell - k_1 - k_2} \eta_i \nu_i,$$

where ν_i's are independent chi-square random variables with one degree of freedom and η_i's are the eigenvalues of the $(2\ell - k_1 - k_2) \times (2\ell - k_1 - k_2)$ matrix

$$\begin{bmatrix} P'_{\mathcal{F}} W^{1/2} V_{\mathcal{F}} W^{1/2} P_{\mathcal{F}} & -P'_{\mathcal{F}} W^{1/2} V_{\mathcal{F}\mathcal{G}} W^{1/2} P_{\mathcal{G}} \\ P'_{\mathcal{G}} W^{1/2} V_{\mathcal{G}\mathcal{F}} W^{1/2} P_{\mathcal{F}} & -P'_{\mathcal{G}} W^{1/2} V_{\mathcal{G}} W^{1/2} P_{\mathcal{G}} \end{bmatrix},$$

where

$$\begin{bmatrix} V_{\mathcal{F}} & V_{\mathcal{F}\mathcal{G}} \\ V_{\mathcal{G}\mathcal{F}} & V_{\mathcal{G}} \end{bmatrix} = \sum_{j=-\infty}^{\infty} E\left[\tilde{m}_t \tilde{m}'_{t+j}\right]$$

with $\tilde{m}_t = \left(m^{\mathcal{F}}_t(\theta_*)', m^{\mathcal{G}}_t(\gamma_*)'\right)'$, and $P_{\mathcal{F}}$ and $P_{\mathcal{G}}$ denote orthonormal matrices with dimensions $\ell \times (\ell - k_1)$ and $\ell \times (\ell - k_2)$ whose columns are orthogonal to $W^{1/2} M_{\mathcal{F}}$ and $W^{1/2} M_{\mathcal{G}}$, respectively, with $M_{\mathcal{F}}$ ($M_{\mathcal{G}}$) being the M matrix for model $\mathcal{F}$ ($\mathcal{G}$) defined above. Since the eigenvalues η_i ($i = 1, ..., 2\ell - k_1 - k_2$) can take on both positive and negative values, the test of the hypothesis $H_0 : \delta^2_{\mathcal{F}} = \delta^2_{\mathcal{G}} = 0$ should be two-sided. If the null hypothesis is rejected, the normal test in (4.13) should be performed.

We now consider the case of nested models. Suppose that, without loss of generality, $\mathcal{F} \subset \mathcal{G}$ and the null hypothesis $H_0 : y^{\mathcal{F}}(\theta_*) = y^{\mathcal{G}}(\gamma_*)$ can be written as a parametric restriction of the form $H_0 : \varphi_{\mathcal{G}}(\gamma_*) = 0_{k_2 - k_1}$ for model $\mathcal{G}$ against $H_1 : \varphi_{\mathcal{G}}(\gamma_*) \neq 0_{k_2 - k_1}$, where $\varphi_{\mathcal{G}}(\cdot)$ is a twice continuously differentiable function in its argument. Define

$$\Psi^{\mathcal{G}}(\gamma) = \frac{\partial \varphi_{\mathcal{G}}(\gamma)}{\partial \gamma'}$$

as a $(k_2 - k_1) \times k_2$ derivative matrix of the parametric restrictions $\varphi_{\mathcal{G}}$. For many models of interest, $y^{\mathcal{F}}(\theta) = y^{\mathcal{G}}(\gamma)$ when a subset of the parameters of model $\mathcal{G}$ is equal to zero. In this case, we can rearrange the parameters so that $\varphi_{\mathcal{G}}(\gamma) = [0_{(k_2-k_1)\times k_1}, I_{k_2-k_1}]\gamma$. Then, $\Psi^{\mathcal{G}}(\gamma) = [0_{(k_2-k_1)\times k_1}, I_{k_2-k_1}]$, which is a selector matrix that selects only the part of the parameter vector γ not contained in model $\mathcal{F}$.

Then, under $H_0 : \varphi_{\mathcal{G}}(\gamma_*) = 0_{k_2-k_1}$,

$$n(\hat{\delta}^2_{\mathcal{F}} - \hat{\delta}^2_{\mathcal{G}}) \xrightarrow{d} \sum_{i=1}^{k_2-k_1} \tilde{\eta}_i \nu_i, \qquad (4.14)$$

where $\tilde{\eta}_i$'s are the eigenvalues (all positive) of $(\Psi_*^{\mathcal{G}} \tilde{H}_{\mathcal{G}} \Psi_*^{\mathcal{G}'})^{-1} \Psi_*^{\mathcal{G}} \Omega_\gamma \Psi_*^{\mathcal{G}'}$, $\Psi_*^{\mathcal{G}} \equiv \Psi^{\mathcal{G}}(\gamma_*)$, and $\tilde{H}_{\mathcal{G}} = (H_{\mathcal{G}} + M_{\mathcal{G}}' W M_{\mathcal{G}})^{-1}$.

This result deserves several remarks. If the parametric constraints implied by the structure of the nested models are not imposed, it can be shown that $n(\hat{\delta}_{\mathcal{F}}^2 - \hat{\delta}_{\mathcal{G}}^2) \xrightarrow{d} \sum_{i=1}^{2\ell+k_1+k_2} \tilde{\eta}_i \nu_i$, where the $(2\ell + k_1 + k_2)$ eigenvalues $\tilde{\eta}_i$ are not all positive and their computation may give rise to numerical problems in small samples. In contrast, the $(k_2 - k_1)$ eigenvalues $\tilde{\eta}$ in (4.14) are guaranteed to be positive. Second, it is typically the case that asset pricing models are evaluated on 25 or 100 test assets, i.e., $\ell = 25$ or 100. It is evident that imposing the parameter constraints delivers a substantial reduction (from $2\ell + k_1 + k_2$ to $k_2 - k_1$) of the computed eigenvalues. This, combined with the fact that all computed eigenvalues are positive by construction, may lead to large improvements in the size and power properties of the test in finite samples. On the other hand, for the test that does not impose these restrictions, there is some internal inconsistency since the test statistic is always positive while the distribution from which the critical and p-values are computed can take on negative values.

Finally, we turn our attention to overlapping models. Let $y^{\mathcal{H}}(\rho)$ be the SDF of model $\mathcal{H}$, where $\mathcal{H}$ is the overlapping part of models $\mathcal{F}$ and $\mathcal{G}$, $\mathcal{H} = \mathcal{F} \cap \mathcal{G}$, and ρ is a $k_3 \times 1$ parameter vector with a pseudo-true value ρ_*. Therefore, $y^{\mathcal{F}}(\theta_*) = y^{\mathcal{G}}(\gamma_*)$ implies $y^{\mathcal{F}}(\theta_*) = y^{\mathcal{H}}(\rho_*)$ and $y^{\mathcal{G}}(\gamma_*) = y^{\mathcal{H}}(\rho_*)$. Suppose that the null hypothesis $H_0 : y^{\mathcal{F}}(\theta_*) = y^{\mathcal{H}}(\rho_*)$ and $y^{\mathcal{G}}(\gamma_*) = y^{\mathcal{H}}(\rho_*)$ can be written as a parametric restriction of the form $H_0 : \varphi_{\mathcal{F}}(\theta_*) = 0_{k_1 - k_3}$ and $\varphi_{\mathcal{G}}(\gamma_*) = 0_{k_2 - k_3}$, where $\varphi_{\mathcal{F}}(\cdot)$ and $\varphi_{\mathcal{G}}(\cdot)$ are some twice continuously differentiable functions of their arguments. Let

$$\Psi^{\mathcal{F}}(\theta) = \frac{\partial \varphi_{\mathcal{F}}(\theta)}{\partial \theta'}$$

and

$$\Psi^{\mathcal{G}}(\gamma) = \frac{\partial \varphi_{\mathcal{G}}(\gamma)}{\partial \gamma'}$$

be $(k_1 - k_3) \times k_1$ and $(k_2 - k_3) \times k_2$ derivative matrices of the parametric restrictions $\varphi_{\mathcal{F}}$ and $\varphi_{\mathcal{G}}$, respectively. As in the case of nested models discussed above, $H_0 : y^{\mathcal{F}}(\theta_*) = y^{\mathcal{H}}(\gamma_*)$ implies that a subset of the parameters of model $\mathcal{F}$ is equal to zero, and $H_0 : y^{\mathcal{F}}(\theta_*) = y^{\mathcal{H}}(\gamma_*)$ implies that a subset of the parameters of model $\mathcal{G}$ is equal to zero. Hence, we can arrange the parameters so that $\Psi^{\mathcal{F}}(\theta) = [0_{(k_1-k_3) \times k_3}, I_{k_1-k_3}]$ and $\Psi^{\mathcal{G}}(\gamma) = [0_{(k_2-k_3) \times k_3}, I_{k_2-k_3}]$. Let $\Omega_{\theta\gamma}$ denote the asymptotic covariance matrix of $(\hat{\theta}', \hat{\gamma}')'$, $\tilde{H}_{\mathcal{F}} = (H_{\mathcal{F}} + M_{\mathcal{F}}' W M_{\mathcal{F}})^{-1}$, $\tilde{H}_{\mathcal{G}} = (H_{\mathcal{G}} + M_{\mathcal{G}}' W M_{\mathcal{G}})^{-1}$, and

$$\Psi_*^{\mathcal{F}\mathcal{G}} = \begin{bmatrix} \Psi^{\mathcal{F}}(\theta_*) & 0_{(k_1-k_3) \times k_2} \\ 0_{(k_2-k_3) \times k_1} & \Psi^{\mathcal{G}}(\gamma_*) \end{bmatrix}.$$

Then, for $\mathcal{F} \cap \mathcal{G} \neq \varnothing$, $\mathcal{F} \not\subset \mathcal{G}$, $\mathcal{G} \not\subset \mathcal{F}$ and under $H_0 : \varphi_{\mathcal{F}}(\theta_*) = 0_{k_1-k_3}$ and $\varphi_{\mathcal{G}}(\gamma_*) = 0_{k_2-k_3}$, we have

$$n(\hat{\delta}_{\mathcal{F}}^2 - \hat{\delta}_{\mathcal{G}}^2) \xrightarrow{d} \sum_{i=1}^{k_1+k_2-2k_3} \bar{\varsigma}_i \nu_i,$$

where $\bar{\varsigma}_i$'s are the eigenvalues of

$$\begin{bmatrix} -(\Psi_*^{\mathcal{F}} \tilde{H}_{\mathcal{F}} \Psi_*^{\mathcal{F}\prime})^{-1} & 0_{(k_1-k_3) \times (k_2-k_3)} \\ 0_{(k_2-k_3) \times (k_1-k_3)} & (\Psi_*^{\mathcal{G}} \tilde{H}_{\mathcal{G}} \Psi_*^{\mathcal{G}\prime})^{-1} \end{bmatrix} \Psi_*^{\mathcal{FG}} \Omega_{\theta\gamma} \Psi_*^{\mathcal{FG}\prime}, \qquad (4.15)$$

where $\Psi_*^{\mathcal{F}} \equiv \Psi^{\mathcal{F}}(\theta_*)$ and $\Psi_*^{\mathcal{G}} = \Psi^{\mathcal{G}}(\gamma_*)$.

Similarly to the nested model case, this testing procedure leads to a potentially significant reduction of the number of computed eigenvalues. But unlike the case of nested models, the eigenvalues of (4.15) are not always positive because $\hat{\delta}_{\mathcal{F}}^2 - \hat{\delta}_{\mathcal{G}}^2$ can take on both positive and negative values and a two-sided test needs to be performed. Since for overlapping models the variance σ_d^2 can be zero when (i) $y^{\mathcal{F}}(\theta_*) = y^{\mathcal{G}}(\gamma_*)$ or (ii) both models are correctly specified, if the null hypothesis $H_0 : \varphi_{\mathcal{F}}(\theta_*) = 0_{k_1-k_3}$ and $\varphi_{\mathcal{G}}(\gamma_*) = 0_{k_2-k_3}$ is rejected, then we need to test whether the two models are both correctly specified as in the case of strictly non-nested models. If the null hypothesis of both models being correctly specified is also rejected, the sequential testing proceeds with the normal test in (4.13).

Exercise 4.9. Show that under the null hypothesis of a correctly specified model $H_0 : \delta_*^2 = 0$,

$$n\hat{\delta}^2 \xrightarrow{d} \sum_{i=1}^{\ell-k_1} \xi_i \nu_i,$$

where ν_i's are independent chi-square random variables with one degree of freedom and ξ_i's are the eigenvalues of the matrix

$$P' W^{1/2} V W^{1/2} P,$$

with $V = \sum_{j=-\infty}^{\infty} E\left[m_t(\theta_*) m_{t+j}(\theta_*)'\right]$ and P being an $\ell \times (\ell - k_1)$ orthonormal matrix whose columns are orthogonal to $W^{1/2} M$.

4.5   Appendix: Solutions to Selected Exercises

Exercise 4.1. The problem

$$\mathcal{KLIC}(\mathbf{e} : f) = E_{\mathbf{e}} \left[\log \frac{\mathbf{e}}{f} \right] = \sum_i \frac{1}{n} \log \frac{1/n}{f(z_i, \theta)} \to \min_{\theta}$$

is equivalent to

$$\sum_{i=1}^{n} \log f(z_i, \theta) \to \max_{\theta},$$

which gives the maximum likelihood estimator in the case where the density $f(z, \theta)$ is correctly specified.

Exercise 4.3. Yes, it does. The density belongs to the linear exponential class, with $\alpha_3(\mu) = \log \mu - \log(a + \mu)$. The form of the skedastic function is immaterial for the consistency property to hold.

Exercise 4.4. The log pseudo-density on which the proposed PML1 estimator is based has the form

$$\log f\,(y, \mu) = -\log \sqrt{2\pi} - \frac{1}{2} \log \mu^2 + \frac{(y - \mu)^2}{2\mu^2},$$

which does not belong to the linear exponential family of densities (the term $y^2/2\mu^2$ does not fit). Therefore, the PML1 estimator is not consistent.

The inconsistency can be shown directly. Consider the special case of estimation of the mean of

$$y \sim \mathcal{N}\left(\theta_0, \sigma^2\right),$$

using the density

$$y \sim \mathcal{N}\left(\theta, \theta^2\right).$$

Then, the pseudo-true value of θ is

$$\theta_* = \arg\max_{\theta} E\left[-\frac{1}{2} \log \theta^2 - \frac{(y - \theta)^2}{2\theta^2}\right]$$

$$= \arg\max_{\theta} \left\{-\frac{1}{2} \log \theta^2 - \frac{\sigma^2 + (\theta_0 - \theta)^2}{2\theta^2}\right\}.$$

It is easy to see by differentiating that θ_* is not θ_0 unless $\theta_0^2 = \sigma^2$.

Exercise 4.5. Indeed, in the example, $w\,(z, \mu, \varsigma)$ reduces to the exponential distribution when $\varsigma = 1$, and the exponential pseudo-density consistently estimates θ_0. When ς is estimated, the vector of parameters is $(\mu, \varsigma)'$, and the pseudo-score is

$$\frac{\partial \log w\,(z, \mu, \varsigma)}{\partial\,(\mu, \varsigma)'} = \frac{\partial}{\partial\,(\mu, \varsigma)'}\left(\log \varsigma + \varsigma \log \Gamma\left(1 + \frac{1}{\varsigma}\right) - \varsigma \log \mu\right.$$

$$\left. + (\varsigma - 1) \log z - \left(\frac{\Gamma\left(1 + \varsigma^{-1}\right) z}{\mu}\right)^{\varsigma}\right)$$

$$= \left(\left(\left(\Gamma\left(1 + \varsigma^{-1}\right) z/\mu\right)^{\varsigma} - 1\right)\varsigma/\mu\right).$$
$$\cdots$$

Observe that the pseudo-score for μ has zero expectation if and only if

$$E\left[\left(\frac{\Gamma\left(1+\varsigma^{-1}\right)z}{\mu}\right)^{\varsigma}\right] = 1.$$

This obviously holds when $\varsigma = 1$, but may not hold for other ς. For instance, when $\varsigma = 2$, we know that $E\left[z^2\right] = \mu^2\Gamma\left(2.5\right)/\Gamma\left(1.5\right)^2 = 1.5\mu^2/\Gamma\left(1.5\right)$, which contradicts the zero expected pseudo-score rule. The pseudo-true value ς_* can be obtained by solving the system of zero expected pseudo-scores, but it is very unlikely that it equals 1. The result can be explained by the presence of an extraneous parameter whose pseudo-true value has nothing to do with the problem and whose estimation adversely affects the estimation of the quantity of interest.

Exercise 4.6. The PML2 estimator based on the normal distribution is the solution to the following problem:

$$\begin{pmatrix}\hat{\alpha}\\\hat{\sigma}^2\end{pmatrix} = \arg\max_{\alpha,\sigma^2}\left\{-\frac{n}{2}\log\sigma^2 - \frac{1}{\sigma^2}\sum_{i=1}^{n}\frac{(y_i-\alpha)^2}{2x_i^2}\right\}.$$

This leads to the estimates

$$\hat{\alpha} = \left(\sum_{i=1}^{n}\frac{1}{x_i^2}\right)^{-1}\sum_{i=1}^{n}\frac{y_i}{x_i^2}, \quad \hat{\sigma}^2 = \frac{1}{n}\sum_{i=1}^{n}\frac{(y_i-\hat{\alpha})^2}{x_i^2}.$$

It can be derived that the asymptotic variances are

$$V_{\hat{\alpha}} = \frac{\sigma^2}{E\left[x^{-2}\right]}, \quad V_{\hat{\sigma}^2} = E\left[\frac{(y-\alpha)^4}{x^4}\right] - \sigma^4.$$

Exercise 4.7. In the exponential model, the log-likelihood for one observation is

$$\log f_1(y|x,\theta) = -\log\theta - \log x - \frac{y}{\theta x},$$

with a first derivative given by

$$\frac{\partial\log f_1(y|x,\theta)}{\partial\theta} = -\frac{1}{\theta} + \frac{y}{\theta^2 x}.$$

Solving out the sample first-order conditions yields

$$\hat{\theta}_1 = \frac{1}{n}\sum_{i=1}^{n}\frac{y_i}{x_i}.$$

As the exponential density belongs to the linear exponential class, this estimator consistently estimates θ_0.

In the lognormal model, the log-likelihood for one observation is

$$\log f_2(y|x,\theta) = -\log y - \log \sqrt{\pi \log 4}$$
$$- \frac{\left(\log y - \log \theta - \log x + \log \sqrt{2}\right)^2}{\log 4},$$

with a first derivative

$$\frac{\partial \log f(y|x,\theta)}{\partial \theta} = \frac{\log y - \log \theta - \log x + \log \sqrt{2}}{\theta \log 2}.$$

It then follows that the estimate of the pseudo-true parameter is

$$\hat{\theta}_2 = \exp\left(\frac{1}{n}\sum_{i=1}^{n}\log\frac{y_i\sqrt{2}}{x_i}\right).$$

The likelihood ratio test statistic has the form

$$\mathcal{LR}(\hat{\theta}_1,\hat{\theta}_2) = \frac{1}{n}\sum_{i=1}^{n}\left(\log f_1(y_i|x_i,\hat{\theta}_1) - \log f_2(y_i|x_i,\hat{\theta}_2)\right)$$

$$= \frac{1}{n}\sum_{i=1}^{n}\left(-\frac{y_i}{\hat{\theta}_1 x_i} + \log\frac{y_i\sqrt{\pi\log 4}}{\hat{\theta}_1 x_i} + \frac{1}{\log 4}\left(\log\frac{y_i\sqrt{2}}{\hat{\theta}_2 x_i}\right)^2\right)$$

$$= \log\sqrt{\pi\log 4} - \log\left(\frac{1}{n}\sum_{i=1}^{n}\frac{y_i}{x_i}\right) - 1 + \frac{1}{n}\sum_{i=1}^{n}\log\frac{y_i}{x_i}$$

$$+ \frac{1}{\log 4}\left(\frac{1}{n}\sum_{i=1}^{n}\left(\log\frac{y_i}{x_i}\right)^2 - \left(\frac{1}{n}\sum_{i=1}^{n}\log\frac{y_i}{x_i}\right)^2\right).$$

Since the two models are strictly non-nested, the studentized statistic constructed as

$$\frac{\sqrt{n}\mathcal{LR}(\hat{\theta}_1,\hat{\theta}_2)}{\hat{\sigma}_Q},$$

where

$$\hat{\sigma}_Q^2 = \frac{1}{n}\sum_{i=1}^{n}\left(-\frac{y_i}{\hat{\theta}_1 x_i} + \log\frac{y_i\sqrt{\pi\log 4}}{\hat{\theta}_1 x_i} + \frac{1}{\log 4}\left(\log\frac{y_i\sqrt{2}}{\hat{\theta}_2 x_i}\right)^2\right)^2,$$

is asymptotically distributed as $\mathcal{N}(0,1)$ under the null hypothesis that the two models are equally good.

When the density is misspecified, the true parameter θ_0 is estimated consistently when the exponential density is used, but inconsistently when the lognormal density is used, because the latter does not belong to the linear exponential family.

Exercise 4.9. Since $\hat{\theta}$ minimizes $\delta_n^2(\theta) = m_n(\theta)'W_n m_n(\theta)$, the first-order conditions for $\hat{\theta}$ are given by

$$0 = \frac{\partial \delta_n^2(\hat{\theta})}{\partial \theta} = 2M_n(\hat{\theta})'W_n m_n(\hat{\theta}), \qquad (4.16)$$

where $M_n(\hat{\theta}) = \partial m_n(\hat{\theta})/\partial \theta$ is an $\ell \times k_1$ matrix.

Take a first-order Taylor series expansion of $m_n(\hat{\theta})$ about θ_*

$$m_n(\hat{\theta}) = m_n(\theta_*) + M_n(\bar{\theta})(\hat{\theta} - \theta_*), \qquad (4.17)$$

where $\bar{\theta}$ is an intermediate point on the line segment joining $\hat{\theta}$ and θ_*. Substituting for $m_n(\hat{\theta})$ into (4.16) yields

$$0 = M_n(\hat{\theta})'W_n\left(m_n(\theta_*) + M_n(\bar{\theta})(\hat{\theta} - \theta_*)\right).$$

Rearranging the above expression gives

$$M_n(\hat{\theta})'W_n M_n(\bar{\theta})(\hat{\theta} - \theta_*) = -M_n(\hat{\theta})'W_n m_n(\theta_*)$$

or

$$\sqrt{n}(\hat{\theta} - \theta_*) = -\left(M_n(\hat{\theta})'W_n M_n(\bar{\theta})\right)^{-1} M_n(\hat{\theta})'W_n \sqrt{n}m_n(\theta_*)$$

$$= -(M'WM)^{-1} M'W\sqrt{n}m_n(\theta_*) + o_P(1).$$

where $M \equiv M(\theta_*)$ and $\sqrt{n}m_n(\theta_*)$ is assumed to satisfy the conditions of the CLT so that $\sqrt{n}m_n(\theta_*) \overset{d}{\to} \mathcal{N}(0, V)$ with $V = \sum_{j=-\infty}^{\infty} E\left[m_t(\theta_*)m_{t+j}(\theta_*)'\right]$.

Substituting for $\sqrt{n}(\hat{\theta} - \theta_*)$ into (4.17) yields

$$\sqrt{n}m_n(\hat{\theta}) = m_n(\theta_*) + M\sqrt{n}(\hat{\theta} - \theta_*) + o_P(1)$$

$$= \left(I_\ell - M(M'WM)^{-1}M'W\right)\sqrt{n}m_n(\theta_*) + o_P(1)$$

$$= W^{-1/2}\left(I_\ell - W^{1/2}M(M'WM)^{-1}M'W^{1/2}\right)W^{1/2}\sqrt{n}m_n(\theta_*)$$

$$\quad + o_P(1)$$

$$= W^{-1/2}PP'W^{1/2}\sqrt{n}m_n(\theta_*) + o_P(1),$$

by using the fact that $I_\ell - W^{1/2}M(M'WM)^{-1}M'W^{1/2} = PP'$, where P is an $\ell \times (\ell - k_1)$ orthonormal matrix whose columns are orthogonal to $W^{1/2}M$.

Therefore,

$$n\delta_n^2(\hat{\theta}) = \sqrt{n}m_n(\hat{\theta})'W_n\sqrt{n}m_n(\hat{\theta})$$

$$= \left(\sqrt{n}m_n(\theta_*)'W^{1/2}PP'W^{-1/2}\right)W\left(W^{-1/2}PP'W^{1/2}\sqrt{n}m_n(\theta_*)\right)$$

$$\quad + o_P(1)$$

$$= \sqrt{n}m_n(\theta_*)'W^{1/2}PP'W^{1/2}\sqrt{n}m_n(\theta_*) + o_P(1)$$

$$\overset{d}{\to} \tilde{z}'V^{\frac{1}{2}}W^{1/2}PP'W^{1/2}V^{\frac{1}{2}}\tilde{z}.$$

where $\tilde{z} \sim \mathcal{N}(0, I_\ell)$. Since $V^{\frac{1}{2}}W^{1/2}PP'W^{1/2}V^{\frac{1}{2}}$ has the same nonzero eigenvalues as $P'W^{1/2}VW^{1/2}P$, we have that for $\hat{\delta}^2 \equiv \delta_n^2(\hat{\theta})$

$$n\hat{\delta}^2 \overset{d}{\to} \sum_{i=1}^{\ell-k_1} \xi_i \nu_i,$$

where ξ_i's are the eigenvalues of $P'W^{1/2}VW^{1/2}P$ and ν_i's are independent chi-square random variables.

References

Akaike, H. (1973) Information theory and an extension of the likelihood ratio principle. In: *Proceedings of the Second International Symposium of Information Theory*, Akademiai Kiado: Budapest, 257–281.

Chen, X., H. Hong and M. Shum (2007) Nonparametric likelihood ratio model selection tests between parametric likelihood and moment condition models. *Journal of Econometrics*, 141, 109–140.

Gospodinov, N., R. Kan and C. Robotti (2010) Chi-squared tests for evaluation and comparison of asset pricing models. Working Paper, Concordia University.

Gourieroux, C., and A. Monfort (1993) Pseudo-likelihood methods. In: *Handbook of Statistics*, Vol. 11, Elsevier: Amsterdam, Chapter 12, 335–362.

Gourieroux, C., A. Monfort and A. Trognon (1984a) Pseudo maximum likelihood methods: Theory. *Econometrica*, 52, 681–700.

Gourieroux, C., A. Monfort and A. Trognon (1984b) Pseudo maximum likelihood methods: Applications to Poisson models. *Econometrica*, 52, 701–720.

Hall, A.R., and A. Inoue (2003) The large sample behaviour of the generalized method of moments estimator in misspecified models. *Journal of Econometrics*, 114, 361–394.

Hansen, L.P., and R. Jagannathan (1997) Assessing specification errors in stochastic discount factor models. *Journal of Finance*, 52, 557–590.

Imbens, G.W., R.H. Spady and P. Johnson (1998) Information theoretic approaches to inference in moment condition models. *Econometrica*, 66, 333–357.

Kitamura, Y. (1998) Comparing misspecified dynamic econometric models using nonparametric likelihood. Working Paper, University of Wisconsin.

Kullback, S., and R.A. Leibler (1951) On information and sufficiency. *Annals of Mathematical Statistics*, 22, 79–86.

Mykland, P.A. (1995) Dual likelihood. *Annals of Statistics*, 23, 396-421.

Schennach, S. (2007) Point estimation with exponentially tilted empirical likelihood. *Annals of Statistics*, 35, 634–672.

Vuong, Q.H. (1989) Likelihood ratio tests for model selection and non-nested hypotheses. *Econometrica*, 57, 307–333.

White, H. (1982) Maximum likelihood estimation of misspecified models. *Econometrica*, 50, 1–25.

White, H. (1994) *Estimation, Inference and Specification Analysis*. Cambridge University Press: Cambridge.

White, H. (2000) A reality check for data snooping. *Econometrica*, 68, 1097–1126.

Part III

Higher-Order and Alternative Asymptotics

Chapter 5

Higher-Order Asymptotic Approximations

5.1 Introduction

The large sample theory is arguably the most popular framework for conducting statistical inference due to its virtually universal applicability and implementational simplicity. There are situations, however, in which the conventional asymptotic methods do not provide satisfactory answers to some important questions. First, a consistent and asymptotically normal estimator may have a significant bias even in very large samples. Second, two asymptotically equivalent estimators may possess very different statistical properties in finite samples. Third, an asymptotically standard normal t-statistic may exhibit severe over- or under-rejection, and ignoring this may result in poor inference. These examples show that the standard asymptotic tools are often insufficient for an adequate econometric analysis.

While the exact distribution theory is designed to provide help in these situations, it is valid under some very strong assumptions on the data generating process and is often not available for more general models. An alternative way to address such issues is to go beyond standard ("first-order") asymptotics by using the so-called *higher-order asymptotic analysis*. This approach has the ability, albeit imperfect, to answer some interesting questions related to the finite sample moments of estimators and sampling distributions of test statistics. This chapter focuses mainly on two types of *asymptotic expansions*: *stochastic expansions* of estimators and *Gram–Charlier, Edgeworth and saddlepoint expansions* of sampling distributions of test statistics. While the stochastic expansions allow the researcher to analyze finite sample moments (such as bias and mean squared error) and compare asymptotically equivalent estimators, the Edgeworth-type approximations are useful in capturing certain characteristics of the distributions of test statistics that are not reflected in the first-order asymptotics.

Tools for improved higher-order asymptotic inference have a long history in statistics but the recent development of new estimators and inference methods in econometrics has led to a renewed interest in higher-order asymptotic analysis for comparing and improving the finite sample properties of different

estimators and test statistics. The higher-order expansions also provide theoretical justification for some popular resampling techniques (such as bootstrap
and jackknife) and are predominantly used for establishing the higher-order
refinements of the bootstrap.

5.2   Stochastic Expansions

5.2.1   Higher-Order Delta Method

As we mentioned in the introduction, higher-order analysis is primarily
used for improved finite sample inference by expanding the moments and
the distributions of estimators and test statistics. In some cases, however,
higher-order asymptotic tools prove indispensable for deriving non-degenerate
asymptotic distributions when the first-order approximation delivers trivial
results.

To introduce the problem, consider a scalar sequence $\{z_n\}_{n=1}^{\infty}$ satisfying
$z_n \overset{p}{\to} z = \text{const}$ and $\sqrt{n}(z_n - z) \overset{d}{\to} \mathcal{N}\left(0, \sigma^2\right)$. Let g be a function which is p
times continuously differentiable at z with $g'(z) = g''(z) = \dots = g^{(p-1)}(z) = 0$
and $g^{(p)}(z) \neq 0$. Suppose we are interested in the asymptotic distribution of
$g(z_n)$.

The standard way to derive this asymptotic distribution is to use the Delta
method. However, because $g'(z) = 0$, this approach will lead to the trivial
result that $\sqrt{n}\left(g(z_n) - g(z)\right) \overset{d}{\to} \mathcal{N}(0,0) = 0$, indicating that the rate of
convergence in this setup is higher than $\sqrt{n}$. Recalling the derivation of the
Delta method, we have to augment the underlying Taylor series expansion by
higher-order terms. In this case, we need to employ a pth-order Taylor series
expansion

$$
\begin{aligned}
g(z_n) &= g(z) + g'(z)(z_n - z) + \frac{1}{2}g''(z^*)(z_n - z)^2 + \dots \\
&\quad + \frac{1}{(p-1)!}g^{(p-1)}(z)(z_n - z)^2 + \frac{1}{p!}g^{(p)}(z^*)(z_n - z)^p \\
&= g(z) + \frac{1}{p!}g^{(p)}(z^*)(z_n - z)^p,
\end{aligned}
$$

where z^* lies between z_n and z, and, hence, $z^* \overset{p}{\to} z$ and $g^{(p)}(z^*) \overset{p}{\to} g^{(p)}(z)$.
Then, by repeatedly using the continuous mapping theorem, we get

$$
\frac{n^{p/2}p!}{\sigma^p}\frac{g(z_n) - g(z)}{g^{(p)}(z)} \overset{d}{\to} (\mathcal{N}(0,1))^p.
$$

We refer to this approach as the *higher-order Delta method*. In some special
cases, this result can be derived from first principles. For example, when

$z = 0$, the asymptotics of z_n^2 is $n z_n^2 = \left(\sqrt{n} z_n\right)^2 \xrightarrow{d} \sigma^2 \left(\mathcal{N}\left(0, 1\right)\right)^2 \sim \sigma^2 \chi_1^2$, but the higher-order asymptotics is still implicit here.

Exercise 5.1. Find the asymptotic distribution of $\cos(z_n)$ when $z = 0$ (a) by using the higher-order Delta method, (b) from first principles using a certain trigonometric identity.

Exercise 5.2. Find the asymptotic distribution of $\bar{x}^p$, where $\bar{x}$ denotes the sample average of a random sample $\{x_i\}_{i=1}^n$ from a population with zero mean.

5.2.2 Stochastic Expansions

One of the main tools for higher-order asymptotic analysis is *stochastic expansions* which, due to the seminal work of Nagar (1959), are sometimes referred to as Nagar-type expansions. These expansions are applied to random variables that are functions of data of length n, around their probability limits. Typically, for parametric estimators or test statistics in IID environments, they are in powers of $n^{-1/2}$, i.e., the zeroth-order term is the probability limit, the first-order term contains a factor $n^{-1/2}$, the second-order term contains a factor n^{-1}, etc. For a regular estimator $\hat{\theta}$ of a scalar parameter θ_0 we have

$$\hat{\theta} = \theta_0 + \frac{a_{1,n}}{\sqrt{n}} + \frac{a_{2,n}}{n} + \frac{a_{3,n}}{n\sqrt{n}} + \dots + \frac{a_{p,n}}{n^{p/2}} + o_P\left(\frac{1}{n^{p/2}}\right),$$

where $a_{1,n}$, $a_{2,n}$, $a_{3,n}$, ... are stochastically bounded random variables having non-trivial limiting distributions. For nonparametric estimators and/or time series processes, the expansion may not be strictly in powers of $n^{-1/2}$.

The degree of accuracy of the expansion is determined by p. The conventional asymptotics corresponds to $p = 0$ and $p = 1$: the notion of consistency corresponds to the stochastic expansion of order zero

$$\hat{\theta} = \theta_0 + o_P\left(1\right),$$

while the asymptotic normality corresponds to the first-order stochastic expansion

$$\hat{\theta} = \theta_0 + \frac{a_{1,n}}{\sqrt{n}} + o_P\left(\frac{1}{n^{1/2}}\right),$$

where $a_{1,n}$ has mean zero and limiting distribution $\mathcal{N}\left(0, \Omega_{\hat{\theta}}\right)$ with $\Omega_{\hat{\theta}}$ being the asymptotic variance of $\hat{\theta}$. Higher-order asymptotics arises when $p \geq 2$. A higher p is usually associated with a higher degree of precision of approximation of the actual statistical properties of $\hat{\theta}$ by asymptotic quantities.

5.2.3 Second-Order Asymptotic Bias

Researchers are often interested in the magnitude of the bias of an asymptotically normal estimator. From the point of view of first-order asymptotics, such an estimator is asymptotically unbiased as $E[a_{1,n}] = 0$. However, to order $1/n$,

$$E[\hat{\theta}] = \theta_0 + \frac{1}{n} \lim_{n \to \infty} E[a_{2,n}] + o\left(\frac{1}{n}\right).$$

Typically, in an *IID* environment, $E[a_{2,n}]$ does not depend on n so that $\lim_{n \to \infty} E[a_{2,n}] = E[a_{2,n}]$ but in a time series context, $E[a_{2,n}]$ may depend on the sample size. The estimator $\hat{\theta}$ is second-order asymptotically biased if this term does not equal zero. The quantity

$$B_{\hat{\theta}} = \frac{1}{n} \lim_{n \to \infty} E[a_{2,n}]$$

is called a *second-order asymptotic bias* (or simply asymptotic bias) of $\hat{\theta}$.

When $B_{\hat{\theta}} = 0$, the estimator $\hat{\theta}$ is said to be *second-order asymptotically unbiased*. Generally, even closed-form estimators in linear models are second-order asymptotically biased. When a formula for the second-order asymptotic bias is available, one may construct a second-order asymptotically unbiased estimator or an *(analytical) bias-corrected estimator*.

Suppose the expression for the second-order asymptotic bias is

$$B_{\hat{\theta}} = \frac{1}{n} B(\theta_0, \varphi_0),$$

where φ_0 is the true value of a vector of other unknown parameters, and $B(\theta, \varphi)$ is continuously differentiable in both arguments. If there is an estimator $\hat{\varphi}$ for φ_0 such that

$$\hat{\varphi} = \varphi_0 + \frac{a_{\varphi,n}}{\sqrt{n}} + o_P\left(\frac{1}{n^{1/2}}\right),$$

then the *bias-corrected estimator* may be constructed as

$$\hat{\theta}^{BC} = \hat{\theta} - \frac{1}{n} B(\hat{\theta}, \hat{\varphi}).$$

Indeed,

$$E[\hat{\theta}^{BC}] = E[\hat{\theta}] - \frac{1}{n} E\left[B(\hat{\theta}, \hat{\varphi})\right]$$

$$= \theta_0 + \frac{1}{n} B(\theta_0, \varphi_0) + o\left(\frac{1}{n}\right)$$

$$- \frac{1}{n} E\left[B(\theta_0, \varphi_0) + \frac{\partial B(\theta_0, \varphi_0)}{\partial \theta} \frac{a_{1,n}}{\sqrt{n}}\right.$$

$$\left. + \frac{\partial B(\theta_0, \varphi_0)}{\partial \varphi} \frac{a_{\varphi,n}}{\sqrt{n}} + o\left(\frac{1}{n^{1/2}}\right)\right]$$

$$= \theta_0 + o\left(\frac{1}{n}\right).$$

Exercise 5.3. Assuming random sampling, consider a consistent and asymptotically normal estimator $\hat{\theta}$ of a scalar parameter θ_0 with asymptotic variance $\Omega_{\hat{\theta}}$ and second-order asymptotic bias $B_{\hat{\theta}}$. Derive the second-order asymptotic bias for $g(\hat{\theta})$ as an estimator of $g(\theta_0)$, where $g(\theta)$ is a smooth nonlinear function.

Exercise 5.4. Assuming random sampling, suppose that the estimator $\hat{\theta}$ of θ_0 admits the following expansion for the mean:

$$E[\hat{\theta}] = \theta + \frac{a_2}{n} + \frac{a_4}{n^2} + o\left(\frac{1}{n^2}\right).$$

Show that the *jackknife estimator*

$$\hat{\theta}^J = n\hat{\theta} - \left(1 - \frac{1}{n}\right)\sum_{i=1}^{n}\hat{\theta}_{-i},$$

where $\hat{\theta}_{-i}$ is a leave-one-out estimator (i.e., the same as $\hat{\theta}$ but computed over the sample excluding the ith observation), is second-order asymptotically unbiased.

The well-known *bootstrap bias correction* is another way to construct second-order asymptotically unbiased estimators. As for the jackknife in Exercise 5.4, it does not require knowledge of the formula for a second-order asymptotic bias.

Below we discuss several important examples of estimators and their second-order asymptotic biases. Some other interesting cases can be found in Rothenberg (1984), Rilstone, Srivastava, and Ullah (1996) and Bao and Ullah (2007).

5.2.3.1 Asymptotic Bias of the OLS Estimator

Let the scalar processes x_t and y_t be jointly stationary and ergodic, and consider the linear projection of y_t on x_t

$$y_t = \theta_0 x_t + e_t, \quad E[x_t e_t] = 0.$$

The OLS estimator of the parameter θ_0 is

$$\hat{\theta} = \frac{\sum_{t=1}^{n} x_t y_t}{\sum_{t=1}^{n} x_t^2} = \theta_0 + \frac{\sum_{t=1}^{n} x_t e_t}{\sum_{t=1}^{n} x_t^2}.$$

Let $\omega = E\left[x_t^2\right]^{-1}$. The first-order stochastic expansion yields the conventional asymptotics:

$$\hat{\theta} - \theta_0 = \frac{1}{\sqrt{n}} \frac{\frac{1}{\sqrt{n}} \sum_{t=1}^{n} x_t e_t}{\frac{1}{n} \sum_{t=1}^{n} x_t^2}$$

$$= \frac{1}{\sqrt{n}} \omega \frac{1}{\sqrt{n}} \sum_{t=1}^{n} x_t e_t + o_P\left(\frac{1}{n^{1/2}}\right),$$

where the remainder term is due to the noise in the sample average of x_t^2. The estimator $\hat{\theta}$ is first-order asymptotically unbiased by virtue of asymptotic normality. Indeed, the first-order asymptotic bias is given by

$$\frac{1}{\sqrt{n}} \omega E\left[\frac{1}{\sqrt{n}} \sum_{t=1}^{n} x_t e_t\right] = 0.$$

The second-order stochastic expansion of the estimator $\hat{\theta}$ can be obtained as

$$\hat{\theta} - \theta_0 = \frac{1}{\sqrt{n}} \omega \frac{\frac{1}{\sqrt{n}} \sum_{t=1}^{n} x_t e_t}{1 + \omega \frac{1}{n} \sum_{t=1}^{n} (x_t^2 - E\left[x_t^2\right])}$$

$$= \frac{1}{\sqrt{n}} \omega \frac{1}{\sqrt{n}} \sum_{t=1}^{n} x_t e_t$$

$$\times \left(1 - \frac{1}{\sqrt{n}} \omega \frac{1}{\sqrt{n}} \sum_{t=1}^{n} (x_t^2 - E\left[x_t^2\right]) + o_P\left(\frac{1}{n^{1/2}}\right)\right)$$

$$= \frac{1}{\sqrt{n}} \omega \frac{1}{\sqrt{n}} \sum_{t=1}^{n} x_t e_t$$

$$- \frac{1}{n} \omega^2 \left(\frac{1}{\sqrt{n}} \sum_{t=1}^{n} (x_t^2 - E\left[x_t^2\right])\right) \left(\frac{1}{\sqrt{n}} \sum_{t=1}^{n} x_t e_t\right) + o_P\left(\frac{1}{n}\right).$$

Note that the expectation of the second-order "coefficient"

$$a_{2,n} = -\omega^2 \left(\frac{1}{\sqrt{n}} \sum_{t=1}^{n} (x_t^2 - E\left[x_t^2\right])\right) \left(\frac{1}{\sqrt{n}} \sum_{t=1}^{n} x_t e_t\right)$$

depends on n under serial dependence. By taking the limit as $n \to \infty$ and turning to the long-run covariance (see section 1.3 in Chapter 1), it is easy to derive the expression for the second-order asymptotic bias:

$$B_{\hat{\theta}} = -\frac{1}{n} \omega^2 \sum_{j=-\infty}^{+\infty} E\left[x_{t-j}^2 x_t e_t\right].$$

When the data are independent, the expectation of $a_{2,n}$ does not depend on the sample size, and we have

$$B_{\hat{\theta}} = -\frac{1}{n}\omega^2 E\left[x_t^3 e_t\right].$$

Furthermore, if the projection is a regression so that $E\left[e_t|x_t\right] = 0$, then $E\left[x_t^3 e_t\right] = 0$ and the second-order asymptotic bias is zero. This is not surprising since the OLS estimator in a linear regression under random sampling is exactly unbiased. In contrast, for time series data, the OLS estimator is biased in models with lagged dependent variables as regressors.

Exercise 5.5. Compute the second-order asymptotic bias of the OLS estimator of the AR coefficient in a linear first-order autoregression with IID innovations (a) when there is no intercept, (b) when there is an intercept. Construct a bias-corrected estimator in both cases.

5.2.3.2 Asymptotic Bias of the 2SLS Estimator

Consider now a linear instrumental variables model with a single endogenous explanatory variable x and ℓ valid instruments z:

$$y = \theta_0 x + e, \quad E\left[e|z\right] = 0,$$

and suppose that the data $\{(x_i, y_i, z_i)\}_{i=1}^n$ constitute a random sample. Assume, for simplicity, conditional homoskedasticity and conditional homocorrelatedness between the right-hand side variable and the instruments:

$$E\left[e^2|z\right] = \sigma_e^2, \quad E\left[ex|z\right] = \rho.$$

Let $M_{xz} = E\left[xz'\right]$, $M_{zz} = E\left[zz'\right]$, $\Pi = M_{xz}M_{zz}^{-1}$ and $\omega = \left(M_{xz}M_{zz}^{-1}M_{xz}'\right)^{-1}$.
The two-stage least squares (2SLS) estimator of θ_0 is given by

$$\hat{\theta} = \frac{\left(\sum\limits_{i=1}^n x_i z_i'\right)\left(\sum\limits_{i=1}^n z_i z_i'\right)^{-1}\left(\sum\limits_{i=1}^n z_i y_i\right)}{\left(\sum\limits_{i=1}^n x_i z_i'\right)\left(\sum\limits_{i=1}^n z_i z_i'\right)^{-1}\left(\sum\limits_{i=1}^n z_i x_i\right)}.$$

Note that $\hat{\theta} - \theta_0$ equals

$$\frac{\left(n^{-1}\sum\limits_{i=1}^n x_i z_i'\right)\left(n^{-1}\sum\limits_{i=1}^n z_i z_i'\right)^{-1}}{\left(n^{-1}\sum\limits_{i=1}^n x_i z_i'\right)\left(n^{-1}\sum\limits_{i=1}^n z_i z_i'\right)^{-1}\left(n^{-1}\sum\limits_{i=1}^n z_i x_i\right)}\frac{1}{n}\sum\limits_{i=1}^n z_i e_i, \qquad (5.1)$$

which is $O_P(1) \cdot o_P(1) = o_P(1)$ rendering consistency of the estimator. The first-order stochastic expansion gives rise to the conventional asymptotics:

$$\hat{\theta} - \theta_0 = \frac{1}{\sqrt{n}} \frac{\left(n^{-1}\sum_{i=1}^{n} x_i z_i'\right)\left(n^{-1}\sum_{i=1}^{n} z_i z_i'\right)^{-1}}{\left(n^{-1}\sum_{i=1}^{n} x_i z_i'\right)\left(n^{-1}\sum_{i=1}^{n} z_i z_i'\right)^{-1}\left(n^{-1}\sum_{i=1}^{n} z_i x_i\right)} \frac{1}{\sqrt{n}}\sum_{i=1}^{n} z_i e_i$$

$$= \frac{1}{\sqrt{n}} \omega \Pi \cdot \xi_n + o_P\left(\frac{1}{n^{1/2}}\right),$$

where $\xi_n \xrightarrow{d} N\left(0, \sigma_e^2 M_{zz}\right)$. The asymptotic normality of $\hat{\theta}$ is directly obtained from this expression. The first-order asymptotic bias, of course, is zero because ξ_n is centered at zero.

Let us now derive a second-order stochastic expansion:

$$\hat{\theta} - \theta_0 = \frac{1}{\sqrt{n}} \frac{\left(M_{xz} + \bar{m}\right)\left(M_{zz} + \bar{p}\right)^{-1}}{\left(M_{xz} + \bar{m}\right)\left(M_{zz} + \bar{p}\right)^{-1}\left(M_{xz}' + \bar{m}'\right)} \frac{1}{\sqrt{n}}\sum_{i=1}^{n} z_i e_i,$$

where $\bar{m}$ and $\bar{p}$ are the sample averages of $m_i = x_i z_i' - M_{xz}$ and $p_i = z_i z_i' - M_{zz}$, respectively. Note that

$$\left(M_{zz} + \bar{p}\right)^{-1} = \left(I_\ell + M_{zz}^{-1}\bar{p}\right)^{-1} M_{zz}^{-1} = \left[I_\ell - M_{zz}^{-1}\bar{p} + o_P\left(\frac{1}{n^{1/2}}\right)\right] M_{zz}^{-1}.$$

Therefore,

$$\hat{\theta} - \theta_0 = \frac{1}{\sqrt{n}} \frac{1}{\omega^{-1}} \frac{\Pi + \bar{m}M_{zz}^{-1} - \Pi\bar{p}M_{zz}^{-1} + o_P\left(n^{-1/2}\right)}{1 + 2\Pi\omega\,\bar{m}' + \Pi\omega\,\bar{p}\,\Pi' + o_P\left(n^{-1/2}\right)} \frac{1}{\sqrt{n}}\sum_{i=1}^{n} z_i e_i$$

$$= \frac{1}{\sqrt{n}}\omega\left[\Pi + \bar{m}M_{zz}^{-1} - \Pi\bar{p}M_{zz}^{-1} + o_P\left(\frac{1}{n^{1/2}}\right)\right]$$

$$\times \left[1 - 2\Pi\omega\,\bar{m}' - \Pi\omega\,\bar{p}\,\Pi' + o_P\left(\frac{1}{n^{1/2}}\right)\right] \frac{1}{\sqrt{n}}\sum_{i=1}^{n} z_i e_i$$

$$= \frac{1}{\sqrt{n}}\Pi\omega \frac{1}{\sqrt{n}}\sum_{i=1}^{n} z_i e_i + \frac{1}{n}\omega\left[\left(\sqrt{n}\bar{m}\right)M_{zz}^{-1} - 2\Pi\omega\left(\sqrt{n}\bar{m}\right)'\Pi\right.$$

$$\left. - \Pi\left(\sqrt{n}\bar{p}\right)M_{zz}^{-1} - \Pi\omega\left(\sqrt{n}\bar{p}\right)\Pi'\Pi\right] \frac{1}{\sqrt{n}}\sum_{i=1}^{n} z_i e_i + o_P\left(\frac{1}{n}\right).$$

Next, we obtain explicit expressions for all components of the second-order asymptotic bias. The first component is caused by the correlatedness of the influence function $n^{-1/2}\sum_{i=1}^{n} z_i e_i$ with the first factor in the numerator of

(5.1):

$$\frac{1}{n}\omega E\left[xz'M_{zz}^{-1}ze\right] = \frac{1}{n}\omega\,E\left[z'M_{zz}^{-1}zE\left[xe|z\right]\right] = \frac{1}{n}\rho\omega\,E\left[z'M_{zz}^{-1}z\right]$$

$$= \frac{1}{n}\rho\omega\,E\left[\mathrm{tr}\left(z'M_{zz}^{-1}z\right)\right] = \frac{1}{n}\rho\omega\,E\left[\mathrm{tr}\left(M_{zz}^{-1}zz'\right)\right]$$

$$= \frac{1}{n}\rho\omega\,\mathrm{tr}\left(M_{zz}^{-1}E\left[zz'\right]\right) = \frac{1}{n}\rho\omega\,\mathrm{tr}\left(I_{\ell}\right)$$

$$= \frac{1}{n}\rho\omega\ell.$$

The second component arises from the correlatedness of $n^{-1/2}\sum_{i=1}^{n}z_ie_i$ with the first and third terms in the denominator of (5.1):

$$-\frac{1}{n}2\Pi\omega^2 E\left[zx\Pi ze\right] = -\frac{1}{n}2\omega^2 E\left[(\Pi z)^2\,E\left[xe|z\right]\right] = -\frac{1}{n}2\omega^2\rho E\left[(\Pi z)^2\right]$$

$$= -\frac{1}{n}2\rho\omega^2 E\left[(\Pi z)\,(z'\Pi')\right] = -\frac{1}{n}2\rho\omega^2\Pi E\left[zz'\right]\Pi'$$

$$= -\frac{1}{n}2\rho\omega.$$

The third component is caused by the correlatedness of $n^{-1/2}\sum_{i=1}^{n}z_ie_i$ with the middle term in the numerator of (5.1):

$$-\frac{1}{n}\Pi\omega E\left[zz'M_{zz}^{-1}ze\right] = -\frac{1}{n}\Pi\omega E\left[zz'M_{zz}^{-1}zE\left[e|z\right]\right]$$

$$= 0.$$

Finally, the fourth component captures the correlatedness of $n^{-1/2}\sum_{i=1}^{n}z_ie_i$ with the middle term in the denominator of (5.1):

$$\frac{1}{n}\Pi\omega^2 E\left[zz'\Pi'\Pi ze\right] - \frac{1}{n}\Pi\omega^2 E\left[zz'\Pi'\Pi zE\left[e|z\right]\right]$$

$$= 0.$$

To summarize, the total second-order bias of the 2SLS estimator is given by

$$B_{\hat{\theta}} = \frac{1}{n}\rho\omega\left(\ell - 2\right).$$

Note that the bias is linearly growing in the number of instruments. It equals zero when there are two instruments, but in this case the second-order asymptotic unbiasedness is coincidental.

Exercise 5.6. Compute the second-order asymptotic bias of the 2SLS estimator in the same setup as above, but when there are $k > 1$ right-hand side variables.

5.2.3.3   Asymptotic Bias of the Maximum Likelihood Estimator

Now we derive the higher-order asymptotic bias of an implicitly given estimator. Suppose we know that a scalar parameter θ_0 solves the ML problem

$$\max_{\theta \in \Theta} E\left[\log f\left(z, \theta\right)\right].$$

Let, as usual,

$$H = -E\left[\frac{\partial^2 \log f\left(z, \theta_0\right)}{\partial \theta^2}\right] = E\left[\left(\frac{\partial \log f\left(z, \theta_0\right)}{\partial \theta}\right)^2\right]$$

be the information matrix. In addition, let

$$K = E\left[\frac{\partial^3 \log f\left(z, \theta_0\right)}{\partial \theta^3}\right],$$

$$L = E\left[\frac{\partial^2 \log f\left(z, \theta_0\right)}{\partial \theta^2}\frac{\partial \log f\left(z, \theta_0\right)}{\partial \theta}\right],$$

and assume, for simplicity, random sampling.

The ML estimator is

$$\hat{\theta} = \arg\max_{\theta \in \Theta} \sum_{i=1}^{n} \log f\left(z_i, \theta\right).$$

The first-order condition for this program, together with its second-order Taylor series expansion around θ_0, is

$$0 = \sum_{i=1}^{n} \frac{\partial \log f(z_i, \hat{\theta})}{\partial \theta}$$

$$= \sum_{i=1}^{n} \frac{\partial \log f\left(z_i, \theta_0\right)}{\partial \theta} + \sum_{i=1}^{n} \frac{\partial^2 \log f\left(z_i, \theta_0\right)}{\partial \theta^2}\left(\hat{\theta} - \theta_0\right)$$

$$+ \frac{1}{2}\sum_{i=1}^{n} \frac{\partial^3 \log f\left(z_i, \bar{\theta}\right)}{\partial \theta^3}\left(\hat{\theta} - \theta_0\right)^2$$

for some mean value $\bar{\theta}$. Ignoring the last, highest-order term gives the first-order stochastic expansion

$$\hat{\theta} = \theta_0 - \frac{1}{\sqrt{n}}\left(\frac{1}{n}\sum_{i=1}^{n} \frac{\partial^2 \log f\left(z_i, \theta_0\right)}{\partial \theta^2}\right)^{-1}\frac{1}{\sqrt{n}}\sum_{i=1}^{n} \frac{\partial \log f\left(z_i, \theta_0\right)}{\partial \theta}$$

$$+ o_P\left(\frac{1}{n^{1/2}}\right)$$

$$= \theta_0 + \frac{1}{\sqrt{n}}H^{-1}\frac{1}{\sqrt{n}}\sum_{i=1}^{n} \frac{\partial \log f\left(z_i, \theta_0\right)}{\partial \theta} + o_P\left(\frac{1}{n^{1/2}}\right).$$

This yields the asymptotic normality of $\hat{\theta}$, and, in particular, the first-order asymptotic unbiasedness as the expected score, evaluated at the true parameter, is zero. Next, if the uniform LLN is applicable to the third derivatives of $\log f$, the highest-order term equals

$$\frac{1}{2} \sum_{i=1}^{n} \frac{\partial^3 \log f\left(z_i, \bar{\theta}\right)}{\partial \theta^3} \left(\hat{\theta} - \theta_0\right)^2$$

$$= \frac{n}{2} \left(K + O_P\left(\frac{1}{n^{1/2}}\right)\right)$$

$$\times \left(\frac{1}{\sqrt{n}} H^{-1} \frac{1}{\sqrt{n}} \sum_{i=1}^{n} \frac{\partial \log f\left(z_i, \theta_0\right)}{\partial \theta} + O_P\left(\frac{1}{n^{1/2}}\right)\right)^2$$

$$= \frac{H^{-2} K}{2} \left(\frac{1}{\sqrt{n}} \sum_{i=1}^{n} \frac{\partial \log f\left(z_i, \theta_0\right)}{\partial \theta}\right)^2 + O_P\left(1\right).$$

Plugging this back into the second-order expansion and also expanding the denominator, we obtain

$$\hat{\theta} = \theta_0 + \frac{1}{\sqrt{n}} H^{-1} \left(1 + \frac{1}{\sqrt{n}} H^{-1} \frac{1}{\sqrt{n}} \sum_{i=1}^{n} \left(\frac{\partial^2 \log f\left(z_i, \theta_0\right)}{\partial \theta^2} + H\right)\right)$$

$$\times \frac{1}{\sqrt{n}} \left(\sum_{i=1}^{n} \frac{\partial \log f\left(z_i, \theta_0\right)}{\partial \theta} + \frac{H^{-2} K}{2} \left(\frac{1}{\sqrt{n}} \sum_{i=1}^{n} \frac{\partial \log f\left(z_i, \theta_0\right)}{\partial \theta}\right)^2\right)$$

$$+ O_P\left(\frac{1}{n}\right)$$

$$= \theta_0 + \frac{1}{\sqrt{n}} H^{-1} \frac{1}{\sqrt{n}} \sum_{i=1}^{n} \frac{\partial \log f\left(z_i, \theta_0\right)}{\partial \theta}$$

$$+ \frac{1}{n} H^{-2} \frac{1}{\sqrt{n}} \sum_{i=1}^{n} \left(\frac{\partial^2 \log f\left(z_i, \theta_0\right)}{\partial \theta^2} + H\right) \frac{1}{\sqrt{n}} \sum_{i=1}^{n} \frac{\partial \log f\left(z_i, \theta_0\right)}{\partial \theta}$$

$$+ \frac{1}{n} \frac{H^{-3} K}{2} \left(\frac{1}{\sqrt{n}} \sum_{i=1}^{n} \frac{\partial \log f\left(z_i, \theta_0\right)}{\partial \theta}\right)^2 + O_P\left(\frac{1}{n}\right).$$

The third and fourth terms in the above expression compose the second-order asymptotic bias that has the form

$$B_{\hat{\theta}} = \frac{1}{n} H^{-2} \left(L + \frac{K}{2}\right).$$

Exercise 5.7. Compute the second-order asymptotic bias of the (conditional) maximum likelihood estimator when the data are not IID but stationary and ergodic.

Exercise 5.8. An analytical bias correction may alternatively be accomplished by modifying the maximum likelihood objective function, or, more conveniently, by changing the first-order condition from

$$\sum_{i=1}^{n} \frac{\partial \log f(z_i, \hat{\theta})}{\partial \theta} = 0,$$

which defines the original estimator $\hat{\theta}$, to

$$\sum_{i=1}^{n} \psi^*(z_i, \hat{\theta}^*) = 0,$$

which defines the corrected estimate $\hat{\theta}^*$, where

$$\psi^*(z_i, \theta) = \frac{\partial \log f(z_i, \theta)}{\partial \theta} + \alpha_n(\theta)$$

for some $\alpha_n(\theta)$. Determine the order (in probability) of $\alpha_n(\theta)$ which would ensure that $\hat{\theta}^*$ is consistent for θ_0 when $\hat{\theta}$ is consistent. Next, determine the order (in probability) of $\alpha_n(\theta)$ which would ensure that $\hat{\theta}^*$ is (first-order) asymptotically equivalent to $\hat{\theta}$. Suggest a formula for $\alpha_n(\theta)$ so that $\hat{\theta}^*$ indeed is second-order unbiased.

Exercise 5.9. Consider the maximum likelihood estimator $\hat{\theta}$ of a scalar parameter θ_0 in a model where the (standardized by n^{-1}) log-likelihood function is $\mathcal{L}(\theta)$ and the data are IID. As we know, $\hat{\theta}$ is consistent, asymptotically normal and (first-order) asymptotically efficient. Let $\hat{\theta}_0$ be another consistent estimator, which is not (first-order) asymptotically efficient. Consider the following estimators that result from applying the Newton–Raphson algorithm for computing $\hat{\theta}$ starting from $\hat{\theta}_0$:

$$\hat{\theta}_{j+1} = \hat{\theta}_j - \frac{\mathcal{L}_1\left(\hat{\theta}_j\right)}{\mathcal{L}_2\left(\hat{\theta}_j\right)},$$

$j = 0, 1, 2, ...$, where $\mathcal{L}_r(\theta) = \partial^r \mathcal{L}(\theta_0) / \partial\theta^r$. Assume that $\sqrt{n}(\hat{\theta}_0 - \hat{\theta})$ has a non-degenerate distribution, and that $\sqrt{n}(\mathcal{L}_r(\theta) - \lambda_r)$, for certain constants λ_r, have normal limits for any r you need.

1. Show that $\hat{\theta}_1$ is (first-order) asymptotically equivalent to $\hat{\theta}$ (and, hence, asymptotically efficient).

2. Show that $\hat{\theta}_2$ is second-order asymptotically equivalent to $\hat{\theta}$.

5.2.3.4 Asymptotic Biases of the Method of Moments Estimators

Section 2.5 in Chapter 2 provides the expressions for the second-order asymptotic biases of GMM and GEL estimators, derived in Newey and Smith (2004) in an IID context, and in Anatolyev (2005) in a time series context. Similarly to the result on the second-order bias of the 2SLS estimator above, these expressions contain several components that are attributed to different sources of bias such as estimation of the parameter given the ideal optimal instrument, estimation of ingredients of the optimal instrument, the first-step estimation of the optimal weighting matrix, etc. In principle, the number of components in an expression for the second-order asymptotic bias may serve as a (rough) measure of biasedness in various comparisons. See section 2.5 in Chapter 2 for a detailed discussion on the higher-order bias properties of GMM and GEL estimators.

Exercise 5.10. Consider estimation of a scalar parameter θ_0 on the basis of the moment conditions $E[x] = E[y] = \theta_0$ and IID data (x_i, y_i), $i = 1, \ldots, n$.

1. Show that the EL estimator of θ_0 is second-order asymptotically unbiased.

2. Derive the second-order asymptotic bias of the two-step GMM estimator of θ_0 using $\bar{x}$ as a first-step estimator.

5.2.4 Higher-Order Asymptotic Variance and MSE

While it may sometimes be desirable to correct for second-order asymptotic bias, taking into account the higher-order asymptotic variance also proves to be an important consideration in inferring finite sample properties of an estimator. Suppose that for a first-order asymptotically normal estimator $\hat{\theta}$ of θ_0, the higher-order asymptotic bias and variance are

$$E[\hat{\theta} - \theta_0] = \frac{b}{n} + o\left(\frac{1}{n}\right)$$

and

$$\text{var}[\hat{\theta}] = \frac{\Omega_{\hat{\theta}}}{n} + \frac{v_1}{n^{3/2}} + \frac{v_2}{n^2} + o\left(\frac{1}{n^2}\right).$$

Then, the asymptotic mean squared error up to order n^{-2} is given by

$$\mathcal{MSE}[\hat{\theta}] = E[\hat{\theta} - \theta_0]^2 + \text{var}[\hat{\theta}] = \frac{\Omega_{\hat{\theta}}}{n} + \frac{v_1}{n^{3/2}} + \frac{b^2 + v_2}{n^2} + O\left(\frac{1}{n^2}\right).$$

The first term in $\mathcal{MSE}[\hat{\theta}]$ is the familiar first-order asymptotic variance. The usual asymptotic quality criterion requires that $\Omega_{\hat{\theta}}$ be as small as possible and (ideally) minimized at the *asymptotic efficiency bound* for $\hat{\theta}$ (see, for example, Chapter 3). Furthermore, the next asymptotic term may be eliminated if v_1 is zero. Finally, $\hat{\theta}$ will be *higher-order asymptotically efficient* if the coefficient in the n^{-2} term is minimized. It is possible to show that there are higher-order superefficient estimators which gain higher-order asymptotic efficiency at a specific value of the true parameter at the expense of second-order asymptotic bias. That is, there is no first-order asymptotically efficient estimator that minimizes the higher-order asymptotic mean squared error.

However, it turns out that in a narrower class of second-order asymptotically unbiased estimators, including bias-corrected estimators, there exist higher-order asymptotically efficient estimators. In particular, bias-corrected maximum likelihood estimators in fully parametric models have this property (Pfanzagl and Wefelmeyer, 1978; Rothenberg, 1984; Newey, Hahn and Kuersteiner, 2005). Furthermore, Newey and Smith (2004) derived the higher-order asymptotic properties of GEL and GMM estimators under random sampling and obtained a semiparametric analog of the higher-order efficiency of ML estimators. They established that the bias-corrected (via analytical, bootstrap or jackknife procedures) EL estimator is higher-order asymptotically efficient (i.e., it has minimal higher-order asymptotic mean squared error) among all bias-corrected GEL and GMM estimators. These nice properties of empirical likelihood estimation must have roots in the nonparametric likelihood interpretation of the EL objective function (see Chapter 2).

Exercise 5.11. Derive a higher-order asymptotic MSE of an instrumental variables estimator in a linear IV regression with a single right-hand side variable and a single instrument, under the assumptions of random sampling, conditional homoskedasticity and conditional homocorrelatedness.

5.3 Higher-Order Approximations of Sampling Distributions

5.3.1 Edgeworth Expansion

5.3.1.1 Introduction and Preliminary Concepts

While the stochastic expansions discussed above are concerned with better approximations of moments of estimators, the accuracy of statistical inference (confidence interval construction, hypothesis testing) depends primarily on the quality of approximation to the distributions of estimators and test statistics. In small samples, approximations based on central limit theorems may be rather inaccurate. This motivates the use of higher-order asymptotic expansions that are more accurate than first-order asymptotics and provide better approximations to the finite sample distribution of the statistic of interest. Also, asymptotic expansions are used in deriving the property of a higher-order accuracy (asymptotic refinement) of bootstrap methods. On a more intuitive level, higher-order expansions deliver some interesting insights and help us understand better how asymptotic theory works. Since these higher-order expansions describe the behavior of the whole distribution of the statistic of interest, approximations to the moments of this statistic can be obtained directly by straightforward calculations. On the other hand, some stochastic expansions that we discussed above can be used to derive more general expansions of the distribution function, as we show later.

To introduce the main ideas, let x be a random variable with probability distribution F and density f and $T(x_1, ..., x_n)$ be a test statistic with a limiting normal distribution and a finite sample distribution $G_n(u) = \Pr\{T(x_1, ..., x_n) \leq u\}$. While the central limit theorem offers a convenient approximation to conduct large sample inference, it provides no information on the magnitude of the approximation error for small n. The Berry–Esseen theorem shows that the accuracy of the asymptotic normal approximation for the sample mean of a random sample is bounded by a term that depends on the magnitude of the third cumulant of the distribution of the data and goes to 0 at rate $n^{-1/2}$. In particular, if the degree of asymmetry is large and the sample size is small, the quality of the central limit approximation is expected to be poor. We show below that, under some regularity conditions, this distribution admits an Edgeworth expansion of the form

$$G_n(u) = \Phi(u) + n^{-1/2}p_1(u)\phi(u) + n^{-1}p_2(u)\phi(u) + ... + n^{-j/2}p_j(u)\phi(u) + ...,$$

where $\Phi(u)$ and $\phi(u)$ are the CDF and PDF of a standard normal variable and $p_j(u)$ is a polynomial of (at most) degree $3j - 1$ in u and is an odd or even function when j is odd or even.

Let us briefly introduce some of the notions that will be used in deriving the higher-order asymptotic expansions of distribution functions. The characteristic function of x is defined as $E\left[\exp(i\lambda x)\right]$ or

$$\varphi(\lambda) = \int_{-\infty}^{+\infty} \exp(i\lambda x)f(x)dx,$$

where $i = \sqrt{-1}$ and $\exp(i\lambda x) = \cos(\lambda x) + i\sin(\lambda x)$. In general, the characteristic function takes complex values, but for random variables with symmetric density around 0 its values are real. The characteristic function always exists and is uniformly continuous. Since distinct probability distributions have distinct characteristic functions, the characteristic function can be inverted (provided that $|\varphi|$ is integrable) to obtain the density

$$f(x) = \frac{1}{2\pi} \int_{-\infty}^{+\infty} \exp(-i\lambda x)\varphi(\lambda)d\lambda.$$

The cumulant generating function of a random variable x is $\mathbb{K}(\lambda) = \log \varphi(\lambda)$, where log is the principal logarithm. The series expansion of $\mathbb{K}(\lambda)$ about $\lambda = 0$, assuming that $\mathbb{K}(\lambda)$ is differentiable at $\lambda = 0$, yields

$$\mathbb{K}(\lambda) = \kappa_1 i\lambda + \frac{1}{2}\kappa_2(i\lambda)^2 + ... + \frac{1}{j!}\kappa_j(i\lambda)^j + ... = \sum_{j=1}^{\infty} \kappa_j \frac{(i\lambda)^j}{j!}, \qquad (5.2)$$

where

$$\kappa_j = \frac{1}{i^j} \left. \frac{\partial^j \mathbb{K}(\lambda)}{\partial \lambda^j} \right|_{\lambda=0}$$

is the jth cumulant of x.

Equivalently, since $\varphi(\lambda)$ can be expanded as

$$\varphi(\lambda) = 1 + E\left[x\right]i\lambda + \frac{1}{2}E\left[x^2\right](i\lambda)^2 + ... + \frac{1}{j!}E\left[x^j\right](i\lambda)^j + ...,$$

$$\mathbb{K}(\lambda) = \log\left(1 + \sum_{j=1}^{\infty} E\left[x^j\right]\frac{(i\lambda)^j}{j!}\right) \qquad (5.3)$$

$$= \sum_{k=1}^{\infty}(-1)^{k+1}\frac{1}{k}\left(\sum_{j=1}^{\infty}E\left[x^j\right]\frac{(i\lambda)^j}{j!}\right)^k$$

and the cumulants can be deduced from equating the coefficients of $(i\lambda)^j$ in expressions (5.2) and (5.3). This gives $\kappa_1 = E\left[x\right]$, $\kappa_2 = E\left[x^2\right] - E\left[x\right]^2 = \text{var}\left[x\right]$, $\kappa_3 = E\left[(x - E\left[x\right])^3\right]$ and $\kappa_4 = E\left[(x - E\left[x\right])^4\right] - 3(\text{var}\left[x\right])^2$. Note that if $x \sim \mathcal{N}(0,1)$, $\kappa_1 = 0$, $\kappa_2 = 1$ and $\kappa_r = 0$ for $r \geq 3$.[1]

5.3.1.2   Edgeworth Expansion for Sums of Random Variables

Let $x_1, ..., x_n$ denote IID observations of a random variable x from a distribution with mean κ_1 and variance κ_2, and $z_i = (x_i - \kappa_1)/\sqrt{\kappa_2}$. By the central limit theorem, $\sqrt{n}\bar{z} \xrightarrow{d} \mathcal{N}(0,1)$ and we refer to this approximation as first-order asymptotics. Suppose that we want to derive higher-order approximations to the density $f_{Z_n}(z)$ and cumulative distribution function $F_{Z_n}(z)$ of the (properly normalized) sample average $Z_n = \sqrt{n}\bar{z} = n^{-1/2}\sum_{i=1}^{n} z_i$.

From (5.2) and using the properties of the cumulants, $\mathbb{K}(\lambda)$ can be expanded as

$$\mathbb{K}_{Z_n}(\lambda) = -\frac{\lambda^2}{2} + \frac{\kappa_3(i\lambda)^3}{6n^{1/2}} + \frac{\kappa_4(i\lambda)^4}{24n} + \frac{\kappa_5(i\lambda)^5}{120n^{3/2}} + \frac{\kappa_6(i\lambda)^6}{720n^2} + ...$$

---

[1] Some useful properties of the cumulant generating function include $\mathbb{K}_{ax+b}(\lambda) = \lambda b + \mathbb{K}_x(a\lambda)$, for some constants a and b, and $\mathbb{K}_{\bar{x}}(\lambda) = n\mathbb{K}_x(\lambda/n)$. Similarly, the cumulants have the properties $\kappa_1(ax+b) = a\kappa_1(x) + b$ and $\kappa_j(ax+b) = a^j\kappa_j(x)$ for $j > 1$, and $\kappa_j\left(\sum_{i=1}^{n} x_i\right) = \sum_{i=1}^{n}\kappa_j(x_i)$.

since $i^2 = -1$, $E[z] = 0$ and $\text{var}[z] = 1$ and, hence, $\kappa_1 = 0$ and $\kappa_2 = 1$. Thus,

$$\varphi_{Z_n}(\lambda) = \exp\left(-\frac{\lambda^2}{2} + \frac{\kappa_3(i\lambda)^3}{6n^{1/2}} + \frac{\kappa_4(i\lambda)^4}{24n} + \frac{\kappa_5(i\lambda)^5}{120n^{3/2}} + \frac{\kappa_6(i\lambda)^6}{720n^2} + \cdots\right)$$

$$= \exp(-\lambda^2/2)\exp\left(\frac{\kappa_3(i\lambda)^3}{6n^{1/2}} + \frac{\kappa_4(i\lambda)^4}{24n} + \frac{\kappa_5(i\lambda)^5}{120n^{3/2}} + \frac{\kappa_6(i\lambda)^6}{720n^2} + \cdots\right).$$

Expanding the second exponential term yields

$$1 + \left(\frac{\kappa_3(i\lambda)^3}{6n^{1/2}} + \frac{\kappa_4(i\lambda)^4}{24n} + \frac{\kappa_5(i\lambda)^5}{120n^{3/2}} + \frac{\kappa_6(i\lambda)^6}{720n^2} + \cdots\right)$$

$$+ \frac{1}{2}\left(\frac{\kappa_3(i\lambda)^3}{6n^{1/2}} + \frac{\kappa_4(i\lambda)^4}{24n} + \frac{\kappa_5(i\lambda)^5}{120n^{3/2}} + \frac{\kappa_6(i\lambda)^6}{720n^2} + \cdots\right)^2 + \cdots$$

$$= 1 + \frac{\kappa_3}{6n^{1/2}}(i\lambda)^3 + \frac{\kappa_4}{24n}(i\lambda)^4 + \frac{\kappa_5}{120n^{3/2}}(i\lambda)^5 + \left(\frac{\kappa_6}{720n^2} + \frac{\kappa_3^2}{72n}\right)(i\lambda)^6 + \cdots,$$

and $\varphi_{Z_n}(\lambda)$ can be more generally rewritten as

$$\varphi_{Z_n}(\lambda) = \exp\left(-\frac{\lambda^2}{2}\right)\sum_{j=0}^{\infty}\frac{(i\lambda)^j}{j!}c_j, \tag{5.4}$$

where $c_0 = 1$, $c_1 = c_2 = 0$, $c_3 = (\kappa_3/n^{1/2})/3!$, $c_4 = (\kappa_4/n)/4!$, $c_5 = (\kappa_5/n^{3/2})/5!$, $c_6 = (\kappa_6/n^2 + 10\kappa_3^2/n)/6!$, etc.

Note that repeated integration by parts of the characteristic function

$$E[\exp(i\lambda Z_n)] = \int_{-\infty}^{+\infty}\exp(i\lambda z)f(z)dz$$

yields

$$\int_{-\infty}^{+\infty}\exp(i\lambda z)f(z)dz = -\frac{1}{i\lambda}\int_{-\infty}^{+\infty}\exp(i\lambda z)\frac{\partial f(z)}{\partial z}dz$$

$$= -\frac{1}{(i\lambda)^2}\int_{-\infty}^{+\infty}\exp(i\lambda z)\frac{\partial^2 f(z)}{\partial z^2}dz$$

$$= \cdots$$

$$= -\frac{1}{(i\lambda)^j}\int_{-\infty}^{+\infty}\exp(i\lambda z)\frac{\partial^j f(z)}{\partial z^j}dz.$$

Since $\exp(-\lambda^2/2)$ is the Fourier transform of the standard normal density $\phi(z)$, then the inverse Fourier transform of $(i\lambda)^j\exp\left(-\lambda^2/2\right)$ is $(-1)^j$ $\partial^j\phi(z)/\partial z^j$. Therefore, multiplying both sides of (5.4) by $\exp(-i\lambda z)/2\pi$ and integrating over λ gives

$$f_{Z_n}(z) = \sum_{j=0}^{\infty}c_j(-1)^j\frac{\partial^j\phi(z)}{\partial z^j} \tag{5.5}$$

since $\frac{1}{2\pi}\int_{-\infty}^{+\infty}\exp(-i\lambda z)\varphi_{Z_n}(\lambda)d\lambda = f_{Z_n}(z)$ by the inversion theorem and $\frac{1}{2\pi}\int_{-\infty}^{+\infty}\exp(-i\lambda z)\exp(-\lambda^2/2)(i\lambda)^j d\lambda = (-1)^j \partial^j \phi(z)/\partial z^j$ from above. Finally, noting that $(-1)^j \partial^j \phi(z)/\partial z^j = H_j(z)\phi(z)$, where $H_j(z)$ denotes a Hermite polynomial of degree j,[2] the expansion of $f_{Z_n}(z)$ has the form

$$f_{Z_n}(z) = \phi(z)\left(1 + \frac{\kappa_3 H_3(z)}{6n^{1/2}} + \frac{\kappa_4 H_4(z)}{24n} + \frac{\kappa_5 H_5(z)}{120n^{3/2}}\right. \tag{5.6}$$

$$\left. + \left(\frac{\kappa_6}{720n^2} + \frac{\kappa_3^2}{72n}\right)H_6(z) + \dots\right).$$

Expression (5.6) is known in the literature as the *Gram–Charlier expansion*. The Gram–Charlier expansion is not an asymptotic expansion[3] since the terms in the approximation of $f_{Z_n}(z)$ do not decrease monotonically. In particular, in expression (5.5), c_3 is $O(n^{-1/2})$, c_4 and c_6 are $O(n^{-1})$, c_5, c_7 and c_9 are $O(n^{-3/2})$ etc.

We can obtain an asymptotic expansion by rearranging the Gram–Charlier expansion and collecting terms with the same order of magnitude. In particular, a third-order asymptotic expansion (called the *Edgeworth expansion*) of the density $f_{Z_n}(z)$ is given by

$$f_{Z_n}(z) = \phi(z)\left(1 + \frac{\kappa_3}{6n^{1/2}}H_3(z) + \frac{3\kappa_4 H_4(z) + \kappa_3^2 H_6(z)}{72n}\right) \tag{5.7}$$

$$+ O\left(\frac{1}{n^{3/2}}\right).$$

After integrating (5.7) and using that

$$\int_{-\infty}^{z}\frac{\partial^j \phi(y)}{\partial y^j}dz = \frac{\partial^{j-1}\phi(z)}{\partial z^{j-1}},$$

we obtain a third-order Edgeworth expansion of the cumulative distribution function of Z_n

$$F_{Z_n}(z) = \Phi(z) - \phi(z)\left(\frac{\kappa_3}{6n^{1/2}}H_2(z) + \frac{3\kappa_4 H_3(z) + \kappa_3^2 H_5(z)}{72n}\right) \tag{5.8}$$

$$+ O\left(\frac{1}{n^{3/2}}\right),$$

---

[2] The Hermite polynomials of degree j for $j = 0, 1, \dots$, are defined as $H_j(x) \equiv \frac{(-1)^j}{\phi(x)}\frac{\partial^j \phi(x)}{\partial x^j}$ with $H_0 = 1$. If x is a standard normal random variable, it is straightforward to verify that the first three Hermite polynomials are given by $H_1(x) = x$, $H_2(x) = x^2 - 1$ and $H_3(x) = x^3 - 3x$. The higher-order Hermite polynomials can be obtained recursively from the differential equation $\frac{\partial^j \phi(x)}{\partial x^j} + \frac{x\partial^{j-1}\phi(x)}{\partial x^{j-1}} + \frac{(j-1)\partial^{j-2}\phi(x)}{\partial x^{j-2}} = 0$. One useful property of the Hermite polynomials is that they are orthogonal to each other, i.e., $E[H_i(x)H_j(x)] = 0$ for $i \neq j$.

[3] An asymptotic expansion is a series with the property that if it is truncated at a given number of terms, the remainder is of smaller order than the last term that has been included (Hall, 1992).

where $F_{Z_n}(z) = \int_{-\infty}^{z} f_{Z_n}(y)\,dy$. Expansion (5.8) is often referred to in the literature as the *Edgeworth-A expansion*.

Several features of Edgeworth expansions (5.7) and (5.8) are worth stressing. The second term (of order $n^{-1/2}$) in (5.7) and (5.8) corrects for the first-order effect of skewness and the third term (of order n^{-1}) corrects for the first-order effect of kurtosis and the second-order effect of skewness. If the distribution is symmetric, i.e., $\kappa_3 = 0$, the central limit theory provides an approximation of order n^{-1}. If, in addition, $\kappa_4 = 0$, the error from the normal approximation goes to 0 at rate $n^{-3/2}$. Finally, the Edgeworth expansion in (5.7) is not a proper probability density function since it does not integrate to one and can take negative values in the tails.

A proper CDF is given by

$$F_{Z_n}(z) = \Phi\left(z - \frac{\kappa_3 H_2(z)}{6n^{1/2}} + \frac{z\kappa_3^2 H_2^2(z) - 3\kappa_4 H_3(z) - \kappa_3^2 H_5(z)}{72n}\right) \quad (5.9)$$
$$+ O\left(\frac{1}{n^{3/2}}\right)$$

or, by substituting for $H_2(z) = z^2 - 1$, $H_3(z) = z^3 - 3z$ and $H_5(z) = z^5 - 10z^3 + 15z$,

$$F_{Z_n}(z) = \Phi\left(z - \frac{\kappa_3(z^2 - 1)}{6n^{1/2}} + \frac{3\kappa_4(3z - z^3) + 2\kappa_3^2(4z^3 - 7z)}{72n}\right) \quad (5.10)$$
$$+ O\left(\frac{1}{n^{3/2}}\right)$$

which is called the *Edgeworth-B expansion*.

The Edgeworth-B expansion can be used to obtain more accurate approximations to the critical values of the statistic Z_n. For a given significance level $\alpha \in (0,1)$, let c_α^* denote the α-level critical value (α-quantile) of the distribution of Z_n defined as $c_\alpha^* = \inf\{z : \Pr\{Z_n \leq z\} \geq \alpha\}$ and c_α be the α-quantile of the standard normal distribution that satisfies $\Phi(c_\alpha) = \alpha$. Then, the asymptotic (*Cornish–Fisher*) expansion of c_α^* has the form

$$c_\alpha^* = c_\alpha + \frac{q_1(c_\alpha)}{n^{1/2}} + \frac{q_2(c_\alpha)}{n} + \dots + \frac{q_j(c_\alpha)}{n^{j/2}} + \dots,$$

where the functions $q_j(c_\alpha)$ are polynomials determined completely by expressions (5.8) and (5.9). For more detailed and comprehensive discussion of the Gram–Charlier, Edgeworth and Cornish–Fisher expansions, see Feller (1971), Rothenberg (1984), Barndorff-Nielsen and Cox (1989), Hall (1992), Zaman (1996) and Ullah (2004).

Exercise 5.12. Suppose that $y_1, y_2, \dots, y_n$ are independent and identically χ_1^2 distributed random variables. Define $x_i = (y_i - 1)/\sqrt{2}$ which is standardized to have mean 0 and variance 1 and $Z_n = n^{-1/2} \sum_{i=1}^{n} x_i$. Derive the third-order Edgeworth expansion of the density of Z_n up to order $O(n^{-3/2})$.

5.3.1.3   General Edgeworth Expansion

The previous section discussed higher-order asymptotic expansions for simple averages of IID random variables. For more general estimators and test statistics, the direct approach for deriving the Edgeworth expansion is no longer available. Instead, we need to develop stochastic (Nagar-type) expansions introduced above for approximating the moments of the statistic, compute the cumulants of the expanded statistic and use them to obtain the Edgeworth expansion to the sampling distribution of the statistic.

More specifically, suppose that the standardized statistic Z_n allows a stochastic expansion

$$Z_n = a_{0,n} + \frac{a_{1,n}}{\sqrt{n}} + \frac{a_{2,n}}{n} + O_P\left(\frac{1}{n^{3/2}}\right),$$

where $a_{0,n}$, $a_{1,n}$ and $a_{2,n}$ are random variables and, as $n \to \infty$, the limiting distribution of Z_n converges to the limiting distribution of $a_{0,n}$, which is assumed to be $\mathcal{N}(0,1)$. Following Rothenberg (1984), let $\tilde{Z}_n = a_{0,n} + a_{1,n}/\sqrt{n} + a_{2,n}/n$ and write $E[\tilde{Z}_n] = \eta_1/\sqrt{n} + o(n^{-1})$ and $\text{var}[\tilde{Z}_n] = 1 + \eta_2/n + o(n^{-1})$ for some η_1 and η_2 that depend on the moments of $a_{0,n}$, $a_{1,n}$ and $a_{2,n}$. The new standardized statistic

$$Z_n^* = \frac{\tilde{Z}_n - \eta_1/\sqrt{n}}{\sqrt{1 + \eta_2/n}}$$

has, up to order n^{-1}, mean zero and variance one, and third and fourth moments given by $E\left[(Z_n^*)^3\right] = \eta_3/\sqrt{n} + o(n^{-1})$ and $E\left[(Z_n^*)^4\right] = 3 + \eta_4/n + o(n^{-1})$, where $\eta_3/\sqrt{n}$ and η_4/n are the approximate third and fourth cumulants of $\tilde{Z}_n$.

Then, using that Z_n^* is asymptotically distributed as a standard normal random variable, we have

$$F_{Z_n}(z) = \Pr\left\{\tilde{Z}_n \leq z\right\} + o\left(\frac{1}{n}\right)$$

$$= \Pr\left\{Z_n^* \leq \frac{z - \eta_1/\sqrt{n}}{\sqrt{1 + \eta_2/n}}\right\} + o\left(\frac{1}{n}\right)$$

$$= \Pr\left\{Z_n^* \leq z - \frac{\eta_1}{n^{1/2}} - \frac{\eta_2 z}{2n} + o(n^{-1})\right\} + o\left(\frac{1}{n}\right)$$

$$= \Phi\left(z + \frac{\gamma_1 + \gamma_2 z^2}{6n^{1/2}} + \frac{\gamma_3 z + \gamma_4 z^3}{72n}\right) + o\left(\frac{1}{n}\right),$$

where $\gamma_1 = \eta_3 - 6\eta_1$, $\gamma_2 = -\eta_3$, $\gamma_3 = 9\eta_4 - 14\eta_3^2 - 36\eta_2 + 24\eta_1\eta_3$ and $\gamma_4 = 8\eta_3^2 - 3\eta_4$ are obtained by matching the corresponding terms of (5.10).

Rothenberg (1984) uses this approach to derive the Edgeworth expansion of the 2SLS estimator considered in section 5.2.3.2 above. Let $u = x - Z\Pi$ with $E\left[u^2|z\right] = \sigma_u^2$, $\bar{\rho} = \rho/(\sigma_e\sigma_u)$, $\mu^2 = \Pi'Z'Z\Pi/\sigma_u^2$ be the concentration parameter (see also section 6.2 in Chapter 6) and $T_n = \sigma_e^{-1}\omega^{-1/2}(\hat{\theta} - \theta_0)$ denote the standardized 2SLS estimator, where Π, ρ, σ_e and ω are defined in section 5.2.3.2. Then, after expanding T_n and calculating the first two moments of the three-term expansion as well as the third and fourth cumulants of the standardized statistic as described above, the Edgeworth expansion of the 2SLS estimator is given by

$$\Pr\{T_n \le x\} = \Phi\left(x + \frac{\bar{\rho}(x^2 + 1 - \ell)}{\mu} + \frac{x(\ell - 1)(1 - \bar{\rho}^2) + x^3(3\bar{\rho}^2 - 1)}{2\mu^2}\right)$$
$$+ o\left(\frac{1}{\mu^2}\right),$$

where μ^2 is of order $O(n)$. By integrating and rearranging the above expression, we can obtain

$$E[\hat{\theta} - \theta_0 | Z] = \frac{1}{n}\rho\omega(\ell - 2),$$

which, by the law of iterated expectations, coincides with the second-order bias of the 2SLS estimator derived in section 5.2.3.2 above.

A similar approach can be used to derive Edgeworth expansions of test statistics that have a non-normal limiting distribution such as the chi-square distribution. For example, Hansen (2006) derives the Edgeworth expansions of the Wald and distance metric ($\mathcal{DM}$) statistics for nonlinear hypotheses in linear regression models of the form $H_0 : d(\theta) = 0$, where $d(\cdot) : \mathbb{R}^k \to \mathbb{R}$. More specifically, Hansen (2006) shows that the second-order Edgeworth-B expansion of the $\mathcal{DM}$ statistic has the form

$$\Pr\{\mathcal{DM} \le x\} = F_\chi\left(x\left(1 - \frac{b_c}{n}\right)\right) + o\left(\frac{1}{n}\right),$$

where $F_\chi(\cdot)$ denotes the CDF of a χ_1^2 random variable and b_c is a function of the first and second derivatives of the nonlinear constraint imposed by the null hypothesis with respect to the model parameters. While the expansion for the Wald statistic shows the presence of extra terms that give rise to the non-invariance of the test to reformulations of the null hypothesis, the Edgeworth expansion of the $\mathcal{DM}$ test demonstrates its invariance. Furthermore, this Edgeworth expansion can be used to Bartlett-correct the original $\mathcal{DM}$ statistic so that the transformed statistic is asymptotically chi-square distributed with an approximation error of $o(n^{-1})$. In particular, the Bartlett-corrected statistic $\mathcal{DM}/(1 - b_c/n)$ can be approximated up to order $o(n^{-1})$ by the chi-square distribution $F_\chi(x)$, where the Bartlett correction factor is $-b_c$.

5.3.2 Saddlepoint Approximation

One drawback of the Edgeworth expansions is that the approximation error associated with the remainder term is absolute. As a result, the error is of the same order of magnitude regardless of whether the approximation is performed at the center or in the tails of the distribution. While the Edgeworth expansion provides a very accurate approximation near $x = 0$ (note that for $x = 0$, all Hermite polynomials of odd degree are zero and the corresponding terms drop out from the expansion), when x is large, the approximation of the density can be rather poor and give rise to negative values. A relative approximation error seems to be a more desirable property of the expansion since it will result in a smaller error in the tails of the density which are of primary importance for computing confidence intervals, critical and p-values. This is achieved by the saddlepoint approximation of a density which can also be related to the theory of large deviations. Furthermore, the Edgeworth expansions are routinely used for establishing the higher-order refinements of the bootstrap. But numerous simulation studies show that the bootstrap performs markedly better than the Edgeworth expansion in the tails of the distribution, which calls for different approximations to explain these results.

Suppose that we are interested in approximating the density of the sample mean $\bar{x} = n^{-1} \sum_{i=1}^{n} x_i$, where $\{x_i\}_{i=1}^{n}$ is a random sample from a distribution with mean κ_1 and variance κ_2. The saddlepoint approximation dates back to Daniels (1954) and can be derived from an Edgeworth expansion not of the density $f_{\bar{x}}(x)$ but of a member of the conjugate exponential family

$$f_{\bar{x}}(x, \tau) = \exp\left[n(\tau x - \mathbb{K}(\tau))\right] f_{\bar{x}}(x),$$

where $\mathbb{K}(\cdot)$ is the cumulant generating function introduced above. Hence,

$$f_{\bar{x}}(x) = f_{\bar{x}}(x, \tau) \exp\left[n(\mathbb{K}(\tau) - \tau x)\right]. \tag{5.11}$$

From expression (5.7), the Edgeworth expansion of the conjugate density $f_{\bar{x}}(x, \tau)$ is given by

$$f_{\bar{x}}(x, \tau) = \frac{\phi(z)}{\sqrt{\mathbb{K}''(\tau)}} \left(1 + \frac{\bar{\kappa}_3(\tau)H_3(z)}{6} + \frac{\bar{\kappa}_4(\tau)H_4(z)}{24}\right. \tag{5.12}$$
$$\left. + \frac{\bar{\kappa}_3(\tau)^2 H_6(z)}{72}\right) + O\left(\frac{1}{n^{3/2}}\right),$$

where $z = (x - \mathbb{K}'(\tau))/\mathbb{K}''(\tau)^{1/2}$, $\mathbb{K}'(\tau) = E_\tau[\bar{x}]$, $\mathbb{K}''(\tau) = \text{var}_\tau[\bar{x}]$, and $\bar{\kappa}_3(\tau) = \mathbb{K}'''(\tau)/\mathbb{K}''(\tau)^{3/2}$ and $\bar{\kappa}_4(\tau) = \mathbb{K}''''(\tau)/\mathbb{K}''(\tau)^2$ are standardized cumulants as functions of τ. Because $\bar{\kappa}_3(\tau) = O(n^{-1/2})$ and $\bar{\kappa}_4(\tau) = O(n^{-1})$, the second term in the brackets is $O(n^{-1/2})$ and the last two terms in the brackets are $O(n^{-1})$ as in (5.7).

Now let us evaluate the Edgeworth expansion (5.12) at the value of τ that makes $z = 0$, which is the solution to the equation

$$x = \mathbb{K}'(\hat{\tau}).$$

The value $\hat{\tau} = \hat{\tau}(x)$ is the mean of the conjugate density and is called the saddlepoint, which gives the name *saddlepoint approximation* to the resulting expansion. Daniels (1954) discusses the existence and properties of real roots of the saddlepoint equation.

Because the terms that involve Hermite polynomials of odd degree vanish when these Hermite polynomials are evaluated at zero, and using that $\phi(0) = (n/2\pi)^{1/2}$, we obtain

$$f_{\bar{x}}(x,\hat{\tau}) = \sqrt{\frac{n}{2\pi \mathbb{K}''(\hat{\tau})}}\left(1 + O\left(\frac{1}{n}\right)\right),$$

where the $O(n^{-1})$ term is $[3\bar{\kappa}_4(\hat{\tau}) - 5\bar{\kappa}_3(\hat{\tau})^2]/24$. Substituting the above expression for $f_{\bar{x}}(x,\tau)$ in (5.11) yields the saddlepoint approximation of the density $f_{\bar{x}}(x)$, evaluated at $\hat{\tau} = \hat{\tau}(x)$,

$$f_{\bar{x}}(x) = \sqrt{\frac{n}{2\pi \mathbb{K}''(\hat{\tau})}}\exp\left(n(\mathbb{K}(\hat{\tau}) - \hat{\tau}x)\right)\left(1 + O\left(\frac{1}{n}\right)\right). \qquad (5.13)$$

Because the leading term does not necessarily integrate to one, the above saddlepoint approximation needs to be renormalized, which leads to a smaller approximation error, although finding the renormalization constant typically requires numerical integration. The saddlepoint approximation can be further used for computing cumulative distribution functions and evaluating tail areas of the distribution. For a detailed discussion on the construction and the statistical properties of saddlepoint approximations, see Barndorff-Nielsen and Cox (1989), Daniels (1954), Field and Ronchetti (1990), Goutis and Casella (1999) and Reid (1988), among others. Finally, Ronchetti and Trojani (2003) and Sowell (2007) provide interesting contributions to the econometric literature by developing saddlepoint approximations to the sampling distributions of the GMM parameter estimates and test for overidentifying restrictions.

Exercise 5.13. As in Exercise 5.12, suppose that $y_1, y_2, ..., y_n$ are independent and identically χ_1^2 distributed random variables and define $Z_n = n^{-1/2}\sum_{i=1}^{n}(y_i - 1)/\sqrt{2}$. Derive the saddlepoint approximation to the density of Z_n.

Exercise 5.14. Using Stirling's approximation to the Gamma function, show that the saddlepoint approximation is identical to the exact finite sample (Gamma) density of Z_n given by

$$\frac{\tilde{n}^{\tilde{n}/2}}{\Gamma(\tilde{n})}\left(z + \sqrt{\tilde{n}}\right)^{\tilde{n}-1}\exp\left(-(z + \sqrt{\tilde{n}})\sqrt{\tilde{n}}\right),$$

where $\tilde{n} = n/2$.

5.3.3 Large Deviations

The saddlepoint approximations discussed above are intimately linked to the large deviations theory where the expansions are developed for possibly expanding sequences (Barndorff-Nielsen and Cox, 1979). One of the major drawbacks of Edgeworth expansions is their unsatisfactory tail behavior. One approach to studying the approximation in tails of the distribution is to allow x to vary with the sample size. If x goes to infinity at a rate faster than $(\log n)^{1/2}$, Hall (1990) shows that the Edgeworth expansion is controlled entirely by the remainder term.

In order to derive the large deviation expansion, rewrite the saddlepoint expression (5.13) as

$$f_{\bar{x}}(x) = \frac{n^{1/2}}{\sqrt{2\pi\mathbb{K}''(\hat{\tau})}} \exp(-nx^2/2)$$

$$\times \exp\left(nx^3(\mathbb{K}(\hat{\tau}) - \hat{\tau}x + x^2/2)x^{-3}\right)\left(1 + O\left(\frac{1}{n}\right)\right).$$

Instead of the fixed value x, suppose that we consider the sequence $x_n = \tilde{x}/\sqrt{n}$ and define the saddlepoint equation as $\mathbb{K}'(\hat{\tau}) = x_n$ with a solution $\hat{\tau} = \hat{\tau}(x_n)$. If $\tilde{x} = o(\sqrt{n})$, then $x_n = o(1)$ and $\hat{\tau}(x_n)$ admits, under some regularity conditions, an absolutely convergent expansion

$$\hat{\tau}(x_n) = x_n - \frac{1}{2}\kappa_3 x_n^2 + \frac{1}{6}(3\kappa_3^2 - \kappa_4)x_n^3 + O(x_n^4),$$

assuming, for simplicity, that $\{x_i\}_{i=1}^n$ is IID with mean 0 and variance 1. Let

$$\gamma(x_n) = (\mathbb{K}(\hat{\tau}(x_n)) - \hat{\tau}(x_n)x_n + x_n^2/2)x_n^{-3}$$

$$= \frac{1}{6}\kappa_3 + \frac{1}{24}(\kappa_4 - 3\kappa_3^2)x_n + ...,$$

which is also absolutely convergent (Hall, 1990).

Then, for $\tilde{x} > 0$ and $\tilde{x} = o(n^{1/2})$, the *large deviation expansion* of the tails of the distribution of the standardized mean is given by (Petrov, 1975)

$$\Pr\left\{n^{1/2}\bar{x} > \tilde{x}\right\} = (1 - \Phi(\tilde{x})) \tag{5.14}$$

$$\times \exp\left(\frac{\tilde{x}^3}{n^{1/2}}\gamma\left(\frac{\tilde{x}}{n^{1/2}}\right)\right)\left(1 + O\left(\frac{\tilde{x}+1}{n^{1/2}}\right)\right)$$

as $n \to \infty$. Unlike Edgeworth expansions, the large deviation approximation (5.14) is guaranteed to be positive in the tails and the relative error vanishes as both $\tilde{x}$ and n grow to infinity, provided that $\tilde{x} = o(n^{1/2})$.

5.3.4   Applications of Higher-Order Asymptotic Expansions

5.3.4.1   Evaluating the Accuracy of Bootstrap Approximations

Let $z_1, z_2, ..., z_n$ be a random sample with distribution $F_0(z) = \Pr\{z_1 \leq z\}$ that belongs to a family of distribution functions $\mathcal{F}$. Also, let $G_n(z, F_0)$ denote the exact finite sample distribution of the t-statistic. Under some regularity conditions, this distribution admits an Edgeworth expansion of the form

$$G_n(z, F_0) = \Phi(z) + \frac{1}{n^{1/2}}p_1(z, F_0)\phi(z) + \frac{1}{n}p_2(z, F_0)\phi(z) + \dots \quad (5.15)$$
$$+ \frac{1}{n^{j/2}}p_j(z, F_0)\phi(z) + \dots,$$

where $p_j(z, F_0)$ is a polynomial of (at most) degree $3j - 1$ in z and is an odd or even function when j is odd or even.[4] We can rewrite (5.15) as

$$G_n(z, F_0) = \Phi(z) + \frac{1}{n^{1/2}}g(z, F_0) + O\left(\frac{1}{n}\right),$$

where $g(z, F_0) = p_1(z, F_0)\phi(z)$. Then, the error from the asymptotic approximation is of order

$$\Phi(z) - G_n(z, F_0) = O\left(\frac{1}{n^{1/2}}\right).$$

Let $F_n(z) = n^{-1}\sum_{i=1}^{n}\mathbb{I}\{z_i \le z\}$ denote the empirical distribution function. The bootstrap distribution of the t-statistic, $G_n(z, F_n)$, admits a similar expansion

$$G_n^*(z) \equiv G_n(z, F_n) = \Phi(z) + \frac{1}{n^{1/2}}g(z, F_n) + O_P\left(\frac{1}{n}\right)$$

and the error from the bootstrap approximation is

$$G_n^*(z) - G_n(z, F_0) = \frac{1}{n^{1/2}}\left(g(z, F_n) - g(z, F_0)\right) + O_P\left(\frac{1}{n}\right).$$

Since F_n converges to F_0 at rate $n^{1/2}$ by the central limit theorem and g is continuous in F, $g(z, F_n) - g(z, F_0)$ also converges to 0 at rate $n^{1/2}$ by the continuous mapping theorem. This can be seen from the first-order Taylor series expansion of $g(z, F_n)$ about F_0

$$g(z, F_n) - g(z, F_0) \approx \frac{\partial g(z, F_0)}{\partial F} \cdot n^{1/2}(F_n - F_0) \cdot \frac{1}{n^{1/2}} = O_P\left(\frac{1}{n^{1/2}}\right)$$

since $\partial g(z, F_0)/\partial F = O(1)$ and $n^{1/2}(F_n - F_0) = O_P(1)$. Then, the error from the bootstrap approximation is of order

$$G_n^*(z) - G_n(z, F_0) = O\left(\frac{1}{n^{1/2}}\right)O_P\left(\frac{1}{n^{1/2}}\right) + O_P\left(\frac{1}{n}\right) = O_P\left(\frac{1}{n}\right),$$

which is smaller than the order of the error from the asymptotic approximation, $O(n^{-1/2})$. Therefore, the bootstrap achieves higher-order accuracy than

---

[4]The explicit expressions of $p_1(z, F_0)$ and $p_2(z, F_0)$ are given above.

the first-order asymptotic approximation, i.e., the bootstrap provides an *asymptotic refinement*. Similar results can be obtained for other asymptotically pivotal statistics ($\mathcal{LR}$, $\mathcal{LM}$ and $\mathcal{W}$ statistics) provided that their bootstrap distributions admit an Edgeworth expansion.

As mentioned above, numerous studies have demonstrated that the bootstrap tends to perform better in the tail areas than the Edgeworth expansion. This challenges the traditional Edgeworth expansion view of the bootstrap. Hall (1990) uses a large deviations expansion, which, similarly to the saddlepoint approximation, is characterized by a relative approximation error, to explain the better performance of the bootstrap over the Edgeworth expansion for moderate and large deviations.

For example, Hall (1990, 1992) shows that the sampling distribution of the standardized sample mean $Z_n = n^{1/2}(\bar{z} - \kappa_1)/\sqrt{\kappa_2}$ can be expanded as

$$\Pr\{Z_n \leq z\} = \Phi(z) \exp\left(\frac{z^3}{n^{1/2}} \gamma\left(\frac{z}{n^{1/2}}\right)\right)$$

$$\times \left(1 + \sum_{j=1}^{m} \frac{\psi_j(z)}{n^{j/2}} + O\left(\left(\frac{1+z}{n^{1/2}}\right)^{m+1}\right)\right),$$

where $\gamma(u) = \frac{1}{6}\kappa_3 + \frac{1}{24}\left(\kappa_4 - 3\kappa_3^2\right) u + \ldots$ and ψ_j is a bounded, continuous function of population moments.

Similarly, the expansion of the bootstrap distribution of $Z_n^* = n^{1/2}(\bar{z}^* - \bar{z})/\hat{\sigma}$ is given by

$$\Pr\{Z_n^* \leq z\} = \Phi(z) \exp\left(\frac{z^3}{n^{1/2}} \hat{\gamma}\left(\frac{z}{n^{1/2}}\right)\right)$$

$$\times \left(1 + \sum_{j=1}^{m} \frac{\hat{\psi}_j(z)}{n^{j/2}} + O\left(\left(\frac{1+z}{n^{1/2}}\right)^{m+1}\right)\right).$$

As $\hat{\gamma} - \gamma = O_P(n^{-1/2})$, one has $\left|n^{-1/2} z^3 \hat{\gamma}(z/n^{1/2}) - n^{-1/2} z^3 \gamma(z/n^{1/2})\right| = O_P(n^{-1} z^3) = o_P(1)$ if $z = o(n^{1/3})$. This implies that the bootstrap approximation has a relative error of order $o_P(1)$ for large deviation probabilities with $z = o(n^{1/3})$, which is not the case for the Edgeworth expansion. For a more detailed discussion, see Hall (1990, 1992).

5.3.4.2   Higher-Order Expansions in AR(1) Models

Consider the autoregressive model

$$y_t = \rho y_{t-1} + u_t,$$

where $|\rho| < 1$ and $u_t \sim IID\,\mathcal{N}(0, \sigma^2)$. The OLS estimator of ρ is given by $\hat{\rho} = \sum_{t=2}^{n} y_t y_{t-1} / \sum_{t=2}^{n} y_{t-1}^2$ and the t-ratio (standardized estimator) $Z_n = n^{1/2}(\hat{\rho} - \rho)/(1 - \rho^2)^{1/2}$ is asymptotically distributed as a standard normal random variable.

Phillips (1977, 1978) derived the Edgeworth expansion for Z_n and showed that the third-order Edgeworth-B expansion is given by

$$\Pr\{Z_n \le z\} = \Phi\left(z + \frac{(z^2+1)\rho}{(1-\rho^2)^{1/2}} \frac{1}{n^{1/2}} + \frac{z(1+\rho^2)+(1+5\rho^2)}{4(1-\rho^2)^{1/2}} \frac{1}{n}\right)$$

$$+ O\left(\frac{1}{n^{3/2}}\right).$$

This expansion of the sampling distribution of Z_n can be used to obtain the higher-order moments of the estimator and, in particular, the higher-order bias discussed in section 5.2.3.

Phillips (1978) also developed a saddlepoint approximation to the density of the OLS estimator $\hat{\rho}$ with a relative approximation error of order $O(n^{-1})$. Unfortunately, the proposed approximation turns out to be undefined in the tails of the density. Lieberman (1994) suggests an alternative saddlepoint approximation and demonstrates its excellent numerical properties.

Finally, Phillips (1986) derived the large deviation expansion of the tails of the distribution of the t-ratio. In particular, for $z > 0$ and $z = O(n^{1/4})$ and as $n \to \infty$,

$$\Pr\{Z_n > z\} = (1 - \Phi(z))\exp\left(-\frac{\rho}{(1-\rho^2)^{1/2}} \frac{z^3}{n^{1/2}} - \frac{1}{4}\left(\frac{1+7\rho^2}{1-\rho^2}\right)\frac{z^4}{n}\right)$$

$$\times \left(1 + O\left(\frac{z+1}{n^{1/2}}\right)\right).$$

The results for the left tail are analogous and achieved by replacing $1 - \Phi(z)$ by $\Phi(-z)$ and switching the sign of the first term in the exponential function.

5.4 Appendix: Solutions to Selected Exercises

Exercise 5.3. The Taylor expansion of $g(\hat{\theta})$ yields

$$g(\hat{\theta}) = g(\theta_0) + g'(\theta_0)(\hat{\theta} - \theta_0) + \frac{g''(\theta_0)}{2}(\hat{\theta} - \theta_0)^2 + o_P\left(\frac{1}{n}\right)$$

$$= g(\theta_0) + g'(\theta_0)\left(\frac{a_{1,n}}{\sqrt{n}} + \frac{a_{2,n}}{n} + o_P\left(\frac{1}{n}\right)\right)$$

$$+ \frac{g''(\theta_0)}{2}\left(\frac{a_{1,n}}{\sqrt{n}} + o_P\left(\frac{1}{n^{1/2}}\right)\right)^2 + o_P\left(\frac{1}{n}\right)$$

$$= g(\theta_0) + \frac{g'(\theta_0)a_{1,n}}{\sqrt{n}} + \frac{1}{n}\left(g'(\theta_0)a_{2,n} + \frac{g''(\theta_0)}{2}a_{1,n}^2\right) + o_P\left(\frac{1}{n}\right).$$

Because $E[a_{1,n}] = 0$, $\lim_{n \to \infty} E[a_{1,n}^2] = \Omega_{\hat{\theta}}$ and $\lim_{n \to \infty} E[a_{2,n}] = B_{\hat{\theta}}$, we obtain that the second-order asymptotic bias for $g(\hat{\theta})$ is

$$\frac{1}{n} \left(g'(\theta_0) B_{\hat{\theta}} + \frac{g''(\theta_0)}{2} \Omega_{\hat{\theta}} \right).$$

Exercise 5.4. Due to symmetry across i and the validity of the expansion for different sample sizes, we have

$$E[\hat{\theta}^J] = nE[\hat{\theta}] - \left(1 - \frac{1}{n} \right) \cdot nE[\hat{\theta}_{-i}]$$

$$= n \left(\theta + \frac{a_2}{n} + \frac{a_4}{n^2} + o\left(\frac{1}{n^2} \right) \right)$$

$$- (n-1) \left(\theta + \frac{a_2}{n-1} + \frac{a_4}{(n-1)^2} + o\left(\frac{1}{n^2} \right) \right)$$

$$= \theta + \left(\frac{a_4}{n} - \frac{a_4}{n-1} \right) + o\left(\frac{1}{n} \right)$$

$$= \theta + o\left(\frac{1}{n} \right).$$

Indeed, $\hat{\theta}^J$ is second-order asymptotically unbiased.

Exercise 5.8. This problem is based on Firth (1993). To keep $\hat{\theta}^*$ consistent for θ_0, the additional term $\alpha_n(\theta)$ should be $o_P(1)$. To keep $\hat{\theta}^*$ asymptotically equivalent to $\hat{\theta}$, the additional term $\alpha_n(\theta)$ should be $o_P(1/\sqrt{n})$. The score function should shift so that the solution shifts from $\hat{\theta}$ to $\hat{\theta} - B_{\hat{\theta}}$. This can be achieved by replacing $\partial \log f(z, \theta)/\partial\theta$ with $\partial \log f(z, \theta)/\partial\theta + \Upsilon B_{\hat{\theta}}$, where Υ is the value of the gradient. The gradient evaluated at θ_0 is minus the information matrix $H(\theta_0)$. Hence, a natural candidate for $\alpha_n(\theta)$ is $-H(\theta) B_{\hat{\theta}}$. Note that $H(\theta)$ and $B_{\hat{\theta}}$ are functions of θ, and whether they will be evaluated at $\hat{\theta}$ or $\hat{\theta}^*$ has no effect on the second-order asymptotic bias. Alternatively, $\alpha_n(\theta)$ can be changed to one where $H(\theta)$ is estimated from the sample rather than evaluated, without altering the second-order asymptotic bias.

Exercise 5.12. This exercise is adapted from Zaman (1996). The characteristic function of a random variable y distributed as Gamma(α, β) is given by $(1 - i\lambda/\beta)^{-\alpha}$. By expanding the cumulant generating function $-\alpha \log(1 - i\lambda/\beta)$ about $\lambda = 0$ as in (5.2), we obtain that $\kappa_1 = \alpha/\beta$, $\kappa_2 = \alpha/\beta^2$, $\kappa_3 = 2\alpha/\beta^3$, $\kappa_4 = 6\alpha/\beta^4$. In general, $\kappa_r = \alpha\beta^{-r}(r-1)!$. Since a $\chi^2(1)$ variable is Gamma($1/2, 1/2$), the values for κ_1, κ_2, κ_3 and κ_4 are 1, 2, 8 and 48, respectively.

Using the properties of cumulants that $\kappa_1(ay+b) = a\kappa_1(y)+b$ and $\kappa_j(ay+b) = a^j\kappa_j(y)$ for $j > 1$, the cumulants of the standardized variable x are $\kappa_j = 0, 1, 2\sqrt{2}, 12$ for $j = 1, 2, 3, 4$. Then, substituting for κ_3 and κ_4 in (5.7), we can conclude that the density of $Z_n = n^{-1/2}\sum_{i=1}^n x_i$ is approximated up to order $O(n^{-3/2})$ by

$$f_{Z_n}(z) = \phi(z)\left(1 + \frac{\sqrt{2/3}}{\sqrt{n}}(z^3 - 3z)\right.$$
$$\left. + \frac{(1/2)(z^4 - 6z^2 + 3) + (1/9)(z^6 - 15z^4 + 45z^2 - 15)}{n}\right).$$

Exercises 5.13 and 5.14. Using that $\mathbb{K}_{ax+b}(\lambda) = \lambda b + \mathbb{K}_x(a\lambda)$ and $\mathbb{K}_x(a\lambda) = -\frac{1}{2}\log(1 - 2\lambda)$ for a chi-square random variable with one degree of freedom, the cumulant function of $z = \sqrt{n/2}(x - 1)$ is given by

$$\mathbb{K}_z(\lambda) = -\sqrt{\frac{n}{2}} - \frac{1}{2}\log\left(1 - \sqrt{2n}\lambda\right)$$

Taking derivatives and solving the saddlepoint equation $\mathbb{K}'_z(\lambda) = z$ yields $\hat{\lambda}(z) = z/\left(n + \sqrt{2n}z\right)$. Then, substituting for $\hat{\lambda}(z)$ in $\mathbb{K}_z(\lambda)$ and $\mathbb{K}''_z(\lambda)$ gives

$$\mathbb{K}_z(\hat{\lambda}) = -\sqrt{\frac{n}{2}}\frac{z}{n + \sqrt{2n}z} - \frac{1}{2}\log\left(\frac{\sqrt{n/2}}{z + \sqrt{n/2}}\right)$$

and

$$\mathbb{K}''_z(\hat{\lambda}) = 2\left(z + \sqrt{n/2}\right)^2.$$

As a result,

$$\exp\left(n(\mathbb{K}(\hat{\lambda}) - \hat{\lambda}z)\right) = \exp\left(\log\left(\frac{z + \sqrt{n/2}}{\sqrt{n/2}}\right)^{n/2} - \sqrt{n/2}z\right)$$
$$= \left(z + \sqrt{n/2}\right)^{n/2}(n/2)^{-n/4}\exp(-\sqrt{n/2}z)$$

and

$$\sqrt{\frac{n}{2\pi\mathbb{K}''(\hat{\lambda})}} = \left(z + \sqrt{n/2}\right)^{-1}\sqrt{\frac{n}{4\pi}}.$$

Hence, the saddlepoint approximation of $f_{Z_n}(z)$ is

$$f_{Z_n}(z) = \frac{(n/2)^{-n/4}}{\sqrt{4\pi/n}}\left(z + \sqrt{n/2}\right)^{n/2-1}\exp\left(-\sqrt{n/2}z\right)$$
$$= \frac{(n/2)^{n/4}\exp(n/2)}{(n/2)^{n/2}\sqrt{4\pi/n}}\left(z + \sqrt{n/2}\right)^{n/2-1}\exp\left(-\sqrt{n/2}\left(z + \sqrt{n/2}\right)\right)$$
$$= \frac{(n/2)^{n/4}}{\Gamma(n/2)}\left(z + \sqrt{n/2}\right)^{n/2-1}\exp\left(-\sqrt{n/2}\left(z + \sqrt{n/2}\right)\right)$$

using Stirling's approximation

$$\Gamma(n/2) = \frac{(n/2)^{n/2}\sqrt{4\pi/n}}{\exp(n/2)}\left(1 + O\left(\frac{1}{n}\right)\right).$$

The last line in the expression for $f_{Z_n}(z)$ is the Gamma density, which is the exact finite sample density of Z_n in this case.

References

Anatolyev, S. (2005) GMM, GEL, serial correlation and asymptotic bias. *Econometrica*, 73, 983–1002.

Andrews, D.W.K. (1991) Heteroskedasticity and autocorrelation consistent covariance matrix estimation. *Econometrica*, 59, 817–858.

Bao, Y., and A. Ullah (2007) The second-order bias and mean squared error of estimators in time-series models. *Journal of Econometrics*, 140, 650–669.

Barndorff-Nielsen, O., and D.R. Cox (1979) Edgeworth and saddle-point approximations with statistical applications (with discussion). *Journal of the Royal Statistical Society B*, 41, 279–312.

Barndorff-Nielsen, O., and D.R. Cox (1989) *Asymptotic Techniques for Use in Statistics*. Chapman and Hall: New York.

Daniels, H.E. (1954) Saddlepoint approximations in statistics. *Annals of Mathematical Statistics*, 25, 631–650.

Feller, W. (1971) *An Introduction to Probability Theory and Its Applications*, Vol. 2, Wiley: New York.

Field, C.A., and E. Ronchetti (1990) *Small Sample Asymptotics*. IMS Monograph Series, Vol. 13, Hayward.

Firth, D. (1993) Bias reduction of maximum likelihood estimates. *Biometrika*, 80, 27–38.

Goutis, C., and G. Casella (1999) Explaining the saddlepoint approximation. *The American Statistician*, 53, 216–224.

Hall, P. (1990) On the relative performance of bootstrap and Edgeworth approximations of a distribution function. *Journal of Multivariate Analysis*, 35, 108–129.

Hall, P. (1992) *The Bootstrap and Edgeworth Expansion*. Springer-Verlag: New York.

Hansen, B.E. (2006) Edgeworth expansions for the Wald and GMM statistics for nonlinear restrictions. In: D. Corbae, S.N. Durlauf and B.E. Hansen (eds.) *Econometric Theory and Practice*. Cambridge University Press: Cambridge.

Lieberman, O. (1994). Saddlepoint approximation for the least squares estimator in first-order autoregression. *Biometrika*, 81, 807–811.

Nagar, A.L. (1959) The bias and moment matrix of the general k-class estimators of the parameters in simultaneous equations. *Econometrica*, 27, 573–595.

Newey, W.K., J. Hahn and G. Kuersteiner (2005) Higher order properties of bootstrap and jackknife bias corrected maximum likelihood estimators. Manuscript, MIT.

Newey, W.K., and R.J. Smith (2004) Higher order properties of GMM and generalized empirical likelihood estimators. *Econometrica*, 72, 219–255.

Petrov, V.V. (1975) *Sums of Independent Random Variables.* Springer-Verlag: New York.

Pfanzagl, J., and W. Wefelmeyer (1978) A third order optimum property of the maximum likelihood estimator. *Journal of Multivariate Analysis*, 8, 1–29.

Phillips, P.C.B. (1977) Approximations to some finite sample distributions associated with a first-order stochastic difference equation. *Econometrica*, 45, 463–485.

Phillips, P.C.B. (1978) Edgeworth and saddlepoint approximations in the first-order noncircular autoregression. *Biometrika*, 65, 91–98.

Phillips, P.C.B. (1986) Large deviation expansions in econometrics. *Advances in Econometrics*, 5, 199–226.

Reid, N. (1988) Saddlepoint methods and statistical inference. *Statistical Science*, 3, 213–227.

Rilstone, P., V. K. Srivastava, and A. Ullah (1996) The second-order bias and mean-squared error of nonlinear estimators. *Journal of Econometrics*, 75, 369–395.

Ronchetti, E., and F. Trojani (2003) Saddlepoint approximations and test statistics for accurate inference in overidentified moment conditions models. National Centre of Competence in Research Financial Valuation and Risk Management, Working Paper 27.

Rothenberg, T. (1984) Approximating the distributions of econometric estimators and test statistics. In: Z. Griliches and M.D. Intriligator (eds.), *Handbook of Econometrics*, Vol. 2, Elsevier: Amsterdam, Chapter 15, 881–935.

Sowell, F. (2007) The empirical saddlepoint approximation for GMM estimators. Unpublished manuscript, Tepper School of Business, Carnegie Mellon University.

Ullah, A. (2004) *Finite Sample Econometrics.* Oxford University Press: Oxford.

Zaman, A. (1996) *Statistical Foundations for Econometric Techniques.* Academic Press: London.

Chapter 6

Asymptotics Under Drifting Parameter Sequences

6.1 Introduction

In many cases, first-order asymptotic theory provides a poor approximation to the finite sample distribution of the statistic of interest, and higher-order expansions also appear to be of limited help. For instance, the validity of the usual asymptotic theory often breaks down near the boundary of the parameter space when the limiting distribution changes discontinuously. Examples include near-integrated and near-cointegrated models, instrumental variable (IV) models with weak instruments, models with time-varying parameters whose variability is close to zero, etc. In these models, conventional asymptotic theory depends discontinuously on some underlying parameter (autoregressive, concentration or variance parameter) while the finite sample distribution of the statistic of interest changes smoothly with the values of this parameter. For instance, if the largest autoregressive (AR) root in dynamic models is strictly less than one, its estimator is asymptotically distributed as a normal random variable but its asymptotic distribution is non-normal (Dickey–Fuller) if the AR root is exactly equal to one. As a result, neither of these asymptotic distributions can provide accurate approximations when the AR root is in the vicinity of (but not exactly at) unity. It has been shown that pretesting (if the parameter is equal to one, for instance) and conventional bootstrap methods also fail to deliver valid inference in this setup.

This chapter discusses alternative asymptotic approximations that do not treat the parameter, which gives rise to potential discontinuity, as fixed but reparameterize it as a drifting sequence that depends explicitly on the sample size. As the sample size increases, this sequence shifts towards the boundary of the parameter space. This artificial statistical device ensures a smooth transition of the asymptotic theory that mimics the behavior of the finite sample distribution. It is now a popular analytical tool in models with highly persistent variables and weak instruments which are frequently encountered in the analysis of economic data. A potential drawback of this asymptotic framework is the introduction of additional nuisance parameters that are not consistently estimable, which complicates the inference procedure. The development of uniformly valid and practically appealing inference methods based on these drifting parameter sequences is an active research topic.

Another important situation where resorting to drifting parameter sequences proves valuable is the analysis of models with many regressors/instruments as well as long-run forecasts and impulse responses. Conventional asymptotic theory assumes that the number of moment conditions or forecast horizons is fixed and the limit is taken only with respect to the sample size. However, when the number of moment conditions or forecast horizons is a nontrivial fraction of the sample size (for example, 20 or 30 with 100 observations), standard asymptotic theory fails to provide a reasonable approximation to the finite sample distribution of interest. It is often beneficial to parameterize this number as a function of the sample size by allowing it to grow at some rate as the sample size approaches infinity. This type of drifting parameterization has become an essential tool in dealing with the many instruments problem as well as conditional forecasting and impulse response analysis at long horizons.[1]

Finally, drifting parameterizations may be useful when conventional asymptotics yields an asymptotic approximation of good quality, but its practical relevance may be hampered if this asymptotic distribution is non-pivotal. An alternative asymptotic result based on drifting parameterization may secure a convenient pivotal asymptotic distribution. This happens, in particular, in threshold and changepoint models.

This chapter provides a detailed review of this alternative asymptotic framework in various models of empirical interest. While the various drifting parameterizations appear seemingly unrelated, the chapter also offers insights that link some of these parameterizations and combine more than one drifting sequence to obtain more precise approximations when several near-boundary problems are simultaneously present.

6.2   Weak Identification and Many Instruments

6.2.1   Weak Instruments

In recent years, the generalized method of moments (GMM) has solidified its position as a predominant framework for estimating economic models. The GMM imposes less structure on the model than the method of maximum likelihood and possesses appealing asymptotic properties, which are reviewed in Chapter 1. The statistical properties of GMM estimators, however, can be seriously affected by instruments that are only weakly correlated with the

---

[1] Excellent surveys of some of the topics discussed in this chapter can be found in Stock (1994, 1997), Stock, Wright and Yogo (2002) and Stock and Watson (2008).

endogenous variables (Staiger and Stock, 1997; Stock and Wright, 2000). For example, the finite sample distribution of the GMM estimator may depart substantially from its asymptotic approximation, and the lack of (or near-) identification can render the estimators inconsistent. In this and the next subsections, we consider an alternative reparameterization of the moment conditions that bridges the fully identified and the unidentified cases and delivers better analytical and limiting approximations.

To illustrate the main idea, consider a linear model

$$y = \theta_0 x + e, \tag{6.1}$$
$$x = \pi z + u,$$

where θ_0 is a parameter of interest, x, y and z are scalars, and e and u are error terms with mean zero, variance one and correlation ρ. Note that $E[e|x] \neq 0$ but $E[e|z] = 0$. This simplified model has one endogenous variable x and one instrument z, and hence is just-identified. A random sample $\{(x_i, y_i, z_i)\}_{i=1}^{n}$ is available for estimating the parameter θ_0.

Suppose now that the instrument is only weakly correlated with the endogenous variable so that the correlation between x and z is very close to zero. To explicitly accommodate for the possibility of a weak instrument, we adopt the *local-to-zero* parameterization $\pi = c/\sqrt{n}$, where c is a fixed constant (Staiger and Stock, 1997). The parameter π is modeled as a function of the sample size, while the standardization factor (as in the other drifting parameter sequences considered below) is chosen to match the rate of convergence of the estimator. This nesting is based on the idea of the Pitman drift used to study the local asymptotic power of hypothesis tests. When $c = 0$, the instrument z carries no information about the endogenous variable x and this parameterization collapses to the non-identified case.

The sequence of non-zero values of c measures the local deviations from the non-identified case and, in combination with the sample size, provides information about the strength of the instrument. A unitless measure of the strength of the instrument is provided by the concentration parameter which, in the context of model (6.1), is defined as $\mu^2 = \pi^2 \sum_{i=1}^{n} z_i^2$. Since $\sum_{i=1}^{n} z_i^2 = O_P(n)$ and $\pi^2 = O(n^{-1})$, the local-to-zero parameterization keeps the concentration parameter constant as $n \to \infty$, $\mu^2 = O_P(1)$. Alternatively, if π is assumed fixed as in the conventional asymptotics, $\mu^2 = O_P(n)$ and using μ as a standardization factor yields standard normal limits (Rothenberg, 1984). As a rule of thumb (Stock and Yogo, 2005), large values of μ^2 are associated with strong instruments and standard asymptotics, while small values of μ^2 indicate the potential presence of weak instruments and possibly non-standard limiting distributions.

Estimation of the parameter of interest θ_0 is typically based on the unconditional moment restriction $E[ez] = 0$ which is obtained by applying the law of iterated expectations to $E[e|z] = 0$. After rewriting and taking expectations, we have

$$E\left[(e + (\theta_0 - \theta)x)\, z\right] = 0 + (\theta_0 - \theta)E\left[xz\right] = O_P(n^{-1/2})$$

for all $\theta \neq \theta_0$, using that $\pi = E[xz]/E[z^2]$. In other words, the population moment condition is nearly uninformative about the parameter θ (the objective function is almost flat over the parameter space) and the parameters are only weakly identifiable. In the extreme case when the instrument is totally uncorrelated with the endogenous variable ($E[xz] = 0$ or $c = 0$), we have identification failure.

The two-stage least squares (2SLS) estimator has the form

$$\hat{\theta} - \theta_0 = \frac{n^{-1/2} \sum_{i=1}^{n} z_i e_i}{n^{-1/2} \sum_{i=1}^{n} z_i x_i} = \frac{n^{-1/2} \sum_{i=1}^{n} z_i e_i}{cn^{-1} \sum_{i=1}^{n} z_i^2 + n^{-1/2} \sum_{i=1}^{n} z_i u_i}$$

by substituting for $x_i = (c/\sqrt{n})z_i + u_i$. Taking limits as $n \to \infty$, we obtain

$$\hat{\theta} - \theta_0 \xrightarrow{d} \frac{\xi_1}{cM_{zz}^{1/2} + \xi_2} = \Lambda, \qquad (6.2)$$

where $M_{zz} = E[z^2]$, and ξ_1 and ξ_2 are two correlated standard normal random variables. As a result, the estimator is inconsistent and has a non-normal distribution. For example, in the non-identified case ($c = 0$), the distribution is a ratio of two correlated standard normal variables which gives rise to a Cauchy-type distribution. Similar results can be obtained for overidentified models and multiple endogenous variables.

Exercise 6.1. Show that the t test of $H_0 : \theta = \theta_0$ also has a non-normal limit given by

$$t_{\theta=\theta_0} \xrightarrow{d} \frac{\xi_1}{\sqrt{\Lambda^2 - 2\rho\Lambda + 1}}.$$

Exercise 6.2. Suppose now that the assumption regarding the instrument strength is changed to $\pi = cn^{-\delta}$, where $\delta \geq 0$. Derive the asymptotic distribution of the 2SLS estimator of the structural parameter. Characterize qualitatively the predictions of this asymptotic theory in the cases (i) $0 \leq \delta < \frac{1}{2}$, (ii) $\delta = \frac{1}{2}$, and (iii) $\delta > \frac{1}{2}$.

While the expression in (6.2) provides the correct asymptotic distribution when the instruments are weak and parameterized as local-to-zero, its practical use is limited due to the presence of the nuisance parameter c, which is not consistently estimable ($\hat{c} - c = O_P(1)$ since $\hat{\pi} - \pi = O_P(n^{-1/2})$ and

$\pi = O(n^{-1/2})$ from the local-to-zero parameterization). Moreover, the presence of weak instruments implies that the asymptotic confidence regions for the weakly identified parameters can be unbounded with positive probability (Dufour, 1997). However, the confidence sets based on the popular Wald-type tests that are bounded by construction can lead to serious size distortions. As a result, most of the recent research has been directed towards developing inference procedures that are robust to weak or completely irrelevant instruments.

Here, we review the properties of the Anderson–Rubin statistic (Anderson and Rubin, 1949), which is also discussed below in the context of many instruments. Consider the more general model

$$y = x\theta_0 + e, \tag{6.3}$$
$$x = Z\Pi + u,$$

where y and x are $n \times 1$ vectors of observations on endogenous variables, $Z = (z_1, ..., z_n)'$ is an $n \times \ell$ matrix of instruments and e and u are $n \times 1$ vectors of disturbance terms. The elements of the errors (e, u) are assumed to be IID across rows with conditional (on Z) mean zero, conditional variance

$$\Sigma = \begin{pmatrix} \sigma_1^2 & \sigma_{12} \\ \sigma_{12} & \sigma_2^2 \end{pmatrix}$$

and finite fourth moments.

Let $e_0 = y - x\theta_0$ be a vector of restricted errors, P_Z denote the projection matrix $P_Z = Z(Z'Z)^{-1}Z'$ and $M_Z = I_n - P_Z$. The Anderson–Rubin ($\mathcal{AR}$) statistic is used to test the joint hypothesis of $H_0 : \theta = \theta_0$ and the validity of the overidentifying restrictions, evaluated at $\theta = \theta_0$, and is given by

$$\mathcal{AR} = (n - \ell) \frac{e_0' P_Z e_0}{e_0' M_Z e_0}.$$

Under the null hypothesis, the Anderson–Rubin test is asymptotically χ_ℓ^2 distributed regardless of the strength of the instruments and possesses other appealing robustness properties (Dufour and Taamouti, 2007). Confidence intervals for θ at level $1 - \alpha$ can be obtained by inverting the $\mathcal{AR}$ test as $CI_{1-\alpha}(\theta) = \{\theta \in \Theta : \mathcal{AR} \leq \chi_\ell^2(1 - \alpha)\}$ and endpoints given by

$$\inf\{\theta \in \Theta : \Pr\left\{\mathcal{AR} \leq \chi_\ell^2(1 - \alpha) \mid H_0\right\} \geq 1 - \alpha\}$$

and

$$\sup\{\theta \in \Theta : \Pr\left\{\mathcal{AR} \leq \chi_\ell^2(1 - \alpha) \mid H_0\right\} \geq 1 - \alpha\}.$$

However, since the number of degrees of freedom of the test is equal to the dimension of the instrument vector, the $\mathcal{AR}$ test can suffer substantial power losses in heavily overidentified models.

Exercise 6.3. Show that the test of $H_0 : \theta = \theta_0$ based on the Anderson–Rubin statistic is inconsistent against the fixed alternative $H_A : \theta = \theta_A \neq \theta_0$ in the weak instrument asymptotic framework.

Exercise 6.4. Consider the classical Lagrange multiplier ($\mathcal{LM}$) statistic for testing the hypothesis $H_0 : \theta = \theta_0$,

$$\mathcal{LM} = \frac{1}{\hat{\sigma}_0^2} \frac{(e_0' P_Z x)^2}{x' P_Z x},$$

where $\hat{\sigma}_0^2 = n^{-1} e_0' e_0$. Derive the asymptotic distribution of $\mathcal{LM}$ under H_0 within the local-to-zero asymptotic framework. Next, refine your answer for the special case when there is only one instrument. Is the $\mathcal{LM}$ test robust?

Kleibergen (2002) and Moreira (2003) developed $\mathcal{LM}$- and $\mathcal{LR}$-type tests that are also robust to weak identification but enjoy better power properties. The $\mathcal{LM}$ test proposed by Kleibergen (2002) has the form

$$K = (n - \ell) \frac{e_0' P_{\tilde{x}(\theta_0)} e_0}{e_0' M_Z e_0},$$

where $\tilde{x}(\theta_0) = Z\tilde{\Pi}(\theta_0)$ and $\tilde{\Pi}(\theta_0) = (Z'Z)^{-1} Z' (y - e_0(e_0' M_Z y)/(e_0' M_Z e_0))$. The only difference with the $\mathcal{AR}$ statistic is that instead of projecting e_0 onto the ℓ columns of matrix Z, the K statistic projects onto the vector $Z\tilde{\Pi}(\theta_0)$ (in general, the column dimension $Z\tilde{\Pi}(\theta_0)$ is determined by the number of endogenous variables) and converges to a χ_1^2 random variable regardless of the strength of the instruments (strong, weak or completely irrelevant). For more details, see Kleibergen (2002).

The construction of Moreira's (2003) conditional likelihood ratio ($\mathcal{CLR}$) test can be best described using the general framework developed by Andrews, Moreira and Stock (2006). Andrews, Moreira and Stock (2006) show that the $\mathcal{AR}$, K and $\mathcal{CLR}$ tests can be expressed conveniently as functions of the 2×2 maximal invariant matrix

$$Q = \begin{bmatrix} Q_S & Q_{SR} \\ Q_{RS} & Q_R \end{bmatrix} = \begin{bmatrix} S'S & S'R \\ R'S & R'R \end{bmatrix},$$

where

$$S = (Z'Z)^{-1/2} Z'Y b_0 (b_0' \Omega b_0)^{-1/2},$$
$$R = (Z'Z)^{-1/2} Z'Y \Omega^{-1} a_0 (a_0' \Omega^{-1} a_0)^{-1/2},$$

$Y = (y \, x)$, $b_0 = (1, -\theta_0)'$, $a_0 = (\theta_0, 1)'$ and $\Omega = Y' M_Z Y/(n - \ell)$. Then, the $\mathcal{AR}$, K and $\mathcal{CLR}$ tests of the hypothesis $H_0 : \theta = \theta_0$ have the form:

$$\mathcal{AR} = Q_S,$$
$$K = \frac{Q_{SR}^2}{Q_R},$$
$$\mathcal{CLR} = \frac{1}{2} \left(Q_S - Q_R + \sqrt{(Q_S - Q_R)^2 + 4Q_{SR}^2} \right).$$

While the $\mathcal{AR}$ and $\mathcal{K}$ tests are asymptotically χ_ℓ^2 and χ_1^2 distributed, the asymptotic distribution of the $\mathcal{CLR}$ test is nonstandard and its critical values need to be obtained numerically (as a function of Q_R.) Also, unlike the other two tests ($\mathcal{AR}$ and $\mathcal{K}$), the extension of $\mathcal{CLR}$ to models with multiple endogenous variables is nontrivial. Despite these disadvantages, the $\mathcal{CLR}$ test enjoys some excellent theoretical properties. Andrews, Moreira and Stock (2006) demonstrate that $\mathcal{CLR}$ is close to being the uniformly most powerful test in the class of invariant similar tests. Mikusheva (2010) compares confidence sets obtained by inverting the $\mathcal{AR}$, $\mathcal{K}$ and $\mathcal{CLR}$ tests and shows that the $\mathcal{CLR}$ confidence sets have the shortest expected length (in spherical coordinates) among similar symmetric invariant confidence sets.

Interestingly, minimizing the $\mathcal{AR}$ statistic with respect to θ produces the limited information maximum likelihood (LIML) estimator

$$\hat{\theta}_{LIML} = (x'(I_n - \mathrm{k}_{LIML} M_Z)x)^{-1} x'(I_n - \mathrm{k}_{LIML} M_Z)y,$$

where k_{LIML} is the smallest characteristic root of $(Y'Y)(Y'M_ZY)^{-1}$ with $Y = (y\ x)$. In fact, the LIML is a member of the k-class of estimators that have the form

$$\hat{\theta}_{\mathrm{k}} = (x'(I_n - \mathrm{k}M_Z)x)^{-1} x'(I_n - \mathrm{k}M_Z)y,$$

where $\mathrm{k} = 1$ gives rise to the 2SLS estimator considered above, and $\mathrm{k} = \mathrm{k}_{LIML} - b/(n - \ell)$, for some positive constant b, delivers Fuller's (1977) estimator. While all estimators in this class are inconsistent under weak instrument (local-to-zero) asymptotics, simulation results reveal that the LIML and Fuller estimators are better behaved and more reliable in the presence of weak instruments than the 2SLS estimator.

Exercise 6.5. In the weak instruments asymptotic framework, derive the probability limit of $\hat{\theta}_{\mathrm{k}}$ for a fixed, data independent $\mathrm{k} \neq 1$.

6.2.2 GMM with Weak Identification

The discussion so far has focused exclusively on linear models. Similar results hold in nonlinear models (Stock and Wright, 2000), although they are more involved and are presented here only briefly. The analysis is performed in the context of the GMM estimator which minimizes a quadratic form in the sample counterparts of a set of ℓ moment conditions $E[m(w, \theta_0)] = 0$ given by

$$Q_n(\theta) = \left(\frac{1}{n}\sum_{i=1}^n m(w_i, \theta)\right)' W_n \left(\frac{1}{n}\sum_{i=1}^n m(w_i, \theta)\right),$$

where W_n is a positive definite weighting matrix consistent with a probability limit W. For example, the 2SLS estimator in the linear model (6.3) can be obtained by setting $m(w, \theta) = (y - \theta x)z$, $w = (x, y, z)$, and $W_n = n(Z'Z)^{-1}$.

The key assumptions that deliver the consistency and asymptotic normality of the GMM estimator are $n^{-1}\sum_{i=1}^{n} m\left(w_i, \theta\right) \overset{p}{\to} E[m\left(w, \theta\right)]$ uniformly in θ and $n^{-1/2}\sum_{i=1}^{n}\{m\left(w_i, \theta\right) - E[m\left(w, \theta\right)]\} \Rightarrow B(\theta)$, where $B(\theta)$ is a zero-mean Gaussian process and $E|m\left(w, \theta\right)| < 0$. In the case of weak identification, the nonlinear analog of the local-to-zero parameterization is the assumption $n^{1/2}E[m\left(w, \theta\right)] = g(\theta)$, a non-random function such that $\sup_{\theta \in \Theta} |g(\theta)| < \infty$, which roughly corresponds to localizing $E[m\left(w, \theta\right)]$ to zero. Then, we have

$$\frac{1}{\sqrt{n}}\sum_{i=1}^{n} m\left(w_i, \theta\right) = \frac{1}{\sqrt{n}}\sum_{i=1}^{n}\left(m\left(w_i, \theta\right) - E[m\left(w, \theta\right)]\right) + \sqrt{n}E[m\left(w, \theta\right)]$$
$$\Rightarrow B(\theta) + g(\theta)$$

and

$$nQ_n\left(\theta\right) \Rightarrow \left(B(\theta) + g(\theta)\right)' W \left(B(\theta) + g(\theta)\right) \equiv Q^*\left(\theta\right).$$

Therefore, the GMM estimator $\hat{\theta}_{GMM} = \arg\min_{\theta \in \Theta} Q_n\left(\theta\right)$ has a non-standard limiting distribution and is inconsistent since its asymptotic limit is

$$\theta^* = \arg\min_{\theta \in \Theta} Q^*\left(\theta\right).$$

An analog of the Anderson–Rubin statistic is Hansen's (1982) $\mathcal{J}$-statistic evaluated at the hypothesized parameter values, and

$$W_n = \left(\frac{1}{n}\sum_{i=1}^{n} m\left(w_i, \theta_0\right) m\left(w_i, \theta_0\right)\right)^{-1}.$$

It provides a robust joint test for parameter restrictions and overidentification. Asymptotically, under the null hypothesis $H_0 : \theta = \theta_0$, the statistic $\mathcal{J} = nQ_n\left(\theta_0\right)$ is distributed as χ^2_ℓ regardless of the degree of identification.

Stock and Wright (2000) also specialized the analysis to the empirically important case where $\theta = \left(\alpha', \beta'\right)'$ and the true β_0 is well identified while α_0 is only weakly identified. The leading example of such a situation is the Hansen and Singleton (1982) consumption-based capital asset pricing model with constant relative risk aversion utility

$$E_t\left[\beta_0 \left(\frac{c_{t+1}}{c_t}\right)^{-\alpha_0} R_{t+1} - 1\right] = 0,$$

where c_t is consumption at time t, R_t is a gross asset return at time t, α_0 is a risk aversion parameter, and β_0 is the discount factor. While the precision of estimation of β_0 is usually quite high, reflecting its good identifiability, the estimates of α_0 vary substantially across different studies, which is a result of its poor identifiability. Stock and Wright (2000) show that in these circumstances, the GMM estimator $\hat{\beta}$ of β_0 is $\sqrt{n}$-consistent, but it has a non-standard asymptotic distribution because of the influence of the GMM estimator of the weakly identified α_0, which is generally inconsistent, and would remain inconsistent even if β_0 were known.

6.2.3 Many Instruments

Consider again model (6.3) but now the number of instruments ℓ represents a nontrivial fraction of the number n of sample observations available for estimation. This setup often arises when instruments are constructed by interacting different variables or using lagged dependent variables in panel data models. It is well documented that in this situation, the asymptotic approximations of the distributions of the IV estimators and various test statistics perform very poorly. As in the previous section, it proves useful to adopt a nesting that allows the dimensionality of Z to depend on the sample size.

If the number of instruments is fixed or grows more slowly than the sample size, the noise that arises from the large dimensionality of Z vanishes in the limit, which validates the use of conventional asymptotics for inference. In order to explicitly recognize the presence of this additional source of sampling variability, Bekker (1994) allows the number of instruments to grow linearly with the sample size. In particular, it is assumed that as $n \to \infty$, $\ell/n \to \lambda$, where $0 < \lambda < 1$. This is often referred to in the literature as *Bekker's asymptotics*.

Interestingly, in both local-to-zero (weak instrument) and Bekker's asymptotic frameworks, the concentration parameter, standardized by the number of instruments, μ^2/ℓ, converges to a constant. Not surprisingly, both frameworks render the 2SLS estimator inconsistent. More specifically, the objective function of the 2SLS estimator is given by

$$(y - x\theta)' P_Z (y - x\theta)$$

with a first-order condition

$$\frac{1}{n} x' P_Z (y - x\hat{\theta}) = 0. \tag{6.4}$$

But the left-hand side of (6.4), evaluated at the true value θ_0, is

$$\frac{x' P_Z e_0}{n} \xrightarrow{p} \lim E\left[\frac{x' P_Z e_0}{n}\right] = \lim E\left[\frac{u' P_Z e_0}{n}\right] \tag{6.5}$$

$$= \lim \frac{1}{n} E[\text{tr}(u' P_Z e_0)] = \lambda \sigma_{12},$$

which is non-zero unless $\sigma_{12} = 0$ or x is exogenous. Therefore, the first-order condition (6.4) forces the 2SLS estimator to satisfy an equality that is not equivalent to the sample analog of (6.5). As a result, the 2SLS estimator is asymptotically biased (Bekker, 1994; Newey, 2004).

Exercise 6.6. In the framework of many instrument asymptotics, consider the following estimator:

$$\tilde{\theta} = \left(x'\left(P_Z - \frac{\ell}{n} I_n\right) x\right)^{-1} x'\left(P_Z - \frac{\ell}{n} I_n\right) y.$$

Show that this estimator is consistent in the framework of many instrument asymptotics. Explain this consistency result using first-order conditions for $\tilde{\theta}$. Explain why and how this estimator may be interpreted as a bias-corrected 2SLS estimator.

Exercise 6.7. In the many instrument asymptotic framework, derive the probability limit of the k-class estimator $\hat{\theta}_k$ assuming that $n^{-1}\Pi'Z'Z\Pi \xrightarrow{p} Q$, where Q is a positive definite matrix. For which value of k is the estimator consistent?

While the 2SLS estimator is asymptotically biased, the LIML estimator turns out to be consistent under the many instrument asymptotic framework. Schematically, let us use its different representation

$$\hat{\theta}_{LIML} = \arg\min_\theta \frac{(y - x\theta)'P_Z(y - x\theta)}{(y - x\theta)'(y - x\theta)},$$

with a first-order condition

$$\frac{x'P_Z(y - x\hat{\theta}_{LIML})}{n} \tag{6.6}$$

$$= \frac{n^{-1}(y - x\hat{\theta}_{LIML})'P_Z(y - x\hat{\theta}_{LIML})}{n^{-1}(y - x\hat{\theta}_{LIML})'(y - x\hat{\theta}_{LIML})} \frac{x'(y - x\hat{\theta}_{LIML})}{n}.$$

We know that the limit of the left-hand side, evaluated at the true parameter θ_0, is $\lambda\sigma_{12}$. The right-hand side, evaluated at θ_0, converges to

$$\frac{\operatorname{plim} n^{-1}e_0'P_Ze_0}{\operatorname{plim} n^{-1}e_0'e_0} \operatorname{plim} \frac{x'e}{n} = \frac{\lambda\sigma_1^2}{\sigma_1^2}\sigma_{12} = \lambda\sigma_{12}.$$

Thus, the left- and right-hand sides of (6.6), evaluated at the true value θ_0, match each other asymptotically and the estimator $\hat{\theta}_{LIML}$ does converge to θ_0. It is possible to show (Bekker, 1994) that the LIML estimator is asymptotically normal, with an asymptotic variance exceeding, possibly substantially for large λ, the conventional asymptotic variance arising in problems with few instruments. Assuming that $n^{-1}\Pi'Z'Z\Pi \xrightarrow{p} Q > 0$ and that the structural error vector e is normally distributed, we have

$$\sqrt{n}\left(\hat{\theta}_{LIML} - \theta_0\right) \xrightarrow{d} \mathcal{N}\left(0, \frac{\sigma_1^2}{Q} + \frac{\lambda}{1-\lambda}\frac{\sigma_1^2\sigma_2^2 - \sigma_{12}^2}{Q^2}\right).$$

Here, the first component of the asymptotic variance corresponds to the conventional one, while the second component, a positive term, is due to the numerosity of instruments. The bias-corrected 2SLS estimator $\tilde{\theta}$ has similar asymptotics but with a plus sign in the numerator of the second component. Next, the LIML estimator is asymptotically efficient in a certain class within the many instrument framework (Anderson, Kunimoto and Matsushita, 2010). van Hasselt (2010) derives the additional components of the asymptotic variances for non-normal errors, and shows that, under certain conditions, the LIML estimator preserves its efficiency gains over the bias-corrected 2SLS estimator.

Anatolyev (2011) studied the impact of a large number of exogenous regressors on existing estimators and their asymptotics. It is assumed that as $n \to \infty$, not only $\ell/n \to \lambda$, but also $\bar{\ell}/n \to \bar{\lambda}$, where $\bar{\ell}$ is the number of exogenous regressors collected in matrix $\bar{Z}$. In particular, the presence of many exogenous regressors inflates the asymptotic variance of the LIML estimator to

$$\frac{1}{1-\bar{\lambda}} \left(\frac{\sigma_1^2}{Q} + \frac{\lambda}{1-\lambda-\bar{\lambda}} \frac{\sigma_1^2\sigma_2^2 - \sigma_{12}^2}{Q^2} \right),$$

although the standard errors of Hansen, Hausman and Newey (2008) are still valid. Further, the conventional bias correction of the 2SLS estimator is no longer valid; the suitably bias-adjusted 2SLS estimator is

$$\tilde{\theta} = \left(x' \left(P_{Z^\perp} - \frac{\ell}{n-\bar{\ell}} M_{\bar{Z}} \right) x \right)^{-1} x' \left(P_{Z^\perp} - \frac{\ell}{n-\bar{\ell}} M_{\bar{Z}} \right) y,$$

where $P_{Z^\perp} = P_{Z\bar{Z}} - P_{\bar{Z}}$, $M_{\bar{Z}} = I_n - P_{\bar{Z}}$, and $P_{Z\bar{Z}}$ and $P_{\bar{Z}}$ denote the projection matrices associated with $(Z, \bar{Z})$ and $\bar{Z}$.

Exercise 6.8. Consider the standard linear model with one endogenous regressor and ℓ instrumental variables in an *IID* environment. The 2SLS estimator can be alternatively rewritten as

$$\hat{\beta}_{2SLS} = \left(\sum_{i,j} P_{ij} x_i x_j \right)^{-1} \sum_{i,j} P_{ij} x_i y_j,$$

where $\sum_{i,j}$ denotes summation in both indexes i and j from 1 to n and P_{ij} denotes the $(i,j)^{th}$ element of the projection matrix P_Z. The idea of the *jackknife instrumental variables estimator* (Angrist, Imbens and Kruger, 1999) is to remove from both summations the terms that correspond to $i = j$:

$$\hat{\beta}_{JIV} = \left(\sum_{i \neq j} P_{ij} x_i x_j \right)^{-1} \sum_{i \neq j} P_{ij} x_i y_j,$$

where $\sum_{i \neq j}$ denotes summation in both indexes i and j from 1 to n only when $i \neq j$. For simplicity, assume that as $\ell/n \to \lambda \geq 0$, the diagonal entries of P_Z, $P_{ii} \equiv z_i' (Z'Z)^{-1} z_i$, converge to λ uniformly in i.

1. Under the standard asymptotics, explain why $\hat{\beta}_{JIV}$ is consistent. What is its asymptotic distribution?

2. Under Bekker's many instrument asymptotics, explain why $\hat{\beta}_{JIV}$ is consistent while $\hat{\beta}_{2SLS}$ is not.

Now we turn our attention to specification testing. When the degrees of freedom of specification tests depend on the number of instruments, the standard asymptotic framework that treats ℓ as fixed is expected to provide a poor approximation. In this case, it seems reasonable to conjecture that asymptotic frameworks which allow ℓ to drift with the sample size would be more accurate. In the case of the $\mathcal{AR}$ test, Andrews and Stock (2007) show that when $\ell^3/n \to 0$ as $\ell, n \to \infty$,

$$\sqrt{\ell} \left(\frac{\mathcal{AR}}{\ell} - 1 \right) \xrightarrow{d} N(0, 2).$$

Anatolyev and Gospodinov (2011) establish that a similar result holds under Bekker's parameterization. In particular, if $\ell/n \to \lambda$ as $n \to \infty$, under suitable conditions, including that $n^{-1}\Pi'Z'Z\Pi$ converges to a fixed positive definite matrix,

$$\sqrt{\ell} \left(\frac{\mathcal{AR}}{\ell} - 1 \right) \xrightarrow{d} N\left(0, \frac{2}{1-\lambda}\right). \tag{6.7}$$

Note the factor $1/(1-\lambda)$ in the asymptotic variance.

Similar results can be obtained for the popular test for overidentifying restrictions. Let $\hat{e} = y - x\hat{\theta}$ and $\hat{\sigma}^2 = \hat{e}'\hat{e}/(n-1)$. The test for overidentifying restrictions has the form

$$\mathcal{J} = \frac{\hat{e}'P\hat{e}}{\hat{\sigma}^2}$$

and, under the null hypothesis of correct moment restrictions $H_0 : E[ez] = 0$, is distributed as $\chi^2_{\ell-k}$ in the conventional asymptotic framework with fixed ℓ. Alternatively, when $\ell^2/n \to 0$ as $\ell, n \to \infty$, Donald, Imbens and Newey (2003) demonstrate that

$$\frac{\mathcal{J} - \ell}{\sqrt{\ell}} \xrightarrow{d} N(0, 2).$$

Finally, Anatolyev and Gospodinov (2011) establish that, under the assumptions listed above (6.7),

$$\sqrt{\ell} \left(\frac{\mathcal{J}}{\ell} - 1 \right) \xrightarrow{d} N(0, 2(1-\lambda)). \tag{6.8}$$

Again, note the factor $1 - \lambda$ in the asymptotic variance.

Using (6.7) and (6.8), it can be shown (Anatolyev and Gospodinov, 2011) that under some conditions imposed on the distribution of instruments, the asymptotic size at level α of the $\mathcal{AR}$ and $\mathcal{J}$ tests is given by $\Phi\left(\Phi^{-1}(\alpha)\sqrt{1-\lambda}\right)$ and $\Phi\left(\Phi^{-1}(\alpha)/\sqrt{1-\lambda}\right)$, respectively, where $\Phi(u)$ is the standard normal cumulative distribution function and $\Phi^{-1}(u)$ is its quantile function. This suggests that the critical values of the $\mathcal{AR}$ and $\mathcal{J}$ tests can be corrected in such a way that their asymptotic size matches the target size α.

More specifically, define the corrected $\mathcal{AR}$ test as the test that rejects the joint hypothesis of $H_0 : \theta = \theta_0$ and the validity of the overidentifying restrictions, evaluated at $\theta = \theta_0$, when

$$\mathcal{AR} > \tau^{\chi^2_\ell}_{\Phi\left(\Phi^{-1}(\alpha)/\sqrt{1-\ell/n}\right)},$$

and the corrected $\mathcal{J}$ test as the test that rejects the null hypothesis of correct moment restrictions when

$$\mathcal{J} > \tau^{\chi^2_{\ell-k}}_{\Phi\left(\Phi^{-1}(\alpha)\sqrt{1-\ell/n}\right)},$$

where $\tau^{\chi^2_p}_\alpha$ denotes the α-quantile of a chi-square distribution with p degrees of freedom. Then, under Bekker's parameterization, the asymptotic size of the corrected $\mathcal{AR}$ and $\mathcal{J}$ tests equals α (Anatolyev and Gospodinov, 2011). It is important to note that these corrected tests bridge the small ℓ (conventional) and large ℓ (Bekker's) extremes and are robust to the numerosity of instruments. For example, note that when $\lambda = 0$, the corrected tests collapse to the standard ones. The implementation of the corrected tests is straightforward, as the only modification that needs to be performed to the conventional procedure is to replace the level of the test α by $\Phi\left(\Phi^{-1}(\alpha)/\sqrt{1-\ell/n}\right)$ or $\Phi\left(\Phi^{-1}(\alpha)\sqrt{1-\ell/n}\right)$.

Suppose $\theta_0 \neq 0$. Hahn and Hausman (2002) proposed a test for strong instruments in the many instrument asymptotic framework. The test statistic is based on the difference between the usual (forward) bias-corrected 2SLS estimator

$$\tilde{\theta} = \left(x'\left(P_Z - \frac{\ell}{n}I_n\right)x\right)^{-1}x'\left(P_Z - \frac{\ell}{n}I_n\right)y$$

and an inverse to its analog

$$\dot{\theta} = \left(x'\left(P_Z - \frac{\ell}{n}I_n\right)y\right)^{-1}y'\left(P_Z - \frac{\ell}{n}I_n\right)y$$

in the "reverse" instrumental variables regression of x on y using the same set of instruments. The difference $\tilde{\theta} - \dot{\theta}$ should be close to zero if the instruments are strong, and far from zero if they are weak. Hahn and Hausman (2002) derive an asymptotic null distribution for the normalized difference and propose valid standard errors. Interestingly, Hahn and Hausman (2002) argue that the alternative many instrument asymptotics leads to similar conclusions as those provided by the higher-order but conventional asymptotic analysis (see Chapter 5). Further, Hausman, Stock, and Yogo (2005) find that the power of the Hahn and Hausman (2002) test is typically low, while Anatolyev (2011) demonstrates what adjustments should be made in the presence of many exogenous regressors.

Earlier we introduced the notion of the concentration parameter, the measure of instrument strength,

$$\mu^2 = \frac{\Pi' Z' Z \Pi}{\sigma_2^2},$$

which effectively shows the degree of explanatory power of the instrument set as a whole. The situation $\mu^2 = o_P(1)$ characterizes the case of irrelevant instruments, $\mu^2 = O_P(1)$ can be classified as a case of weak instruments, while $\mu^2 = O_P(n)$ corresponds to the case of strong instruments in the classical sense. The instruments as a set may be strong while some individual instruments may be weak if there are many of them, so, for example, one group of relatively strong instruments may be followed by a group of weaker instruments. An interesting line of recent literature on many weak instruments (Chao and Swanson, 2005; Hansen, Hausman and Newey, 2008; Newey and Windmeijer, 2009) investigates the possibilities of intermediate degrees of identification. In particular, conditions are derived for consistent estimation and asymptotic normality of the LIML and k-class estimators, and valid inference procedures are proposed. In this more general framework, μ, the square root of the concentration parameter, plays the role of rate of convergence and μ^2 becomes an effective sample size.

6.2.4 Many Regressors

Sometimes applied researchers run regressions where the number of regressors is large and even comparable to the number of observations, e.g., cross-sectional growth regressions. A researcher may be willing to test, for instance, that a particular coefficient is zero, or to test for joint significance of a big or small subset of regression parameters. Typically, the t-, F or one of the trinity of asymptotic tests (Wald, likelihood ratio, Lagrange multiplier) is applied. The problems with classical tests when there are many regressors and especially many restrictions in the null hypothesis have been reported and studied in the literature. For example, Berndt and Savin (1977) document huge conflicts between the classical tests when the number of restrictions is comparable to the sample size. Anatolyev (2012) shows that not accounting for numerosity of regressors may lead to erroneous inference and suggests modifications that are valid irrespective of whether there are many or few regressors and/or restrictions.

Consider the standard linear regression model

$$y = x'\theta_0 + e,$$

where $E[e|x] = 0$ and $E[e^2|x] = \sigma^2$. Assume that $\{(x_i, y_i)\}_{i=1}^{n}$ is a random sample. The special feature of this setup is that the dimensionality of x may be large and comparable to the number of observations. Suppose that one wants to test r parameter restrictions on the $k \times 1$ vector of parameters, and r may also be large. In this case, the appropriate asymptotic framework is similar to Bekker's (1994): it is assumed that as $n \to \infty$, $k/n \to \gamma$ and $r/n \to \rho$, where $0 \leq \rho \leq \gamma < 1$. Of course, under such circumstances, the OLS estimator $\hat{\theta}$ of θ_0 is inconsistent (the number of observations per parameter is asymptotically fixed), but tests may or may not be valid.

It turns out that under suitable conditions, both the asymptotic and finite sample t tests (using the normal or Student's distribution tables) are still asymptotically valid in this framework. The reason is that the number of restrictions equals one and hence $\rho = 0$. The conclusions are sharply different when $\rho \neq 0$. In particular, the asymptotic Wald test $\mathcal{W}$ moderately overrejects the null hypothesis in large samples, while the $\mathcal{LR}$ and $\mathcal{LM}$ tests exhibit severe size distortions. It is possible to modify these tests and make them robust to the number of parameter restrictions. For example, the asymptotic size at level α of the asymptotic Wald test is given by $\Phi\left(\Phi^{-1}(\alpha)/\sqrt{1 + \rho/(1 - \gamma)}\right)$, which suggests (see also section 6.2.3) that the corrected $\mathcal{W}$ test rejects the parameter restrictions imposed by the null hypothesis when

$$\mathcal{W} > \tau^{\chi_r^2}_{\Phi\left(\Phi^{-1}(\alpha)\sqrt{1 + r/(n-k)}\right)}$$

instead of when $\mathcal{W} > \tau^{\chi_r^2}_{\alpha}$, and is asymptotically valid in the framework with many regressors and restrictions. It is easy to see that the corrected Wald test is also valid under conventional asymptotics when $r/(n - k) \to 0$ and the correction factor disappears. The $\mathcal{LR}$ and $\mathcal{LM}$ tests can be corrected in a similar fashion, although obtaining these corrections is more involved (see Anatolyev, 2012). Anatolyev (2012) also shows that the finite sample F test (i.e., using the tables of Fisher's distribution) is valid under conventional and many regressor asymptotics. That is, this test automatically accounts for the numerosity of regressors and restrictions asymptotically, no matter what the error distribution is.

6.2.5 Nearly-Singular Design

Caner (2008) considers a situation where the asymptotic variance of moment conditions is invertible, but almost singular. This may occur, for example, in IV regressions when the instruments are closely tied to each other but do not repeat themselves, or when the conditional orthogonality restrictions are closely related but are not collinear. In these situations, the finite sample properties of conventional estimators and test statistics are expected to deteriorate.

To investigate the consequences of such configurations in the framework of moment conditions $E[m(w, \theta_0)] = 0$, Caner (2008) introduced alternative asymptotics of *nearly-singular design* by assuming that

$$n^{\kappa} \left(\frac{1}{n} \sum_{i=1}^{n} m\left(w_i, \theta\right) m\left(w_i, \theta\right)' - E\left[m\left(w, \theta\right) m\left(w, \theta\right)' \right] \right) \xrightarrow{p} D\left(\theta\right)$$

uniformly over θ, where $D\left(\theta\right)$ is continuous in θ and positive definite on the null space of the limit inside the brackets for all θ, and the constant $0 < \kappa < 1$ indexes the degree of severity of nearly-singular design. Caner (2008) shows that under this assumption and other suitable conditions, the GMM estimator is consistent and asymptotically normal, but the rate of convergence is lower than the conventional root-n rate and is equal to $n^{(1-\kappa)/2}$. Moreover, the higher-order asymptotic expansion is expressed in powers of $n^{(1-\kappa)/2}$. This slower convergence signals, in particular, larger biases in finite samples compared to those obtained under the non-singular design. However, the asymptotic variance of the GMM estimator and the asymptotic distribution of the test for overidentifying restrictions are the same as in the standard case. Similar conclusions hold for the class of GEL estimators. To detect the presence of nearly-singular design, Caner (2008) suggests keeping track of minimal eigenvalues of the sample variance matrix of moments, and proposes a downward testing procedure of moment selection to avoid a nearly-singular design.

One approach to dealing with the nearly-singular design is using regularization procedures. Knight (2008) considers various penalized least squares estimators (bridge, ridge, lasso and others) in a linear regression with a nearly-singular design, i.e., near collinearity. The asymptotic drifting data generating process (DGP) is similar to the one above and, for some sequence $\{a_n\}$ that tends to infinity, is given by

$$a_n \left(\frac{1}{n} \sum_{i=1}^{n} x_i x_i' - E\left[xx' \right] \right) \xrightarrow{p} D,$$

where D is positive definite on the null space of the limit inside the brackets. Knight (2008) shows that under this assumption and other suitable conditions, the penalized least squares estimators are b_n-consistent, where $b_n = \sqrt{n/a_n}$, and their asymptotic distributions are non-standard.

6.2.6 Drifting Parameterizations in Threshold and Change-point Models

Alternative asymptotic approximations resulting from drifting parameterizations are used, although more rarely, for a different purpose than getting a better quality of approximation. Sometimes the goal is to get a more convenient asymptotic distribution, which is not possible under the conventional asymptotic paradigm. This is the case, for example, in threshold and change-point models.

Consider a simple threshold model

$$y_t = x_t' \left(\theta_1 \mathbb{I} \{ q_t \leq \gamma_0 \} + \theta_2 \mathbb{I} \{ q_t > \gamma_0 \} \right) + \varepsilon_t,$$

where the series (y_t, x_t, q_t) is stationary, q_t is a threshold variable, γ is a threshold parameter, and $\varepsilon_t \sim IID(0, \sigma^2)$. Chan (1993) derived an asymptotic distribution for the n-consistent least squares estimator $\hat{\gamma}$ of γ_0 which is non-pivotal and hard to implement. Hansen (1997, 2000) adapted a drifting parameterization for the difference $\theta_2 - \theta_1$ as $\theta_2 - \theta_1 = cn^{-\alpha}$ for $c \neq 0$ and $0 < \alpha < \frac{1}{2}$. To comply with this assumption in practice, the data generating mechanism must be such that the difference in parameters across regimes is, at most, moderate. Hansen (1997) showed that under suitable conditions,

$$n \left(\theta_2 - \theta_1 \right)' V \left(\theta_2 - \theta_1 \right) \left(\hat{\gamma} - \gamma_0 \right) \xrightarrow{d} \arg\max_{r \in \mathbb{R}} \left\{ W(r) - \frac{|r|}{2} \right\}, \tag{6.9}$$

where $V = E \left[x_t x_t' | q_t = \gamma_0 \right] \sigma^{-2} f (\gamma_0)$, $f(\cdot)$ is the density of q_t, and $W(r)$ is a standard Wiener process on $(-\infty, +\infty)$. The limiting representation in (6.9) is pivotal and possesses a distribution function with a known closed form. Still, this result is not very convenient to use because of the presence of nuisance parameters in the factor V that need to be explicitly estimated. A practically more appealing approach to constructing interval estimates of γ_0 is based on the $\mathcal{LR}$ test of the hypothesis $H_0 : \gamma_0 = \bar{\gamma}$. Let

$$\sigma_n^2(\gamma) = \frac{1}{n} \sum_{t=1}^{n} \left(y_t - x_t' (\hat{\theta}_1 \mathbb{I} \{ q_t \leq \gamma \} + \hat{\theta}_2 \mathbb{I} \{ q_t > \gamma \}) \right)^2.$$

Then, the asymptotic distribution of

$$\mathcal{LR} = n \cdot \frac{\sigma_n^2 (\bar{\gamma}) - \sigma_n^2 (\hat{\gamma})}{\sigma_n^2 (\hat{\gamma})}$$

is given by

$$\mathcal{LR} \xrightarrow{d} \xi \equiv \max_{r \in \mathbb{R}} \left\{ 2W(r) - |r| \right\}.$$

The density of the random variable ξ is known in a closed form and can be used to obtain a confidence interval for γ_0 as $CI_{1-\alpha}(\gamma_0) = \left\{ \bar{\gamma} : \mathcal{LR} \leq \tau_{1-\alpha}^{\xi} \right\}$, where $\tau_{1-\alpha}^{\xi}$ is the $(1-\alpha)$-quantile of the distribution of ξ. For more details and some complications arising under conditional heteroskedasticity, see Hansen (1997, 2000). A similar drifting parameterization can be employed in models with structural breaks where the analog of a threshold parameter is the fraction of observations before the break. See, for example, Bai (1997).

6.2.7 Weak Identification Under the Null Hypothesis

Non-standard asymptotics may arise in models, other than those discussed above, that are characterized by weak identification. Consider the model

$$y_t = x_t' \alpha_0 + h_1 \left(z_t, \gamma_0 \right)' \theta_0 + h_2 \left(z_t, \gamma_0 \right)' \varphi_0 + \varepsilon_t,$$

where the data are stationary, ε_t is a homoskedastic martingale difference sequence with variance σ^2 and $H_0 : \varphi_0 = 0$ is the null hypothesis of interest. If $\theta_0 = 0$, the parameter γ is not identified under the null hypothesis, and it is well known (Hansen, 1996) that a valid inference procedure requires the use of test statistics with non-standard asymptotic distributions.

Anatolyev (2004) considers a slightly different setup where the parameter γ is weakly identified under the null hypothesis as a consequence of low variability of $h_1 (z_t, \gamma)' \theta$ as γ changes. This situation can be modeled as one with a drifting parameter sequence $\theta_0 = c/\sqrt{n}$, where $c \neq 0$. Note that the case $c = 0$ corresponds to a complete lack of identification. A leading example of this framework is the two-regime self-exciting threshold autoregressive model

$$y_t = \varepsilon_t + \begin{cases} (\mu - \Delta\mu/2) + (\phi - \Delta\phi/2)\, y_{t-1} & \text{if } y_{t-1} \leq \gamma, \\ (\mu + \Delta\mu/2) + (\phi + \Delta\phi/2)\, y_{t-1} & \text{if } y_{t-1} > \gamma, \end{cases}$$

where $\theta_0 = \Delta\mu$ and $\varphi_0 = \Delta\phi$. The hypothesis of interest is the test of equality of the AR coefficients in the two regimes, $H_0 : \Delta\phi = 0$.

The model is estimated by minimizing the average squared residuals (ASR) via the concentration method: the ASR is first minimized with respect to the unknown parameters for fixed values of γ and the resulting ASR function is then minimized with respect to γ. The minimizer $\hat{\gamma}$ of ASR converges almost surely to

$$\gamma^* = \arg\sup_{\gamma} \left\{ (\Psi(\gamma) + Q(\gamma, \gamma_0)J_1 c)'\, Q(\gamma, \gamma)^{-1}\, (\Psi(\gamma) + Q(\gamma, \gamma_0)J_1 c) \right\},$$

where J_1 is a selector matrix (see Anatolyev, 2004), $\Psi(\gamma)$ is a $(k_x + k_1 + k_2)$-variate Gaussian process with covariance kernel

$$\sigma^2 Q(\gamma_1, \gamma_2) \equiv \sigma^2 E \left[h_t (\gamma_1)\, h_t (\gamma_2)' \right]$$

and $h_t (\gamma) = (x_t', h_1 (z_t, \gamma)', h_2 (z_t, \gamma)')'$. As in the case of weak instruments, the limit γ^* is different from γ_0 and is random. Under full non-identification when $c = 0$, the true γ_0 does not enter into the objective function at all. The asymptotic distribution of the other estimates under H_0 is given by

$$\sqrt{n} \begin{pmatrix} \hat{\alpha} - \alpha_0 \\ \hat{\theta} - \theta_0 \\ \hat{\varphi} \end{pmatrix} \xrightarrow{d} Q(\gamma^*, \gamma^*)^{-1} [\Psi(\gamma^*) + (Q(\gamma^*, \gamma_0) - Q(\gamma^*, \gamma^*))\, J_1 c],$$

which is non-normal.

Similar arguments can be used to derive the asymptotic distributions of the $\mathcal{W}$, $\mathcal{LM}$ and $\mathcal{LR}$ tests. The null distributions for these tests are nonstandard and depend on a host of nuisance parameters, including the localizing constant c, which is not consistently estimable. In simulations, the $\mathcal{LR}$ test, in contrast to the other two tests, exhibits remarkable robustness to the degree of identification. For more details, see Anatolyev (2004).

6.3 Local-to-Unity and Local-to-Zero Parameterizations in Nearly Nonstationary Models

6.3.1 Local-to-Unity Parameterization

So far, we have analyzed only models with IID and stationary data. It turns out that similar drifting parameterizations can also be used in the context of nonstationary models, although the setup of these sequences and the theory need to be modified accordingly. Consider the $AR(p)$ process

$$y_t^* = \mu_1 + \mu_2 t + y_t, \qquad (6.10)$$
$$\Gamma(L)y_t = e_t,$$

where $\Gamma(L) = 1 - \gamma_1 L - \gamma_2 L^2 - ... - \gamma_p L^p$ with roots on or outside the unit circle, $y_{-p+1}, ..., y_0$ are assumed fixed and e_t is a martingale difference sequence with $E[e_t^2] = \sigma^2$ and $\sup_t E[e_t^{2+\epsilon}] < \infty$ for some $\epsilon > 0$. The polynomial $\Gamma(L)$ can be factorized as (Stock, 1991)

$$\Gamma(L) = \psi(L)(1 - \phi L), \qquad (6.11)$$

where ϕ denotes the largest root of the AR polynomial and $\psi(L) = 1 - \sum_{j=1}^{p-1} \psi_j L^j$ is a lag polynomial describing the short-run dynamics of the process with no roots near or on the unit circle.

Many economic time series, including interest rates, unemployment, real exchange rates and asset volatility extracted from option prices, are characterized by high persistence, although imposing an exact unit root on the process may not be consistent with economic theory. This corresponds to the case where ϕ is near, but not exactly, one. The model can also be rewritten using the augmented Dickey–Fuller (ADF) representation

$$y_t = \rho y_{t-1} + \varphi_1 \triangle y_{t-1} + ... + \varphi_{p-1} \triangle y_{t-p+1} + e_t, \qquad (6.12)$$

where $\rho = \gamma_1 + \gamma_2 + ... + \gamma_p$ and $\varphi_j = -(\gamma_{j+1} + ... + \gamma_p)$ for $j = 1, ..., p - 1$. This form of the model is often used in empirical work for estimation, testing and forecasting. Model (6.12) is typically estimated by OLS and the OLS estimator $(\hat{\rho}, \hat{\varphi}_1, ..., \hat{\varphi}_{p-1})$ is asymptotically jointly normally distributed provided that $\rho < 1$.

To account explicitly for the high persistence of the process, it is convenient to adopt the *local-to-unity* parameterization (Chan and Wei, 1987; Phillips, 1987) of the largest AR root

$$\phi_n = 1 + \frac{c}{n},$$

where c is a fixed constant and n is the sample size. Typically, it is assumed that $c \leq 0$, with $c = 0$ corresponding to the exact unit root case, but mildly explosive processes ($c > 0$) can also be allowed. As a result, this parameterization nests a range of possible values for ϕ which is particularly useful when there is uncertainty about the exact magnitude of the largest AR root. This nesting implies that in the ADF representation of process (6.12), $\rho_n = 1 + c\psi(1)/n$, where $\psi(1) = 1 - \psi_1 - \ldots - \psi_{p-1}$.

The local-to-unity framework expresses the parameter space as a shrinking neighborhood of unity as the sample size increases. As mentioned in the introduction, this statistical construction ("asymptotic fiction") removes the discontinuity of the distribution theory and gives an excellent approximation to the finite sample distribution of $\hat{\rho}$ in model (6.12). Also, it facilitates the analysis of continuous asymptotic limits since $\lim_{n\to\infty}(\phi_n)^n = \exp(c)$. Finally, another important feature of this nesting is worth stressing. While the last two decades have witnessed the development of powerful asymptotic tests for distinguishing between stationary and unit root processes, the decision rule from this pre-testing procedure is dichotomous and requires the researcher to commit to a particular asymptotic (standard normal or Dickey–Fuller) framework. In contrast, the local-to-unity parameterization accounts for the uncertainty associated with the largest root of the process and allows a valid approximation (indexed by the localizing constant c) over the whole parameter space. In what follows, we suppress the dependence of ϕ_n and ρ_n on n for notational convenience.

The limiting distribution of the estimator $\hat{\rho}$ can be obtained by appealing to the functional central limit theorem. In particular, we have (Phillips, 1987)

$$n(\hat{\rho} - \rho) \Rightarrow \psi(1) \frac{\int_0^1 J_c^\tau(s)dW(s)}{\int_0^1 J_c^\tau(s)^2 ds},$$

where $\Rightarrow$ denotes weak convergence, $J_c(r)$ is an Ornstein–Uhlenbeck process generated by the stochastic differential equation $dJ_c(r) = cJ_c(r)dr + dW(r)$, $\{W(r) : r \in [0,1]\}$ is a standard Brownian motion and $J_c^\tau(r) = J_c(r)$ if (6.10) does not contain any deterministic components ($\mu_1 = 0$, $\mu_2 = 0$), $J_c^\tau(r) = J_c(r) - \int_0^1 J_c(s)ds$ if (6.10) includes only a constant term ($\mu_1 \neq 0$, $\mu_2 = 0$) and $J_c^\tau(r) = J_c(r) - \int_0^1 (4 - 6s)J_c(s)ds - r\int_0^1 (12s - 6)J_c(s)ds$ if (6.10) includes both a constant and a linear trend ($\mu_1 \neq 0$, $\mu_2 \neq 0$).

Also, the studentized estimator (t statistic) has a limit

$$t_\rho = \frac{\hat{\rho} - \rho}{\text{se}(\hat{\rho})} \Rightarrow \frac{\int_0^1 J_c^\tau(s)dW(s)}{\sqrt{\int_0^1 J_c^\tau(s)^2 ds}}. \tag{6.13}$$

The limiting distributions of $\hat{\rho}$ and t_ρ are functions of the local-to-unity parameter, which is not consistently estimable since $\hat{c} - c = O_P(1)$, where $\hat{c} = n(\hat{\rho} - 1)/\hat{\psi}(1)$ and $\hat{\psi}(1) = 1 - \sum_{j=1}^{p-1} \hat{\varphi}_j$. This complicates inference in these models. But the local-to-unity parameterization provides a uniform asymptotic approximation to the distribution of t_ρ for all values of ρ in the interval $(0, 1]$ (Mikusheva, 2007). In particular, if the localizing constant c approaches $-\infty$, the limiting distribution approaches the standard normal distribution (Phillips, 1987). When $c = 0$, the limiting distribution collapses to the Dickey–Fuller distribution. All intermediate values of c bridge continuously the standard normal and Dickey–Fuller asymptotics.

Even though the parameter c is not consistently estimable, valid methods for constructing confidence intervals for c and ρ are readily available. They are based on inversion of asymptotic (Stock, 1991), bootstrap (Hansen, 1999) or Monte Carlo (Andrews, 1993) tests on a grid of possible values for c (or ρ). Mikusheva (2007) shows that these three methods provide asymptotically valid confidence intervals for ρ.

To describe the construction of $100(1 - \alpha)\%$ confidence intervals for the parameter ρ (or equivalently c) as in Stock (1991), let $\tau_c(\alpha)$ denote the α-quantile of the asymptotic distribution in (6.13). Then, the $100(1 - \alpha)\%$ confidence interval for ρ is given by $CI_\rho = \{\rho : \tau_c(\alpha/2) \le t_\rho \le \tau_c(1 - \alpha/2)\}$. The asymptotic quantile functions $\tau_c(\alpha/2)$ and $\tau_c(1 - \alpha/2)$ are typically obtained by simulation. Next, for a particular sample size n, these quantile functions can be associated with an implicit value of ρ. The statistic t_ρ can then be computed for a sequence of null hypotheses on a grid of values for ρ and the intersections of the test statistic and the quantile functions produce the endpoints of the $100(1 - \alpha)\%$ confidence interval. Andrews' (1993) and Hansen's (1999) methods are based on the same idea by replacing the asymptotic quantile functions with their Monte Carlo and bootstrap analogs.

The local-to-unity framework also proves to be very useful for analyzing the consequences of misspecification of the underlying processes. To illustrate this, rewrite the process (6.10)–(6.11) as

$$(1 - \phi L)y_t = a(L)e_t,$$

where $a(L) = \psi^{-1}(L) = \sum_{i=0}^{\infty} a_i L^i$ with $a_0 = 1$, $\sum_{i=0}^{\infty} i|a_i| < \infty$ and $\sum_{i=0}^{\infty} a_i \ne 0$, and assuming no deterministic component.

Let $u_t = a(L)e_t$ and $S_t = \sum_{j=1}^{t} e_j$. By the Beveridge–Nelson (BN) decomposition, $u_t = (a(1) + (1 - L)a^*(L)) e_t$, where $a(1) = \sum_{i=0}^{\infty} a_i$, $a^*(L) = \sum_{i=1}^{\infty} a_i^* L^{i-1}$ and $a_i^* = -\sum_{j=i}^{\infty} a_j$. Then, using recursive substitution and summation by parts,

$$
\begin{aligned}
y_t &= \sum_{j=1}^{t} \phi^{t-j} a(L) e_j \\
&= (a(1) + (1 - L)a^*(L)) S_t \\
&\quad + \sum_{j=1}^{t-1} (a(1) + (1 - L)a^*(L)) S_{j-1} \left(\phi^{t-j+1} - \phi^{t-j} \right).
\end{aligned}
$$

Denoting $v_t = a^*(L)e_t$, we have

$$y_t = a(1)S_t + v_t + \sum_{j=1}^{t-1} a(1)S_{j-1} \left(\phi^{t-j+1} - \phi^{t-j} \right)$$

$$+ \sum_{j=1}^{t-1} v_{j-1} \left(\phi^{t-j+1} - \phi^{t-j} \right)$$

$$= a(1)S_t + v_t + \frac{c}{n} \sum_{j=1}^{t-1} a(1)\phi^{t-j} S_{j-1} + \frac{c}{n} \sum_{j=1}^{t-1} \phi^{t-j} v_{j-1}, \qquad (6.14)$$

Expression (6.14) is an algebraic decomposition of the process y_t and contains the standard BN decomposition for exact unit root processes as a special case $(c = 0)$. Interestingly, while the standard BN decomposition is given by the components $a(1)S_t$ (permanent) and v_t (transitory), decomposition (6.14) contains two additional terms. The fourth term

$$\frac{c}{n} \sum_{j=1}^{t-1} \phi^{t-j} v_{j-1}$$

is asymptotically negligible but the term

$$\frac{c}{n} \sum_{j=1}^{t-1} a(1)\phi^{t-j} S_{j-1}$$

is not and is of the same order $O_P(n^{1/2})$ as $a(1)S_t$. Therefore, (6.14) contains two permanent component terms (i.e., terms of order $O_P(n^{1/2})$) and omitting one of them (by wrongly assuming an exact unit root, for example) will lead to biased estimators and size distortions of the test statistics. This will also have important bias implications for the standard trend-cycle decomposition based on the assumption of an exact unit root.

Let $\lfloor \cdot \rfloor$ denote the greatest integer function and $t = \lfloor rn \rfloor$ for $r \in [0, 1]$. Then, dividing both sides of (6.14) by $\sqrt{n}$ and taking limits as $n \to \infty$ gives

$$\frac{1}{\sqrt{n}} y_{\lfloor rn \rfloor} \Rightarrow \sigma^2 a(1) \left(W(r) + c \int_0^r \exp((r-s)c)W(s)ds \right) \equiv J_c(r), \qquad (6.15)$$

where $J_c(r)$ denotes an Ornstein–Uhlenbeck process and $W(r)$ is a standard Brownian motion. The limiting result (6.15) confirms that both sides of (6.14) converge to the same Ornstein–Uhlenbeck process.

It is instructive to perform a similar analysis in multivariate models. Now let y_t denote a multivariate process

$$(I_m - \Phi L)y_t = A(L)e_t,$$

where $\Phi = I_m + C/n$, $C = \text{diag}\{c_1, c_2, ..., c_m\}$ and $c_1, c_2, ..., c_m$ are fixed constants. Using similar arguments as above, we have

$$y_t = A(1)S_t + v_t + \frac{C}{n}A(1)\sum_{j=1}^{t-1}\Phi^{t-j}S_{j-1} + \frac{C}{n}\sum_{j=1}^{t-1}\Phi^{t-j}v_{j-1}$$

and imposing restrictions on $A(1)$ is not sufficient to remove the permanent component because there is another $O_P(n^{1/2})$ term, $Cn^{-1}\sum_{j=1}^{t-1}\Phi^{t-j}S_{j-1}$.

More specifically, one can study the cointegrated model

$$x_{1,t} = \beta x_{2,t} + e_{1,t},$$
$$x_{2,t} = (1 + c/n)x_{2,t-1} + e_{2,t}$$

considered by Elliott (1998), and obtain a similar representation as the one above. In this case, the restriction $\beta A(1) = 0$ does not annihilate the permanent component. As a result, the reduced rank regressions that impose only this restriction are not valid and would lead to biased estimates and test size distortions, as shown by Elliott (1998). Furthermore, restrictions imposed on the "misspecified" permanent component when $C \neq 0_{m \times m}$ are also expected to adversely affect the impulse response analysis and variance decomposition based on long-run identifying restrictions.

Exercise 6.9 Consider the model

$$y_t = \alpha + \beta x_{t-1} + \varepsilon_{1t},$$
$$x_t = \mu + v_t, \quad \psi(L)(1 - \phi L)v_t = \varepsilon_{2t},$$

where $\phi = 1 + c/n$, $\varepsilon_t = (\varepsilon_{1t}, \varepsilon_{2t})'$ is a homoskedastic martingale difference sequence with finite fourth moments and $\text{corr}(\varepsilon_{1t}, \varepsilon_{2t}) = \delta$. Show that the t statistic of $H_0 : \beta = 0$ is asymptotically distributed as

$$t_\beta \Rightarrow \delta \frac{\int_0^1 J_c^\mu(s)dW(s)}{\sqrt{\int_0^1 J_c^\mu(s)^2 ds}} + \sqrt{1 - \delta^2}\, \tilde{z},$$

where $J_c^\mu(r) = J_c(r) - \int_0^1 J_c(s)ds$, and $\tilde{z}$ is a standard normal random variable distributed independently of (W, J_c).

6.3.2 Inference with Local-to-Unity Processes at Long Forecast Horizons

Tracing the effects of structural shocks on the future dynamics of endogenous economic variables has become one of the major tools for policy analysis and evaluation. Often interest lies in testing hypotheses about the magnitude and the shape of the impulse response at long horizons; for instance,

$\theta_l \equiv \partial y_{t+l}/\partial e_t$ at lead time l. Alternatively, one might want to measure how long it takes for a non-explosive series to complete $100w\%$ of the adjustment to the initial shock, $\sup_{l \in \mathbb{N}} |\partial y_{t+l}/\partial e_t| \geq 1 - w$ for some fixed $w \in (0, 1]$. In both cases, the restrictions imposed by the null hypothesis are polynomials of order l in the parameters of the model. In the AR(1) model, the structure of the adjustment is monotonic and $l = \log(1 - w)/\log(\rho)$ or $l = \lfloor \delta n \rfloor$, where $\delta = \log(1 - w)/c$ is a fixed positive constant if $c < 0$. For higher-order AR models with a root near unity, Rossi (2005) showed that $l = \lfloor \delta n \rfloor + o(1)$. Therefore, the order of the polynomial constraint increases linearly with the sample size as the process approaches the unit root boundary.

For this reason, we adopt the parameterization $l = \lfloor \delta n \rfloor$ for some fixed $\delta > 0$ which has been used previously in the literature for impulse response analysis and long-horizon forecasting of nearly nonstationary processes (Stock, 1996; Phillips, 1998; Gospodinov, 2002a; Rossi, 2005). This nesting, which bears a strong resemblance to the many instruments parameterization in section 6.2.3, allows the asymptotic approximation to preserve parameter estimation uncertainty present in the finite sample distribution. By contrast, in the fixed forecast horizon case, parameter estimation uncertainty vanishes asymptotically as n goes to ∞.

Now consider the estimation of the parameters in model (6.12) with $\rho_n = 1 + c/n$ imposing the restriction that θ_l is equal to a particular value $\theta_{0,l}$, where $l = \lfloor \delta n \rfloor$. Interestingly, Gospodinov (2004) shows that the restricted estimator of ρ is converging at a faster rate ($n^{3/2}$-consistency) than the (n-consistent) unrestricted estimator. As a result, the localizing constant c can be consistently estimated under the imposed restriction. The result appears to be driven by the parameterization of the lead time of the impulse response as a function of the sample size. This parameterization forces the parameter on the (near-) nonstationary component to satisfy a highly nonlinear polynomial constraint whose degree increases with the sample size, which in turn accelerates the rate of convergence of the estimator.

To illustrate this result, consider the AR(2) model

$$y_t = \rho y_{t-1} + \varphi \triangle y_{t-1} + e_t.$$

We can rewrite this model as

$$\begin{pmatrix} y_t \\ \triangle y_t \end{pmatrix} = \begin{pmatrix} \rho & \varphi \\ \rho - 1 & \varphi \end{pmatrix} \begin{pmatrix} y_{t-1} \\ \triangle y_{t-1} \end{pmatrix} + \begin{pmatrix} e_t \\ e_t \end{pmatrix}$$

or

$$Y_t = \Lambda Y_{t-1} + \bar{e}_t.$$

Then, $Y_{t+l} = \Lambda^{l+1} Y_{t-1} + \Lambda^l \bar{e}_t + \Lambda^{l-1} \bar{e}_{t+1} + ... + \bar{e}_{t+l}$ and the impulse response at lead time l is

$$\theta_l \equiv \frac{\partial y_{t+l}}{\partial e_t} = (1, 0) \Lambda^l \begin{pmatrix} 1 \\ 1 \end{pmatrix}.$$

Since $\rho - 1 = c/n = o_P(1)$,

$$(1,0) \begin{pmatrix} \rho & \varphi \\ o_P(1) & \varphi \end{pmatrix}^l \begin{pmatrix} 1 \\ 1 \end{pmatrix}$$

$$= (1,0) \begin{pmatrix} \rho^l + o_P(1) & \rho^{l-1}\varphi + \rho^{l-2}\varphi^2 + \ldots + \varphi^l + o_P(1) \\ o_P(1) & \varphi^l + o_P(1) \end{pmatrix} \begin{pmatrix} 1 \\ 1 \end{pmatrix}$$

$$= \rho^l + \rho^{l-1}\varphi + \rho^{l-2}\varphi^2 + \ldots + \varphi^l + o_P(1)$$

$$= \rho^l \left(1 + \frac{\varphi}{\rho} + \ldots + \left(\frac{\varphi}{\rho} \right)^l \right) + o_P(1).$$

Further, if $l = \lfloor \delta n \rfloor$ and as $n \to \infty$, we have that $\rho^l = \exp(c\delta)$, $1 + \varphi/\rho + \ldots + (\varphi/\rho)^l = \rho/(\rho - \varphi) = (1 - \varphi)^{-1} + o_P(1)$ and $\theta_l \to (1 - \varphi)^{-1} \exp(c\delta)$ (Rossi, 2005).

Let $\tilde{c}$ and $\tilde{\varphi}$ denote the restricted OLS estimates of c and φ subject to the constraint $\theta_l = \theta_{0,l}$. Then, it follows from the expression above that the restricted estimate $\tilde{c}$ is a nonlinear function of $\tilde{\varphi}$,

$$\tilde{c} = \frac{\log(\theta_{0,l}(1 - \tilde{\varphi}))}{\delta} \equiv g(\tilde{\varphi}).$$

Taking a first-order Taylor series expansion of $\tilde{c}$ about c, we have

$$\sqrt{n} \, (\tilde{c} - c) = \frac{\partial g(\varphi)}{\partial \varphi} \sqrt{n} \, (\tilde{\varphi} - \varphi_0) + o_P(1),$$

i.e., the estimator of $\tilde{c}$ has to share the rate of convergence of the estimator $\tilde{\varphi}$. Gospodinov (2004) further develops an asymptotic procedure for constructing pointwise confidence bands for impulse responses based on inverting the $\mathcal{LR}$ test.

A related model framework arises in the context of conditional forecasting of local-to-unity processes at long horizons. To introduce the main idea, consider the zero-mean AR(1) model

$$y_t = \rho y_{t-1} + e_t, \quad t = 1, 2, \ldots, n.$$

Suppose we are interested in constructing forecasts for the future value y_{n+l} conditional on the last observation y_n when ρ is near one, parameterized as $\rho_n = 1 + c/n$, and l is a nontrivial fraction of the sample size, parameterized as $l = \lfloor \lambda n \rfloor$.

In AR models, the dependence between the data used for estimation and the data used for prediction introduces some difficulties in assessing the effects of parameter variability and the properties of the estimators on forecasts (Phillips, 1979). Unlike the stationary case, the dependence between $\hat{\rho}$ and y_n does not vanish asymptotically for AR processes with a root on or near the unit circle. This can be seen from the joint limiting representations of the OLS estimator of ρ and the last observed value of the series, which is given by (Phillips, 1987)

$$
\left(n(\hat{\rho} - \rho), n^{-1/2} y_n \right) \Rightarrow \left(\frac{1}{2} \frac{J_c(1)^2 - J_c(0)^2 - 2c \int_0^1 J_c(s)^2 ds - 1}{\int_0^1 J_c(s)^2 ds}, J_c(1) \right).
$$

Let the true l-step ahead future value of y be denoted by

$$
y_{n+l} = \rho^l y_n + \sum_{j=0}^{l-1} \rho^j e_{n+l-j},
$$

the true conditional mean by $\bar{y}_{n+l|n} = E\left[y_{n+l}|y_n\right] = \rho^l y_n$ and the predictive conditional mean by $\hat{y}_{n+l|n} = \hat{\rho}^l y_n$, where $\hat{\rho}$ is the OLS estimator. The objective is to approximate the distributions of $\hat{y}_{n+k|n} - \bar{y}_{n+k|n}$ and the forecast errors $\hat{y}_{n+k|n} - y_{n+k}$, conditional on the value of y_n. Since y_n is $O_P(n^{1/2})$, it diverges as $n \to \infty$. Thus, it will be more appropriate to condition on the rescaled terminal value $n^{-1/2} y_n = x$.

The conditional asymptotic representation of the appropriately normalized difference $\hat{y}_{n+k|n} - \bar{y}_{n+k|n}$ is given by (Gospodinov, 2002a)

$$
\left(n^{-1/2} \left(\hat{y}_{n+k|n} - \bar{y}_{n+k|n} \right) | x \right)
$$

$$
\Rightarrow \exp(\lambda c) \left(\exp \left(\frac{\lambda}{2} \frac{x^2 - J_c(0)^2 - 2c \int_0^1 J_{c|x}(s)^2 ds - 1}{\int_0^1 J_{c|x}(s)^2 ds} \right) - 1 \right) x,
$$

where $J_{c|x}(r)$ is the path consistent with the scaled terminal value x. The conditional limiting representation of the normalized forecast errors

$$
n^{-1/2} \left(\hat{y}_{n+k|n} - y_{n+k} \right)
$$

has an additional term $\mathcal{N}\left(0, (\exp(2c\lambda) - 1)/2c\right)$ (Gospodinov, 2002a).

These limiting results are obtained when the lead time l is modeled as a fraction of the sample size, i.e., it approaches infinity at the same rate as n. Letting the forecast horizon grow linearly with the sample size is better suited for long-term forecasting. As in the impulse response example, this parameterization also allows the asymptotic approximation to preserve the parameter estimation uncertainty present in the finite sample distribution, whereas in the fixed forecast horizon case this uncertainty vanishes asymptotically as l/n goes to 0. Since the limiting distribution depends on c, which is not consistently estimable, Gospodinov (2002a) proposed a conditional grid bootstrap method and established its asymptotic validity under the local-to-unity and long-horizon parameterizations.

Finally, there are other setups in which the drifting parameterization $\lfloor \delta n \rfloor$ proves useful. For instance, the standard approach to heteroskedasticity and autocorrelation consistent (HAC) variance-covariance estimation, reviewed in section 1.3 of Chapter 1, requires that the bandwidth parameter $b \to \infty$ as $n \to \infty$ but $b/n \to 0$. It is well documented, however, that the finite sample properties of the t-statistic that employs this conventional HAC estimator are rather poor when the serial correlation is strong. Kiefer and Vogelsang (2005) propose an alternative approximation that adopts the asymptotic nesting $b = \lfloor \delta n \rfloor$ for $\delta \in (0, 1]$. In this framework, the HAC variance estimator converges weakly to a random variable which gives rise to a non-standard asymptotic distribution of the t- and F statistics. Kiefer and Vogelsang (2005) demonstrate substantial improvements in the finite sample size properties of the t-test based on this alternative approximation.

6.3.3 Nearly Non-Invertible Moving Average Processes and Local-to-Zero Signal-to-Noise Ratio

The local-to-unity and local-to-zero parameterizations also play an important role for modeling nearly non-invertible and nearly constant local level models. To introduce the main ideas, consider the stochastic process $\{y_t\}_{t=1}^n$ generated from the first-order moving average (MA(1)) model

$$y_t = e_t - \theta e_{t-1},$$

where $|\theta| \le 1$ and $e_t \sim IID(0, \sigma^2)$ with $E[e_t^4] < \infty$.

Let θ be the parameter of interest and η denote a possibly infinite dimensional nuisance parameter vector that completely characterizes the distribution of e. If $|\theta|$ is strictly less than one, the process y_t is invertible and the maximum likelihood (ML) estimator of θ is asymptotically normally distributed with mean θ and variance $(1 - \theta^2)/n$. When θ is close to the unit circle, the Gaussian distribution provides a rather inaccurate approximation to the limiting behavior of the ML estimator. Moreover, in finite samples the estimator takes values exactly on the boundary of the invertibility region with positive probability ("pile-up" effect) when the true MA parameter is in the vicinity of one. The observed point probability mass at unity results from the symmetry of the likelihood function around one and the small sample deficiency to identify all critical points near the unit circle.

The distribution of the ML estimator of θ in the presence of an MA unit root is nonstandard and has been derived by Davis and Dunsmuir (1996). Recasting the MA parameter into a local-to-unity form, $\theta_n = 1 + c/n$ for a finite constant $c \le 0$, provides a useful framework for analyzing the limiting behavior of the ML estimator and allows a smooth transition from the normal approximation to the asymptotic distribution in the non-invertible case.

A very flexible reparameterization of the MA(1) model is given by the local level model:

$$x_t = \alpha_t + u_t,$$
$$\alpha_t = \alpha_{t-1} + \tau \xi_t,$$

where α_t is an unobserved, time-varying parameter, u_t and ξ_t are mutually uncorrelated white noise disturbances, and τ is the signal-to-noise ratio.

Taking differences and defining $\Delta x_t = y_t$, we obtain $y_t = \tau \xi_t + \Delta u_t$. It is straightforward to show that this model possesses the same autocorrelation structure as the restricted MA(1) model $\triangle x_t = e_t - \theta e_{t-1}$ with the constraint that $0 \le \theta \le 1$. In fact, there exists a one-to-one mapping between the parameters of the two representations τ and θ; namely, $\tau = \sqrt{(1-\theta)^2/\theta}$ and $\theta = (\tau^2 + 2 - \sqrt{\tau^4 + 4\tau^2})/2$, which are monotonic in θ and τ, respectively. This implies that testing for an MA unit root $\theta = 1$ is equivalent to testing for constancy of α, that is, $H_0 : \tau = 0$ against $H_1 : \tau > 0$. The local-to-unity parameterization of the MA parameter $\theta_n = 1 + c/n$ in the restricted MA(1) model corresponds to a local-to-zero parameterization of the signal-to-noise ratio $\tau_n = \lambda/n$ in the local level model. Gospodinov (2002b) proposed a bootstrap method for confidence interval construction and median unbiased estimation of θ and τ and established its validity under the local-to-unity and local-to-zero nesting.

6.3.4   Possibly Cointegrated Models with Local-to-Zero Error Variance

The drifting parameterizations introduced above also prove useful in the analysis of multivariate processes. Consider the triangular system

$$y_t = \beta x_t + u_{y,t}, \tag{6.16}$$
$$x_t = u_{x,t},$$

and

$$\begin{pmatrix} (1-\rho L)u_{y,t} \\ (1-L)u_{x,t} \end{pmatrix} = \begin{pmatrix} \varepsilon_{y,t} \\ \varepsilon_{x,t} \end{pmatrix},$$

where $(\varepsilon_{y,t}, \varepsilon_{x,t})'$ is a vector of IID random variables with mean zero. Higher-order AR dynamics in the errors, higher-dimensional systems and presence of deterministic components are not explicitly considered for presentational simplicity. Note that the case of no cointegration between y_t and x_t arises when $\rho = 1$ while y_t and x_t are cointegrated if $-1 < \rho < 1$. Now suppose that $\mathrm{var}(\varepsilon_{y,t}) \ll \mathrm{var}(\varepsilon_{x,t})$, where $\mathrm{var}(\varepsilon_{x,t}) = 1$, for simplicity.

This modeling framework can be motivated in the context of forward premium regressions that describe the dynamics of the spot and 1-month forward exchange rates and their difference (forward premium). Despite the voluminous literature on testing for cointegration between spot and forward exchange rates, the plot of their dynamic behavior over time clearly reveals that these two series follow each other extremely closely and do not exhibit any tendency to drift apart. At the same time, the high persistence (near unit root behavior) in the marginal process of the cointegrated errors could often lead to statistical rejections of the cointegration hypothesis that may create tension with economic intuition. The joint process, however, suggests that the possibly unit root component is so small that it does not cause the variables to deviate over a reasonably long horizon. So how do we model and analyze this system? In order to mimic the observed characteristics of the data, we resort to and combine some of the drifting parameterizations discussed above.

To capture the high persistence and small variance of the cointegrated errors (forward premium), $u_{y,t}$ is parameterized as a dampened near-unit root process. It involves the dual localization

$$\rho_n = 1 + \frac{c}{n}$$

for some fixed constant $c \leq 0$ (local-to-unity process) and

$$\varepsilon_{y,t} = \tau v_t, \ \tau = \frac{\lambda}{\sqrt{n}}$$

for some fixed constant $\lambda > 0$ and $v_t \sim IID(0,1)$.

Let $\{(V_1(r), V_2(r))' : r \in [0,1]\}$ be a bivariate Brownian motion with correlation δ. It is interesting to note that even though $u_{y,t}$ is near-integrated, it is a bounded stochastic process

$$u_{y,t} = \frac{\lambda}{\sqrt{n}} \sum_{i=1}^{t} \left(1 + \frac{c}{n}\right)^{t-i} v_i$$
$$\Rightarrow \lambda J_c(r),$$

where $J_c(r)$ is an Ornstein–Uhlenbeck process generated by the stochastic differential equation $dJ_c(r) = cJ_c(r)dr + dV_2(r)$.

We now investigate the effects of this parameterization on the properties of the estimators in the cointegrated model (6.16). Using a control variable approach, an efficient estimator of β can be obtained from the regression

$$y_t = \beta x_t + \omega \triangle x_t + e_t,$$

where ω is the regression coefficient of $u_{y,t}$ on $\varepsilon_{x,t}$ and e_t are errors in this regression. The OLS estimator of β from this regression is equivalent to the MLE (Phillips, 1991).

Then, the estimator $\hat{\beta}$ is asymptotically distributed as (Gospodinov, 2009a,b)

$$\sqrt{n}\left(\hat{\beta} - \beta_0\right) \Rightarrow \lambda \frac{\int_0^1 J_c(s)V_1(s)ds}{\int_0^1 V_1(s)^2 ds}.$$

This estimator is consistent but its rate of convergence is slower than n. Also, the conventional t-statistic of $H_0 : \beta = \beta_0$ diverges at rate $n^{1/2}$ as in spurious regressions.

The vector error-correction (VEC) representation of model (6.16) is given by

$$\begin{pmatrix} \triangle y_t \\ \triangle x_t \end{pmatrix} = (\rho - 1) \begin{pmatrix} 1 & -\beta \\ 0 & 0 \end{pmatrix} \begin{pmatrix} y_{t-1} \\ x_{t-1} \end{pmatrix} + \begin{pmatrix} 1 & \beta \\ 0 & 1 \end{pmatrix} \begin{pmatrix} \varepsilon_{y,t} \\ \varepsilon_{x,t} \end{pmatrix},$$

and the single-equation conditional VEC model (VECM) has the form

$$\triangle y_t = \gamma u_{y,t-1} + \bar{\omega} \triangle x_t + \varepsilon_{y,t}, \tag{6.17}$$

where $\gamma = \rho - 1$, and the null hypothesis of no cointegration is $H_0 : \gamma = 0$. Let $\tilde{\gamma}$ denote the OLS estimator of γ in (6.17).

Taking limits reveals that the asymptotic behavior of the estimator $\tilde{\gamma}$ in the conditional VECM is the same as in Hansen (1995) and Zivot (2000):

$$n\left(\tilde{\gamma} - \gamma\right) \Rightarrow \delta \frac{\int_0^1 J_c(s)dW_1(s)}{\int_0^1 J_c(s)^2 ds} + \sqrt{1 - \delta^2} \frac{\int_0^1 J_c(s)dV_2(s)}{\int_0^1 J_c(s)^2 ds}$$

and

$$t_{\tilde{\gamma}} \Rightarrow \delta \tilde{z} + \sqrt{1 - \delta^2} \frac{\int_0^1 J_c(s)dV_2(s)}{\left(\int_0^1 J_c(s)^2 ds\right)^{1/2}},$$

where $\tilde{z}$ is a standard normal random variable and W_1 is a standard Brownian motion independent of V_2.

It is often the case that the VECM is defined (for predictive purposes or as in the forward premium literature, for instance) as

$$\triangle y_t = \gamma u_{y,t-1} + \xi_t, \tag{6.18}$$

where $\gamma = \rho - 1$ and $\xi_t = \bar{\omega} \triangle x_t + \varepsilon_{y,t}$. Let $\hat{\gamma}$ denote the OLS estimator of γ in (6.18). In this case,

$$\sqrt{n}\left(\hat{\gamma} - \gamma\right) \Rightarrow \frac{1}{\lambda} \left(\delta \frac{\int_0^1 J_c(s)dV_2(s)}{\int_0^1 J_c(s)^2 ds} + \sqrt{1 - \delta^2} \frac{\int_0^1 J_c(s)dW_1(s)}{\int_0^1 J_c(s)^2 ds} \right)$$

and

$$t_{\hat{\gamma}} \Rightarrow \delta \frac{\int_0^1 J_c(s)dV_2(s)}{\left(\int_0^1 J_c(s)^2 ds\right)^{1/2}} + \sqrt{1 - \delta^2} \, \tilde{z}.$$

One difference between model (6.18) and the conditional model is the slower rate of convergence of the estimator. Also, unlike the conditional VECM, the localizing constant λ from the parameterization of the signal-to-noise ratio appears in the limiting distribution of the estimator. Since λ shows up in the denominator, values of λ close to zero make the estimator highly volatile. Finally, when $\delta \to 0$, the asymptotic distribution of the t-statistic in the unconditional VECM approaches the standard normal distribution, while in the conditional VECM, it approaches the Dickey–Fuller type of distribution. The result is the opposite when $\delta \to 1$.

Simulation results show that the bias of the estimator of β in the unconditional VECM can be very large and negative when the correlation between the error terms δ approaches one, while the estimator in the conditional VECM remains unbiased. Moreover, the variability of the unconditional estimator can exceed manyfold the variability of the conditional estimator and the t-test based on the unconditional estimator $\hat{\gamma}$ lacks power against the null hypothesis. For details, see Gospodinov (2009a,b).

6.3.5 Local-to-Unity and Weak Identification

This section illustrates that there exists a close connection between the local-to-unity and weak identification frameworks in structural time series models. To see this, consider the bivariate vector autoregressive (VAR) process $\tilde{y}_t = (y_{1,t}, y_{2,t})'$ of order $p + 1$

$$\Psi(L)(I_2 - \Phi L)\tilde{y}_t = u_t,$$

where the matrix Φ contains the largest roots of the system and

$$\Psi(L) = I_2 - \sum_{i=1}^{p} \Psi_i L^i = \begin{bmatrix} \psi_{11}(L) & \psi_{12}(L) \\ \psi_{21}(L) & \psi_{22}(L) \end{bmatrix}$$

is a p-order polynomial with roots outside the unit circle. The errors u_t are assumed to be a two-dimensional martingale difference sequence with $E[u_t u_t' | u_{t-1}, u_{t-2}, ...] = \Sigma > 0$ and $\sup_t E[\|u_t\|^{2+\xi}] < \infty$ for some $\xi > 0$, and the initial values are assumed fixed.

The matrix of largest roots Φ is parameterized as

$$\Phi_n = \begin{bmatrix} 1 & 0 \\ 0 & 1 + c/n \end{bmatrix} = I_2 + \frac{C}{n},$$

where

$$C = \begin{bmatrix} 0 & 0 \\ 0 & c \end{bmatrix}$$

and $c \leq 0$ is a fixed constant. The off-diagonal elements of Φ_n are set to 0 to rule out the case in which any of the two processes are (near-) $I(2)$ (Elliott, 1998; Phillips, 1988). The structure of the matrix also implies that the two processes are not cointegrated.

It proves useful to impose the exact unit root on the first variable so that $\triangle y_{1,t}$ is a stationary process. In this case, let $y_t = (\triangle y_{1,t}, y_{2,t})'$ and

$$D(L) = \Psi(L) \begin{bmatrix} 1 & 0 \\ 0 & 1 - (1 + c/n)L \end{bmatrix}.$$

Then, the reduced form VAR model is given by

$$D(L)y_t = u_t, \tag{6.19}$$

or

$$y_t = D_1 y_{t-1} + ... + D_{p+1} y_{t-p-1} + u_t.$$

Premultiplying both sides of (6.19) by the matrix

$$B_0 = \begin{bmatrix} 1 & -b_{12}^{(0)} \\ -b_{21}^{(0)} & 1 \end{bmatrix}$$

yields the structural VAR model

$$B(L)y_t = \varepsilon_t,$$

where $B(L) = B_0 D(L)$ and $\varepsilon_t = B_0 u_t$ denote the structural shocks $(\varepsilon_{1,t}, \varepsilon_{2,t})'$ which, following typical practice, are assumed to be orthogonal with variances $\sigma_{\varepsilon_1}^2$ and $\sigma_{\varepsilon_2}^2$. The long-run identifying restriction that the shocks ε_2 have no long-run effect on y_1 imposes a lower triangular structure on the moving average matrix $D(1)^{-1}B_0^{-1}$. Hence, under this identifying restriction, the matrix of long-run multipliers in the structural model, $B(1) = B_0 D(1)$, is also lower triangular.

For presentational purposes, let us simplify the model by assuming that $\Psi(L) = I_2$. The reduced form of this first-order model can be rewritten as

$$\triangle y_{1,t} = u_{1,t}, \tag{6.20}$$

$$y_{2,t} = \left(1 + \frac{c}{n}\right) y_{2,t-1} + u_{2,t}.$$

The structural form of the model is

$$\triangle y_{1,t} = b_{12}^{(0)} y_{2,t} + b_{12}^{(1)} y_{2,t-1} + \varepsilon_{1,t}, \tag{6.21}$$

$$y_{2,t} = b_{21}^{(0)} \triangle y_{1,t} + b_{22}^{(1)} y_{2,t-1} + \varepsilon_{2,t},$$

where $b_{12}^{(1)} = -b_{12}^{(0)}(1 + c/n)$ and $b_{22}^{(1)} = 1 + c/n$.

In order to identify the structural parameters of model (6.21) from the reduced form (6.20), we impose the long-run restriction that $B(1)$ is a lower triangular matrix. To be more precise, by adding and subtracting $b_{12}^{(0)} y_{2,t-1}$ from the first equation of (6.21) and imposing the long-run restriction that the long-run multiplier $b_{12}^{(0)} + b_{12}^{(1)}$ is zero, the first equation of the structural model reduces to

$$\triangle y_{1,t} = b_{12}^{(0)} \triangle y_{2,t} + \varepsilon_{1,t}. \tag{6.22}$$

Since $\triangle y_{2,t}$ is endogenous, the unknown parameter $b_{12}^{(0)}$ can be estimated by instrumental variables using $y_{2,t-1}$ as an instrument. The relationship between the endogenous variable and the instrument is given by the second equation of the reduced VAR (6.20)

$$\triangle y_{2,t} = \frac{c}{n} y_{2,t-1} + u_{2,t}. \tag{6.23}$$

Note that the local-to-unity parameterization automatically produces a local-to-zero correlation between the endogenous variable and the instrument. This bears some similarities with Staiger and Stock's (1997) analytical framework, discussed in section 6.2.1 of this chapter, but here the correlation between the endogenous regressor and the instrument shrinks to zero at rate n due to the (near-) nonstationarity.

After substituting (6.22) and (6.23) in the IV estimator of $b_{12}^{(0)}$,

$$\hat{b}_{12}^{(0)} = \frac{\sum_{t=2}^{n} y_{2,t-1} \triangle y_{1,t}}{\sum_{t=2}^{n} y_{2,t-1} \triangle y_{2,t}},$$

we have

$$\hat{b}_{12}^{(0)} - b_{12}^{(0)} = \frac{n^{-1} \sum_{t=2}^{n} y_{2,t-1}\varepsilon_{1,t}}{cn^{-2} \sum_{t=2}^{n} y_{2,t-1}^2 + n^{-1} \sum_{t=2}^{n} y_{2,t-1}u_{2,t}}.$$

The limiting distribution of the IV estimator of $b_{12}^{(0)}$ is given by (Gospodinov, 2010)

$$\hat{b}_{12}^{(0)} - b_{12}^{(0)} \Rightarrow \frac{\sigma_{\varepsilon_1}}{\sigma_{u_2}} \frac{\delta \int_0^1 J_c(s)dV_1(s) + \sqrt{1-\delta^2} \int_0^1 J_c(s)dV_2(s)}{c \int_0^1 J_c(s)^2 ds + \int_0^1 J_c(s)dV_1(s)},$$

where $V_1(r)$ and $V_2(r)$ are independent standard Brownian motions,

$$J_c(r) = \exp(cr) \int_0^r \exp(-cs)dV_1(s)$$

is an Ornstein–Uhlenbeck process, δ is the correlation coefficient between ε_1 and u_2, and $\sigma_{\varepsilon_1}/\sigma_{u_2}$ is the ratio of the standard deviations of ε_1 and u_2.

This result shows that the IV estimator of $b_{12}^{(0)}$ is inconsistent. The reason for the inconsistency is that $y_{2,t-1}$ is a weak instrument in the sense that it provides very little information about the endogenous variable $\triangle y_{2,t}$. This in turn arises from the highly persistent nature of the process $y_{2,t}$, which in this chapter is modeled as local-to-unity. Furthermore, the limiting distribution of $\hat{b}_{12}^{(0)} - b_{12}^{(0)}$ is nonstandard. First, the numerator of the limiting representation is a mixture of a Gaussian random variable and a functional of an Ornstein–Uhlenbeck process where the weights are determined by the correlation between the first structural shock and the reduced form errors from the second equation. Second, it is a ratio of two random variables since the denominator is also a random variable that involves functionals of the Ornstein–Uhlenbeck process.

It is instructive to consider the situation when $y_{2,t}$ approaches an exact unit root process ($c \to 0$). In this case, the distribution of $\hat{b}_{12}^{(0)} - b_{12}^{(0)}$ has a limit

$$\frac{\sigma_{\varepsilon_1}}{\sigma_{u_2}} \left(\delta + \sqrt{1-\delta^2} \frac{\int_0^1 V_1(s)dV_2(s)}{\int_0^1 V_1(s)dV_1(s)} \right).$$

Furthermore, if $\delta = 1$, the limiting distribution of $\hat{b}_{12}^{(0)} - b_{12}^{(0)}$ approaches a point probability mass at the constant $\sigma_{\varepsilon_1}/\sigma_{u_2}$. At the other extreme, if $\delta = 0$, the asymptotic distribution of $\hat{b}_{12}^{(0)} - b_{12}^{(0)}$ converges to a random variable that is a ratio of a standard normal $\left(\int_0^1 V_1^2(s)ds\right)^{-1/2}\int_0^1 V_1(s)dV_2(s)$ and Dickey–Fuller $\left(\int_0^1 V_1^2(s)ds\right)^{-1/2}\int_0^1 V_1(s)dV_1(s)$ distributed random variables.

The asymptotic distributions of the estimators of the remaining structural parameters and impulse response function can be obtained using similar arguments (Gospodinov, 2010). It turns out that the weak instrument problem that causes inconsistency in $\hat{b}_{12}^{(0)}$ also contaminates the estimation of $b_{21}^{(0)}$ and impulse response functions and renders them inconsistent. For more details and an improved inference procedure, see Gospodinov (2010).

6.4   Appendix: Solutions to Selected Exercises

Exercise 6.2. This exercise is based on Hahn and Kuersteiner (2002). Irrespective of δ, we have $n^{-1}\sum_{i=1}^n z_i^2 \xrightarrow{p} M_{zz}$, and $n^{-1/2}\sum_{i=1}^n z_i e_i \xrightarrow{d} M_{zz}^{1/2}\xi_1$. Next,

$$\sum_{i=1}^n z_i x_i = cn^{-\delta}\sum_{i=1}^n z_i^2 + \sum_{i=1}^n z_i u_i,$$

so the suitable normalization is

$$n^{\delta-1}\sum_{i=1}^n z_i x_i = cn^{-1}\sum_{i=1}^n z_i^2 + n^{\delta-1}\sum_{i=1}^n z_i u_i.$$

Then,

$$\hat{\theta} - \theta_0 = \frac{n^{\delta-1}}{n^{-1/2}}\frac{n^{-1/2}\sum_{i=1}^n z_i e_i}{cn^{-1}\sum_{i=1}^n z_i^2 + n^{\delta-1}\sum_{i=1}^n z_i u_i},$$

and, thus asymptotically, $\hat{\theta} - \theta_0$ is equal in distribution to

$$n^{\delta-1/2}\frac{\xi_1}{cM_{zz}^{1/2} + n^{\delta-1/2}\xi_2}.$$

The three cases are:

(i) When $0 \le \delta < \frac{1}{2}$, the asymptotics is close to the conventional one and is given by

$$n^{1/2-\delta}\left(\hat{\theta} - \theta_0\right) \xrightarrow{d} \frac{\xi_1}{cM_{zz}^{1/2}} \sim \mathcal{N}\left(0, \frac{1}{c^2 M_{zz}}\right).$$

The 2SLS estimator is consistent, asymptotically normal, but the rate of convergence is $n^{1/2-\delta}$. The implied approximate distribution is

$$\mathcal{N}\left(0, \frac{n^{2\delta-1}}{c^2 M_{zz}}\right)$$

or

$$\mathcal{N}\left(0, \frac{1}{n\pi^2 M_{zz}}\right),$$

which is the same as the standard asymptotics would predict.

(ii) When $\delta = \frac{1}{2}$, we have the standard weak instrument asymptotics:

$$\hat{\theta} - \theta_0 \xrightarrow{d} \frac{\xi_1}{cM_{zz}^{1/2} + \xi_2}.$$

The 2SLS estimator is inconsistent and has a random limit.

(iii) When $\delta > \frac{1}{2}$, we have

$$\hat{\theta} - \theta_0 \xrightarrow{d} \frac{\xi_1}{\xi_2}.$$

The 2SLS estimator is again inconsistent and has a random limit which is equal to one in the case of irrelevant instruments (i.e., when $c = 0$).

Exercise 6.3. Consider the simplified model (6.1). The $\mathcal{AR}$ test statistic under the alternative hypothesis is

$$\mathcal{AR} = \frac{n - \ell}{n} \frac{n^{-1/2}\left((\theta_A - \theta_0)x + e\right)' Z \left(n^{-1}Z'Z\right)^{-1} n^{-1/2} Z' \left((\theta_A - \theta_0)x + e\right)}{n^{-1}\left((\theta_A - \theta_0)x + e\right)' \left(I_n - Z(Z'Z)^{-1}Z'\right)\left((\theta_A - \theta_0)x + e\right)}.$$

The denominator has the following limit:

$$n^{-1}\left((\theta_A - \theta_0)x + e\right)' \left(I_n - Z(Z'Z)^{-1}Z'\right)\left((\theta_A - \theta_0)x + e\right)$$
$$\xrightarrow{p} (\theta_A - \theta_0)^2 + 2(\theta_A - \theta_0)\rho + 1,$$

since the part associated with $Z(Z'Z)^{-1}Z'$ is zero in the limit. The numerator has the following limit:

$$n^{-1/2}\left((\theta_A - \theta_0)x + e\right)' Z \left(n^{-1}Z'Z\right)^{-1} n^{-1/2} Z' \left((\theta_A - \theta_0)X + e\right)$$
$$\xrightarrow{p} \left((\theta_A - \theta_0)(M_{zz}c + M_{zz}^{1/2}\xi_2) + M_{zz}^{1/2}\xi_1\right)' M_{zz}^{-1}$$
$$\times \left((\theta_A - \theta_0)(M_{zz}c + M_{zz}^{1/2}\xi_2) + M_{zz}^{1/2}\xi_1\right).$$

So, under the alternative hypothesis in the weak instrument asymptotic framework, the $\mathcal{AR}$ statistic has a stochastic limit

$$\varkappa = \frac{\left((\theta_A - \theta_0)(M_{zz}^{1/2}c + \xi_2) + \xi_1\right)'\left((\theta_A - \theta_0)(M_{zz}^{1/2}c + \xi_2) + \xi_1\right)}{(\theta_A - \theta_0)^2 + 2(\theta_A - \theta_0)\rho + 1}$$

which follows a non-central chi-square distribution and consequently $\Pr\{\varkappa > \tau_{1-\alpha}^{\chi_l^2}\} \nrightarrow 1$. Thus, the $\mathcal{AR}$ test is inconsistent against fixed alternatives.

Exercise 6.7. Note that

$$\hat{\theta}_k = \theta + \frac{(1-k)\,x'e + kx'P_Ze}{(1-k)\,x'x + kx'P_Zx}.$$

In the many instruments asymptotic framework,

$$\frac{x'e}{n} \xrightarrow{p} \sigma_{12}, \quad \frac{x'P_Ze}{n} \xrightarrow{p} \lambda\sigma_{12}, \quad \frac{x'x}{n} \xrightarrow{p} Q + \sigma_2^2 \quad \text{and} \quad \frac{X'P_ZX}{n} \xrightarrow{p} Q + \lambda\sigma_2^2.$$

Hence,

$$\hat{\theta}_k \xrightarrow{p} \theta + \frac{((1-k)+k\lambda)\,\sigma_{12}}{Q + ((1-k)+k\lambda)\,\sigma_2^2}.$$

It can be easily seen that the estimator is consistent when $k = 1/(1-\lambda)$. In this case, it is equivalent to the "bias-corrected 2SLS" in Exercise 6.6.

References

Anatolyev, S. (2004) Inference when a nuisance parameter is weakly identified under the null hypothesis. *Economics Letters*, 84, 245–254.

Anatolyev, S. (2011) Instrumental variables estimation and inference in the presence of many exogenous regressors. Unpublished Manuscript, New Economic School.

Anatolyev, S. (2012) Inference in regression models with many regressors. *Journal of Econometrics*, forthcoming.

Anatolyev, S., and N. Gospodinov (2011) Specification testing in models with many instruments. *Econometric Theory*, 27, 427–441.

Anderson, T.W., N. Kunimoto and Y. Matsushita (2010) On the asymptotic optimality of the LIML estimator with possibly many instruments. *Journal of Econometrics*, 157, 191–204.

Anderson, T.W., and H. Rubin (1949) Estimation of the parameters of a single equation in a complete system of stochastic equations. *Annals of Mathematical Statistics*, 20, 46–63.

Andrews, D.W.K. (1993) Exactly median-unbiased estimation of first order autoregressive / unit root models. *Econometrica*, 61, 139–165.

Andrews, D.W.K., M.J. Moreira and J.H. Stock (2006) Optimal two-sided invariant similar tests for instrumental variables regression. *Econometrica*, 74, 715–752.

Andrews, D.W.K., and J.H. Stock (2007) Testing with many weak instruments. *Journal of Econometrics*, 138, 24–46.

Angrist, J.D., G.W. Imbens and A. Kruger (1999) Jackknife instrumental variables estimation. *Journal of Applied Econometrics*, 14, 57–67.

Bai, J. (1997) Estimation of a change point in multiple regressions. *Review of Economics and Statistics*, 79, 551–563.

Bekker, P.A. (1994) Alternative approximations to the distributions of instrumental variable estimators. *Econometrica*, 62, 657–681.

Berndt, E.R., and N.E. Savin (1977) Conflict among criteria for testing hypotheses in the multivariate linear regression model. *Econometrica*, 45, 1263–1277.

Caner, M. (2008) Nearly-singular design in GMM and generalized empirical likelihood estimators. *Journal of Econometrics*, 144, 511–523.

Chan, K.S. (1993) Consistency and limiting distribution of the least squares estimator of a threshold autoregressive model. *Annals of Statistics*, 21, 520–533.

Chan, N.H., and C.Z. Wei (1987) Asymptotic inference for nearly nonstationary AR(1) processes. *Annals of Statistics*, 15, 1050–1063.

Chao, J., and N. Swanson (2005) Consistent estimation with a large number of weak instruments. *Econometrica*, 73, 1673–1692.

Davis, R.A., and W.T.M. Dunsmuir (1996) Maximum likelihood estimation for MA(1) processes with a root on or near the unit circle. *Econometric Theory*, 12, 1–29.

Donald, S.G., G.W. Imbens and W.K. Newey (2003) Empirical likelihood estimation and consistent tests with conditional moment restrictions. *Journal of Econometrics*, 117, 55–93.

Dufour, J. M. (1997) Some impossibility theorems in econometrics, with applications to structural and dynamic models. *Econometrica*, 65, 1365-1387.

Dufour, J.M., and M. Taamouti (2007) Further results on projection-based inference in IV regressions with weak, collinear or missing instruments. *Journal of Econometrics*, 139, 133–153.

Elliott, G. (1998) On the robustness of cointegration methods when regressors almost have unit roots. *Econometrica*, 66, 149–158.

Fuller, W.A. (1977) Some properties of a modification of the limited information estimator. *Econometrica*, 45, 939–954.

Gospodinov, N. (2002a) Median unbiased forecasts for highly persistent autoregressive processes. *Journal of Econometrics*, 111, 85–101.

Gospodinov, N. (2002b) Bootstrap-based inference in models with a nearly noninvertible moving average component. *Journal of Business & Economic Statistics*, 20, 254–268.

Gospodinov, N. (2004) Asymptotic confidence intervals for impulse responses of near-integrated processes. *Econometrics Journal*, 7, 505–527.

Gospodinov, N. (2009a) A new look at the forward premium puzzle. *Journal of Financial Econometrics*, 7, 312–338.

Gospodinov, N. (2009b) Inference in nearly cointegrated systems. Unpublished Manuscript, Concordia University.

Gospodinov, N. (2010) Inference in nearly nonstationary SVAR models with long-run identifying restrictions. *Journal of Business & Economic Statistics*, 28, 1–12.

Hahn, J., and J. Hausman (2002) A new specification test for the validity of instrumental variables. *Econometrica*, 70, 163–189.

Hahn, J., and G. Kuersteiner (2002) Discontinuities of weak instrument limiting distributions. *Economics Letters*, 75, 325–331.

Hansen, B.E. (1995) Rethinking the univariate approach to unit root tests: How to use covariates to increase power. *Econometric Theory*, 11, 1148–1171.

Hansen, B.E. (1996) Inference when a nuisance parameter is not identified under the null hypothesis. *Econometrica*, 64, 413–430.

Hansen, B.E. (1997) Inference in TAR models. *Studies in Nonlinear Dynamics & Econometrics*, 2, 1–14.

Hansen, B.E. (1999) The grid bootstrap and the autoregressive model. *Review of Economics and Statistics*, 81, 594–607.

Hansen, B.E. (2000) Sample splitting and threshold estimation. *Econometrica*, 68, 575–603.

Hansen, L.P. (1982) Large sample properties of generalized method of moments estimators. *Econometrica*, 50, 1029–1054.

Hansen, L.P., and K.J. Singleton (1982) Generalized instrumental variables estimation of nonlinear rational expectations models. *Econometrica*, 50, 1269–1286.

Hansen, C., J. Hausman and W.K. Newey (2008) Estimation with many instrumental variables. *Journal of Business & Economic Statistics*, 26, 398–422.

Hausman, J., J.H. Stock and M. Yogo (2005) Asymptotic properties of the Hahn–Hausman test for weak instruments. *Economics Letters*, 89, 333–342.

Kiefer, N.M., and T.J. Vogelsang (2005) A new asymptotic theory for heteroskedasticity-autocorrelation robust tests. *Econometric Theory*, 21, 1130–1164.

Kleibergen, F.R. (2002) Pivotal statistics for testing structural parameters in instrumental variables regression. *Econometrica*, 70, 1781–1803.

Knight, K. (2008) Shrinkage estimation for nearly singular designs. *Econometric Theory*, 24, 323–337.

Mikusheva, A. (2007) Uniform inference in autoregressive models. *Econometrica*, 75, 1411–1452.

Mikusheva, A. (2010) Robust confidence sets in the presence of weak instruments. *Journal of Econometrics*, 157, 236–247.

Moreira, M.J. (2003) A conditional likelihood ratio test for structural models. *Econometrica*, 71, 1027–1048.

Newey, W.K. (2004) Many instrument asymptotics. Unpublished Manuscript, MIT.

Newey, W.K., and F. Windmeijer (2009) Generalized method of moments with many weak moment conditions. *Econometrica*, 77, 687–719.

Phillips, P.C.B. (1979) The sampling distribution of forecasts from a first-order autoregression. *Journal of Econometrics*, 9, 241–261.

Phillips, P.C.B. (1987) Towards a unified asymptotic theory for autoregression. *Biometrika*, 74, 535–547.

Phillips, P.C.B. (1988) Regression theory for near-integrated time series. *Econometrica*, 56, 1021–1043.

Phillips, P.C.B. (1991) Optimal inference in cointegrated systems. *Econometrica*, 59, 283–306.

Phillips, P.C.B. (1998) Impulse response and forecast error variance asymptotics in nonstationary VARs. *Journal of Econometrics*, 83, 21–56.

Rossi, B. (2005) Confidence intervals for half-life deviations from purchasing power parity. *Journal of Business & Economic Statistics*, 23, 432–442.

Rothenberg, T. (1984) Approximating the distributions of econometric estimators and test statistics. In: Z. Griliches and M. D. Intriligator (eds.), *Handbook of Econometrics*, Vol. 2, Elsevier: Amsterdam, Chapter 15, 881–935.

Staiger, D., and J.H. Stock (1997) Instrumental variables regression with weak instruments. *Econometrica*, 65, 557–586.

Stock, J.H. (1991) Confidence intervals for the largest autoregressive root in U.S. macroeconomic time series. *Journal of Monetary Economics*, 28, 435–459.

Stock, J.H. (1994) Unit roots, structural breaks and trends. In: R.F. Engle and D. McFadden (eds.), *Handbook of Econometrics*, Vol. 4, Elsevier: Amsterdam, Chapter 46, 2739–2841.

Stock, J.H. (1996) VAR, error-correction and pretest forecasts at long horizons. *Oxford Bulletin of Economics and Statistics*, 58, 685–701.

Stock, J.H. (1997) Cointegration, long-run comovements and long horizon forecasting. In: D. Kreps and K.F. Willis (eds.), *Advances in Econometrics: Proceedings of the Seventh World Congress of the Econometric Society*, Cambridge University Press: Cambridge, 34–60.

Stock, J.H., and M.W. Watson (2008) What's new in econometrics – time series. *NBER Summer Institute*.

Stock, J.H., and J.H. Wright (2000) GMM with weak identification. *Econometrica*, 68, 1055–1096.

Stock, J.H., J.H. Wright and M. Yogo (2002) A survey of weak instruments and weak identification in generalized method of moments. *Journal of Business & Economic Statistics*, 20, 518–529.

Stock, J.H., and M. Yogo (2005) Testing for weak instruments in linear IV regression. In: J.H. Stock and D.W.K. Andrews (eds.), *Identification and Inference for Econometric Models: Essays in Honor of Thomas J. Rothenberg*, Cambridge University Press: Cambridge, Chapter 5, 80–108.

van Hasselt, M. (2010) Many instruments asymptotic approximations under nonnormal error distributions. *Econometric Theory*, 26, 633–645.

Zivot, E. (2000) The power of single equation tests for cointegration when the cointegrating vector is prespecified. *Econometric Theory*, 16, 407–439.

Part IV

Appendix

Appendix A

Results from Linear Algebra, Probability Theory and Statistics

This Appendix provides a short review of some basic concepts and results from linear algebra, probability and distribution theory, statistics and time series analysis. Most of these results are adapted from and discussed in greater detail in Feller (1971), Amemiya (1985), Spanos (1986), Brockwell and Davis (1991), Hall (1992), Davidson (1994), Zaman (1996), White (2001) and Carrasco, Florens and Renault (2007).

A.1 Spaces and Norms

A.1.1 Inner Product Space

Definition (inner product space): An inner product space is a vector space $\mathbb{S}$ with an inner product of x and y, denoted by $\langle x, y \rangle$, such that

(i) $\langle x, x \rangle \geq 0$ for all $x \in \mathbb{S}$ with $\langle x, x \rangle = 0$ if and only if $x = 0$,

(ii) $\langle x, y \rangle = \overline{\langle y, x \rangle}$, where $\overline{\langle \cdot, \cdot \rangle}$ denotes the complex conjugate,

(iii) $\langle ax, y \rangle = a \langle x, y \rangle$ for all $x, y \in \mathbb{S}$ and $a \in \mathbb{C}$ ($a \in \mathbb{R}$),

(iv) $\langle x + y, z \rangle = \langle x, z \rangle + \langle y, z \rangle$ for all $x, y, z \in \mathbb{S}$.

A.1.2 Vector Norms

Definition (vector norm): The norm of an element x of an inner product space is defined as
$$|x| = \langle x, x \rangle^{1/2}.$$

Definition (Euclidean norm): The norm of the vector x in the Euclidean space $\mathbb{R}^m$ is defined as
$$|x| = \left(\sum_{i=1}^{m} x_i^2 \right)^{1/2}.$$

Definition (properties of norms): If $\mathbb{S}$ is an inner product space and $|x|$ is a norm as defined above, then

    (i) $|x| \geq 0$ for all $x \in \mathbb{S}$, with $|x| = 0$ if and only if $x = 0$,

    (ii) $|ax| = |a|\,|x|$ for all $x \in \mathbb{S}$ and $a \in \mathbb{C}$ ($a \in \mathbb{R}$),

    (iii) $|x + y| \leq |x| + |y|$ (triangle inequality) for all $x, y \in \mathbb{S}$.

Definition (convergence in norm): A sequence $\{x_n, n = 1, 2, ...\}$ is said to converge in norm to $x \in \mathbb{S}$ if

$$|x_n - x| \to 0 \text{ as } n \to \infty.$$

Definition (Cauchy sequence): A sequence $\{x_n, n = 1, 2, ...\}$ is said to be a Cauchy sequence if

$$|x_n - x_m| \to 0 \text{ as } m, n \to \infty.$$

Definition (complete inner product space): An inner product space $\mathbb{S}$ is complete if every Cauchy sequence $\{x_n\}$ of elements of this inner product space converges in norm to some element $x \in \mathbb{S}$.

A.1.3 Hilbert Space

Let π be the PDF of a distribution that is absolutely continuous with respect to Lebesgue measure on $\mathbb{R}^s$, admits all its moments and $\pi(\tau) > 0$ for all $\tau \in \mathbb{R}^s$. The Hilbert space is a complex inner product space

$$L^2(\pi) = \left\{ g : \mathbb{R}^s \to \mathbb{C} \mid \left(\int |g(\tau)|^2 \pi(\tau) d\tau \right)^{1/2} \right\}$$

which is complete in the induced norm. The inner product defined on $L^2(\pi)$ is given by

$$\langle f, g \rangle = \int f(\tau)\overline{g(\tau)}\pi(\tau)d\tau,$$

where $\overline{g(\tau)}$ denotes the complex conjugate of $g(\tau)$. The norm induced by the inner product $\langle \cdot, \cdot \rangle$ on $L^2(\pi)$ is the real-valued function

$$|g| = \langle g, g \rangle^{1/2}.$$

A.1.4 Matrix Norms

Definition (matrix norm): The norm of an $n \times m$ matrix is a functional $\|\cdot\|$ that satisfies

(i) $\|A\| \geq 0$ for all $A \in \mathbb{R}^{n \times m}$, with $\|A\| = 0$ if and only if $A = 0$,

(ii) $\|aA\| = |a|\,\|A\|$ for all $a \in \mathbb{R}$ and $A \in \mathbb{R}^{n \times m}$

(iii) $\|A + B\| \leq \|A\| + \|B\|$ (triangle inequality) for all $A, B \in \mathbb{R}^{n \times m}$.

Definition (Frobenius or Euclidean norm): The Frobenius norm (often referred to as the Euclidean norm in the econometric literature) of an $n \times m$ matrix A is defined as

$$\|A\| = \operatorname{tr}\left(A'A\right)^{1/2} = \left(\operatorname{vec}(A)'\operatorname{vec}(A)\right)^{1/2} = \left(\sum_{i=1}^{n}\sum_{j=1}^{m} a_{ij}^2\right)^{1/2}.$$

A.2 Matrix Notation and Definitions

Definition (null space of a matrix): The null space of matrix A is the space of all vectors x for which $Ax = 0$.

Definition (orthonormal matrix): An $n \times m$ matrix A is orthonormal if $A'A = I_m$.

Definition (projection matrix): Let A be an $n \times m$ matrix with rank m. The projection matrix associated with A is $P = A(A'A)^{-1}A'$.

Properties of projection matrix P:

(i) P is symmetric and idempotent, i.e., $P = P' = P^2$,

(ii) $\operatorname{rank}(P) = m$,

(iii) the eigenvalues of P consist of m ones and $n - m$ zeros,

(iv) if $x = Ac$ for some vector c, then $Px = x$,

(v) $M = I_n - P$ is idempotent with rank $n - m$, with the eigenvalues consisting of $n - m$ ones and m zeros, and if $x = Ac$, then $Mx = 0$,

(vi) P can be written as $G'G$, where G' is an orthonormal matrix.

Definition (differentiation of an inverse matrix): If a is an element of A,

$$\frac{\partial A^{-1}}{\partial a} = -A^{-1}\frac{\partial A}{\partial a}A^{-1}.$$

A.3   Inequalities

Cauchy–Schwartz inequality:

$$E|XY| \leq \left(E|X|^2\right)^{1/2} \left(E|Y|^2\right)^{1/2}.$$

Generalized Chebyshev's inequality: For $\varepsilon > 0$, $r > 0$ and $E|X|^r < \infty$,

$$\Pr\{|X| \geq \varepsilon\} \leq \frac{E|X|^r}{\varepsilon^r}.$$

When $r = 1$, we have Markov's inequality and when $r = 2$ we have the familiar form of Chebyshev's inequality.

Jensen's inequality: If $h(.)$ is a convex function and $E(X)$ exists, then

$$h[E(X)] \leq E[h(X)].$$

A.4   Some Distributional Results

Definition (chi-square distribution): Let z be a vector of n random variables distributed as $\mathcal{N}(0, I_n)$ and A be an $n \times n$ symmetric and idempotent matrix of rank n. Then,

$$z'Az \sim \chi_n^2,$$

where χ_n^2 denotes chi-square distribution with n degrees of freedom.

Definition (weighted chi-square distribution): Let x be a vector of n random variables distributed as $\mathcal{N}(0, \Omega)$, where $\mathrm{rk}(\Omega) \leq n$, and A be an $n \times n$ symmetric matrix. Then,

$$x'Ax \sim \sum_{i=1}^{n} \xi_i z_i^2,$$

where z_i are independent standard normal random variables and ξ_i $(i = 1, ..., n)$ are the eigenvalues of the matrix $A\Omega$.

A.5 Convergence of Sequences of Random Variables

A.5.1 Modes of Convergence

Definition (convergence in probability): A sequence of random variables $\{X_n\}$ converges to a random variable X in probability, $X_n \overset{p}{\to} X$, if for any $\varepsilon > 0$

$$\lim_{n \to \infty} \Pr\{|X_n - X| > \varepsilon\} = 0.$$

Definition (convergence in mean square): A sequence of random variables $\{X_n\}$ converges to a random variable X in mean square, $X_n \overset{m.s.}{\to} X$, if

$$\lim_{n \to \infty} E[(X_n - X)^2] = 0.$$

Theorem: $X_n \overset{m.s.}{\to} X \implies X_n \overset{p}{\to} X$.

Definition (convergence in L_p norm): A sequence of random variables $\{X_n\}$ converges to a random variable X in L_p norm, $X_n \overset{L_p}{\to} X$, if for some $p > 0$,

$$\lim_{n \to \infty} E\left[(|X_n - X|^p)\right] = 0.$$

Convergence in mean square is when $p = 2$.

Definition (almost sure convergence): A sequence of random variables $\{X_n\}$ converges to a random variable X almost surely, $X_n \overset{a.s.}{\to} X$, if

$$\Pr\left\{\lim_{n \to \infty} X_n = X\right\} = 1.$$

Theorem: $X_n \overset{a.s.}{\to} X \implies X_n \overset{p}{\to} X$.

Definition (convergence in distribution): A sequence of random variables $\{X_n\}$ with distribution functions $\{F_n\}$ converges in distribution to a random variable X with distribution function F, $X_n \overset{d}{\to} X$, if $F_n \to F$ at all continuity points of F.

Theorem: Let $\{X_n\}$ be a sequence of random variables with characteristic functions $\{\varphi_n(\lambda)\}$. If $X_n \overset{d}{\to} X$, then for every λ, $\varphi_n(\lambda) \to \varphi(\lambda)$. Further, if for every λ, $\varphi_n(\lambda) \to \varphi(\lambda)$ and $\varphi(\lambda)$ is continuous at $\lambda = 0$, then

$$X_n \overset{d}{\to} X.$$

Theorem: $X_n \overset{p}{\to} X \implies X_n \overset{d}{\to} X$.

A.5.2   Convergence of Functions

Definition (pointwise convergence): A sequence of functions $\{h_n(x)\}$ converges pointwise to a limit function $h(x)$, $h_n(x) \to h(x)$, if for each x

$$\lim_{n \to \infty} h_n(x) = h(x).$$

Definition (uniform convergence): A sequence of functions $\{h_n(x)\}$ is said to converge uniformly to a limit function $h(x)$ if

$$\lim_{n \to \infty} \sup_x |h_n(x) - h(x)| = 0.$$

Definition (stochastic equicontinuity): A sequence of functions $\{h_n(x)\}$ is said to be stochastically equicontinuous at x if for all $\varepsilon > 0$ and $\eta > 0$ there exists $\delta > 0$ such that

$$\lim_{n \to \infty} \Pr \left\{ \sup_{x \in B_\delta(x)} |h_n(x) - h(x)| > \eta \right\} < \varepsilon,$$

where $B_\delta(x)$ denotes a ball of radius δ about x.

Lemma: If $\lim_{n \to \infty} h_n(x) = h(x)$ for all x and $h_n(x)$ is stochastically equicontinuous, then

$$\lim_{n \to \infty} \sup_x |h_n(x) - h(x)| = 0.$$

A.5.3   Convergence of Transformations

Theorem (Mann–Wald): If $X_n \overset{d}{\to} X$ and $g(X)$ is continuous with probability 1, then,

$$g(X_n) \overset{d}{\to} g(X).$$

Theorem (Delta method): Let $\{a_n\}$ be a sequence of constants with $a_n \to \infty$ and $a_n(X_n - \beta) \overset{d}{\to} X$. If the function $g(.)$ is continuously differentiable at β and $\|\partial g(\beta)/\partial \beta'\| < \infty$, then

$$a_n \left(g(X_n) - g(\beta) \right) \overset{d}{\to} \frac{\partial g(\beta)}{\partial \beta'} X.$$

Theorem (Slutsky): If $X_n \overset{d}{\to} X$ and $Y_n \overset{p}{\to} \alpha$, where α is a constant, then

(i) $X_n + Y_n \overset{d}{\to} X + \alpha$

(ii) $X_n Y_n \overset{d}{\to} \alpha X$

(iii) $X_n / Y_n \overset{d}{\to} X / \alpha$, provided that $\alpha \neq 0$.

A.6 Orders of Magnitude

Let $\{a_n\}$ be a sequence of real numbers, $\{X_n\}$ be a sequence of random variables and $\{g_n\}$ be a sequence of positive real numbers. Then,

(i) a_n is of smaller order (in magnitude) than g_n, denoted $a_n = o(g_n)$, if

$$\lim_{n \to \infty} \frac{a_n}{g_n} = 0.$$

(ii) a_n is at most of order (in magnitude) g_n, denoted $a_n = O(g_n)$, if there exists a real number B such that $|a_n|/g_n \le B$ for all n.

(iii) X_n is of smaller order (in probability) than g_n, denoted $X_n = o_P(g_n)$, if

$$\frac{X_n}{g_n} \xrightarrow{p} 0.$$

(iv) X_n is at most of order (in probability) g_n, denoted $X_n = O_P(g_n)$, if there exists a nonstochastic sequence $\{c_n\}$ such that $c_n = O(1)$ and

$$\frac{X_n}{g_n} - c_n \xrightarrow{p} 0.$$

A.7 Laws of Large Numbers

Theorem (Kolmogorov): If $\{X_i\}$ is an *IID* sequence of random variables with $E|X_i| < \infty$, then

$$\bar{X} = \frac{1}{n} \sum_{i=1}^{n} X_i \xrightarrow{a.s.} E[X].$$

Theorem (Markov): If $\{X_i\}$ is a sequence of independent random variables with finite means $E(X_i) = \mu_i$ and for some $\delta > 0$, $\sum_{i=1}^{\infty} (E|X_i - \mu_i|^{1+\delta})/i^{1+\delta} < \infty$, then

$$\bar{X} - \bar{\mu} \xrightarrow{a.s.} 0,$$

where $\bar{\mu} = n^{-1} \sum_{i=1}^{n} \mu_i$.

Theorem (Glivenko–Cantelli): If $\{X_i\}$ is an *IID* sequence of random variables with empirical distribution function $\widehat{F}_n(x) = n^{-1} \sum_{i=1}^{n} \mathbb{I}\{X_i \le x\}$, where $\mathbb{I}\{\cdot\}$ is the indicator function, then

$$\sup_{x \in \mathbb{R}} \left| \widehat{F}_n(x) - F(x) \right| \xrightarrow{a.s.} 0.$$

Theorem (uniform weak law of large numbers): Let $\{X_i\}$ be an *IID* sequence of random variables and $f(X, \theta)$ be measurable in X for all $\theta \in \Theta$ and continuous in θ for almost all X. If $|f(X, \theta)| < B(X)$ with $E[B(X)] < \infty$ and Θ is compact, then

$$\sup_{\theta \in \Theta} \left| \frac{1}{n} \sum_{i=1}^{n} f(X_i, \theta) - E\left[f(X_i, \theta)\right] \right| \xrightarrow{p} 0.$$

A.8   Central Limit Theorems

Theorem (Lindeberg–Levy): If $\{X_i\}$ is an *IID* sequence of random variables with $E[X_i] = \mu$, $\operatorname{var}[X_i] = \sigma^2 < \infty$ and $\sigma^2 \neq 0$, then

$$\frac{\sqrt{n}\left(\bar{X} - \mu\right)}{\sigma} \xrightarrow{d} \mathcal{N}(0, 1).$$

Theorem: If $\{X_i\}$ is a sequence of independent random variables with $E[X_i] = \mu_i$, $\operatorname{var}[X_i] = \sigma_i^2 < \infty$, $\sigma_i^2 \neq 0$, $\bar{\sigma}^2 = n^{-1} \sum_{i=1}^{n} \sigma_i^2$ and distribution functions F_i, then

$$\frac{\sqrt{n}\left(\bar{X} - \bar{\mu}\right)}{\bar{\sigma}} \xrightarrow{d} \mathcal{N}(0, 1)$$

and

$$\lim_{n \to \infty} \max_{1 \le i \le n} \frac{\sigma_i^2}{\bar{\sigma}^2} = 0 \tag{A.1}$$

if and only if for every $\varepsilon > 0$,

$$\lim_{n \to \infty} \bar{\sigma}^{-2} n^{-1} \sum_{i=1}^{n} \int_{(x-\mu_i)^2 > \varepsilon n \bar{\sigma}^2} (x - \mu_i)^2 dF_i(x) = 0. \tag{A.2}$$

Condition (A.2), known in the literature as the Lindeberg condition, requires that the average contribution of the extreme tails to the variance of X_i is 0 in the limit. The Lindeberg condition implies the asymptotic negligibility condition in (A.1), which says that none of the variances of X_i, $1 \le i \le n$, dominates the variance of $\bar{X}$. Since the Lindeberg condition is difficult to verify in practice, it can be replaced by the slightly stronger but more intuitive condition $E |X_i - \mu_i|^{2+\delta} < \infty$ for some $\delta > 0$. This condition, called the Lyapunov condition, is sufficient for the Lindeberg condition to hold (see White, 2001).

The accuracy of the CLT is given by the following result.

Theorem (Berry–Esseen): Suppose that $X_1, ... X_n$ are $IID(0, \sigma^2)$ and $E|X_i|^3 = m_3 < \infty$. Let $\Phi(x)$ be the CDF of a standard normal random variable and $F_n(x)$ be the CDF of $(1/\sqrt{n}) \sum_{i=1}^{n} X_i/\sigma$. Then,

$$\sup_x |F_n(x) - \Phi(x)| \leq \frac{0.7975 m_3}{\sigma^3 \sqrt{n}}.$$

A.9   Characteristic and Cumulant Generating Functions

Definition (characteristic function): Let X be a random variable with probability distribution F and density f. The characteristic function of X is defined as $E \exp(i\lambda X)$ or

$$\varphi(\lambda) = \int_{-\infty}^{+\infty} \exp(i\lambda x) dF(x) \tag{A.3}$$

$$\varphi(\lambda) = \int_{-\infty}^{+\infty} \exp(i\lambda x) f(x) dx, \tag{A.4}$$

where $i = \sqrt{-1}$ and $\exp(i\lambda x) = \cos(\lambda x) + i \sin(\lambda x)$.

The expression in (A.4) is also known as the Fourier transform of $f(x)$. In general, the characteristic function is a complex number but for random variables with symmetric density around 0 it is a real number. The characteristic function always exists and is uniformly continuous. The characteristic function of $\mathcal{N}(0, 1)$ is $\exp(-\lambda^2/2)$.

Theorem: Distinct probability distributions have distinct characteristic functions.

Theorem (Fourier inversion): Let φ be the characteristic function of the distribution F and $|\varphi|$ be integrable over $(-\infty, +\infty)$. Then, F has a bounded continuous density f given by

$$f(x) = \frac{1}{2\pi} \int_{-\infty}^{+\infty} \exp(-i\lambda x) \varphi(\lambda) d\lambda.$$

Definition (cumulant generating function): The cumulant generating function of a random variable X is $\mathbb{K}(\lambda) = \log \varphi(\lambda)$, where log is the principal logarithm[1].

---

[1] The principal logarithm of a complex number $r \exp(i\theta)$ is defined as $\log(r) + i\theta$.

The series expansion of $\mathbb{K}(\lambda)$ about $\lambda = 0$ yields

$$\mathbb{K}(\lambda) = \kappa_1 i\lambda + \frac{1}{2}\kappa_2(i\lambda)^2 + ... + \frac{1}{j!}\kappa_j(i\lambda)^j + ...,$$

where $\kappa_j = \partial^j g(\lambda)/\partial\lambda^j\big|_{\lambda=0}/i^j$ is the jth cumulant of X and assuming that $g(\lambda)$ is differentiable at $\lambda = 0$.

A.10   Dependent Sequences

A.10.1   Stationarity and Ergodicity

Definition (strict stationarity): A stochastic process $\{X_t, t \in \mathbb{N}\}$ is strictly stationary if for any subset $(t_1, t_2, ..., t_k)$ of $\mathbb{N}$ and any real number h such that $t_i + h \in \mathbb{N}$,

$$F(X_{t_1}, X_{t_2}, ..., X_{t_k}) = F(X_{t_1+h}, X_{t_2+h}, ..., X_{t_k+h}),$$

where $F(.)$ is the joint distribution function of the k values.

Definition (weak stationarity): A stochastic process $\{X_t, t \in \mathbb{N}\}$ is weakly stationary if

(i) $E(X_{t_i}) = E(X_{t_i+h}) = \mu < \infty,$

(ii) $E(X_{t_i}^2) = E(X_{t_i+h}^2) = \mu_2 < \infty,$

(iii) $E(X_{t_i} X_{t_j}) = E(X_{t_i+h} X_{t_j+h}) = \mu_{ij} < \infty.$

Definition (ergodicity): A stationary process $\{X_t, t \in \mathbb{N}\}$ is ergodic if for any two bounded functions $f : \mathbb{R}^k \to \mathbb{R}$ and $g : \mathbb{R}^l \to \mathbb{R}$,

$$\lim_{n\to\infty} |E\left[f\left(X_t, ..., X_{t+k}\right) g\left(X_{t+n}, ..., X_{t+n+l}\right)\right]|$$

$$= |E\left[f\left(X_t, ..., X_{t+k}\right)\right]| \, |E\left[g\left(X_{t+n}, ..., X_{t+n+l}\right)\right]|.$$

Heuristically, ergodicity can be thought of as "asymptotic independence." In addition, if the process is Gaussian, a sufficient but not necessary condition for ergodicity is $\text{cov}(X_t, X_{t+h}) \to 0$ as $h \to \infty$.

Theorem (Birkhoff–Khinchin ergodic theorem): Let $\{X_t\}$ be a stationary ergodic sequence with $E|X_t| < \infty$. Then,

$$\bar{X} \overset{a.s.}{\to} E[X_t].$$

A.10.2   Mixing Sequences

Definition (uniform and strong mixing): Let $\mathcal{F}_n^k$ denote the sigma-field generated by a random sequence $\{X_t\}$ and

$$\phi(m) = \sup_n \sup_{A\in\mathcal{F}_{-\infty}^n, B\in\mathcal{F}_{n+m}^\infty, \Pr\{A\}>0} |\Pr\{B|A\} - \Pr\{B\}|$$

$$\alpha(m) = \sup_n \sup_{A\in\mathcal{F}_{-\infty}^n, B\in\mathcal{F}_{n+m}^\infty} |\Pr\{A\cap B\} - \Pr\{A\}\Pr\{B\}|.$$

Then, $\{X_t\}$ is ϕ- (or uniform) mixing if $\phi(m) \to 0$ as $m \to \infty$ and α- (or strong) mixing if $\alpha(m) \to 0$ as $m \to \infty$. ϕ and α are of size $-\lambda$ ($\lambda \in \mathbb{R}$) if $\phi(m) = O(m^{-\lambda-\delta})$ and $\alpha(m) = O(m^{-\lambda-\delta})$ for some $\delta > 0$. If $\phi(m) \to 0$ as $m \to \infty$, then $\alpha(m) \to 0$ as $m \to \infty$.

Theorem: Let $\{X_t\}$ be a stationary sequence. If $\alpha(m) \to 0$ as $m \to \infty$, then $\{X_t\}$ is ergodic.

Theorem (McLeish LLN): Let $\{X_t\}$ be a sequence of scalars with finite means $E(X_t) = \mu_t$ and suppose that for some δ, $0 < \delta \le r$ where $r \ge 1$, $\sum_{t=1}^\infty (E|X_t - \mu_t|^{r+\delta}/t^{r+\delta})^{1/r} < \infty$. If ϕ is of size $-r/(2r-1)$ or α is of size $-r/(r-1)$, then

$$\bar{X} - \bar{\mu} \overset{a.s.}{\to} 0,$$

where $\bar{\mu} = n^{-1}\sum_{t=1}^n \mu_t$.

Theorem (Wooldridge–White CLT): Let $\{X_t\}$ be a sequence of scalars with $E(X_t) = \mu_t$ and $\text{var}(X_t) = \sigma_t^2$ such that $E|X_t|^r < \Delta < \infty$ for some $r \ge 2$ and all t. If ϕ is of size $-r/(2r-1)$ or α is of size $-r/(r-1)$, then

$$\frac{\sqrt{n}(\bar{X} - \bar{\mu})}{\bar{\sigma}} \overset{d}{\to} N(0,1),$$

where $\bar{\sigma}^2 = \text{var}[n^{-1/2}\sum_{t=1}^n X_t] > 0$.

A.10.3   Martingale Difference Sequences

Definition (MDS): Let $\{\mathcal{X}_t\}$ be a random sequence and $\{\mathcal{F}_t\}$ be a sequence of σ-fields $\mathcal{F}_t \subset \mathcal{F}$ such that $\mathcal{F}_{t-1} \subset \mathcal{F}_t$ for all t (i.e., $\{\mathcal{F}_t\}$ is an increasing sequence of σ-fields, also called a filtration). Let $\mathcal{X}_t$ be measurable with respect to $\mathcal{F}_t$, i.e., $\{\mathcal{X}_t, \mathcal{F}_t\}$ is an adapted stochastic sequence. Then, $\{\mathcal{X}_t, \mathcal{F}_t\}$ is a martingale difference sequence (MDS) if

$$E(\mathcal{X}_t|\mathcal{F}_{t-1}) = 0 \text{ for all } t \ge 1.$$

Law of Iterated Expectations: Let $\mathcal{X}$ be measurable with respect to $\mathcal{F}$, $E|\mathcal{X}| < \infty$ and $\mathcal{G}$ is a σ-field contained in $\mathcal{F}$. Then,

$$E\left[E(\mathcal{X}|\mathcal{G})\right] = E(\mathcal{X}).$$

Theorem (LLN for MDS): Let $\{X_t, \mathcal{F}_t\}$ be a martingale difference sequence. If $\sum_{t=1}^{\infty}(E|X_t|^{2r})/t^{1+r} < \infty$ for some $r \geq 1$, then

$$\bar{X} \overset{a.s.}{\to} 0.$$

Theorem (CLT for MDS): Let $\{X_t, \mathcal{F}_t\}$ be a martingale difference sequence such that $E[X_t^2] = \sigma_t^2 < \infty$, $\sigma_t^2 \neq 0$, $\bar{\sigma}^2 = n^{-1}\sum_{t=1}^{n}\sigma_t^2$ and distribution functions F_t. If for every $\varepsilon > 0$,

$$\lim_{n\to\infty} \bar{\sigma}^{-2}n^{-1}\sum_{t=1}^{n}\int_{x^2>\varepsilon n\bar{\sigma}^2} x^2 dF_t(x) = 0$$

and

$$\bar{\sigma}^{-2}n^{-1}\sum_{t=1}^{n} X_t^2 - 1 \overset{p}{\to} 0,$$

then

$$\frac{\sqrt{n}\bar{X}}{\bar{\sigma}} \overset{d}{\to} \mathcal{N}(0,1).$$

A.11   Nonstationary Processes

Let S_t denote a partial sum of the form

$$S_t = \sum_{j=1}^{t} e_j = e_1 + e_2 + ... + e_t$$

and $\lfloor a \rfloor$ denote the largest integer that is less than or equal to a. Define the standardization

$$W_{T,t} = \frac{1}{\sqrt{T}\sigma} S_t = \frac{1}{\sqrt{T}\sigma}\sum_{j=1}^{t} e_j$$

Next, consider a transformation that maps a sequence of random variables on the increasing interval $[0, T]$ onto a random function on the fixed interval $[0, 1]$. In particular, for some $r \in [0, 1]$, we have the partial sum process

$$W_T(r) = W_{T,\lfloor Tr \rfloor} = \frac{1}{\sqrt{T}\sigma} S_{\lfloor Tr \rfloor} = \frac{1}{\sqrt{T}\sigma}\sum_{j=1}^{\lfloor Tr \rfloor} e_j \qquad (A.5)$$

As r varies from 0 to 1, $\lfloor Tr \rfloor$ varies from 0 to T on the integers and $W_T(r)$ varies from $W_{T,1}$ to $W_{T,T}$. As $T \to \infty$, $W_T(r)$ becomes increasingly dense on the interval $[0,1]$ and can be regarded as a continuous analog of the random walk process.

Properties of $W_T(r)$:

(i) $W_T(0) = 0$ (normalization).

(ii) $W_T(r) \overset{d}{\to} \mathcal{N}(0, r)$ for any given r as $T \to \infty$.

(iii) If $s < r$, $W_T(s)$ and $W_T(r) - W_T(s)$ are independent.

Definition (Wiener process): A stochastic process $W(r)$ is a standard Brownian motion (Wiener process) if

(i) $W(0) = 0$,

(ii) $W(r) \sim \mathcal{N}(0, r)$ for $\forall r$,

(iii) it has independent increments.

   The sample paths of the Wiener process are continuous but nowhere differentiable. Also, $W_T(r)$ is a random function that lives in a function space.[2] It is fundamentally different from the random variables and random vectors that we considered before. Thus, we need a different type of limit theorem in which the limit is a function of r.

Functional Central Limit Theorem (FCLT): Let $e_t \sim IID(0, \sigma^2)$ with $\sigma^2 < \infty$. Then,
$$W_T(r) \Rightarrow W(r),$$
where $W(r)$ is a standard Brownian motion, $W_T(r)$ is defined in (A.5) and $\Rightarrow$ denotes weak convergence for random functions.

   This is also known as Donsker's FCLT or invariance principle. By relaxing the dependence and moment conditions on $\{e_t\}$, we can obtain the Lindeberg–Feller, Lyapunov, stationary ergodic, heterogeneous mixing and martingale difference versions of the FCLT.

Continuous Mapping Theorem: If $W_T \Rightarrow W$ and $h(\cdot)$ is continuous, then
$$h(W_T) \Rightarrow h(W).$$

Corollary: Let $e_t \sim IID(0, \sigma^2)$ with $\sigma^2 < \infty$. Then,

---

[2] This is the space of real valued functions on the interval $[0,1]$ that are right continuous at each point in $[0,1]$ and have finite left limit (*cadlag* functions).

(i) $\dfrac{1}{T^{3/2}\sigma}\displaystyle\sum_{t=1}^{T} S_t \Rightarrow \displaystyle\int_{0}^{1} W(r)dr,$

(ii) $\dfrac{1}{T^2\sigma^2}\displaystyle\sum_{t=1}^{T} S_t^2 \Rightarrow \displaystyle\int_{0}^{1} W(r)^2 dr,$

(iii) $\dfrac{1}{\sigma\sqrt{T}} S_T \Rightarrow W(1).$

Definition (Ornstein–Uhlenbeck process): The Ornstein–Uhlenbeck process is defined as

$$J_c(r) = \int_{0}^{r} \exp((r-c)s)dW(s).$$

The Ornstein–Uhlenbeck process is generated by the stochastic differential equation

$$dJ_c(r) = cJ_c(r)dr + dW(r)$$

with $J_c(0) = 0$. Also,

$$J_c(r) \sim \mathcal{N}\left(0, \frac{\exp(2rc)-1}{2c}\right).$$

References

Amemiya, T. (1985) *Advanced Econometrics*. Harvard University Press: Cambridge, MA.

Brockwell, P.J., and R.A. Davis (1991) *Time Series: Theory and Methods*, second edition. Springer: New York.

Carrasco, M., J.P. Florens and E. Renault (2007) Linear inverse problems and structural econometrics: Estimation based on spectral decomposition and regularization. In: J.J. Heckman and E.E. Leamer (eds.), *Handbook of Econometrics*, Vol. 6/2, Elsevier: Amsterdam, Chapter 77, 5633–5751.

Davidson, J. (1994) *Stochastic Limit Theory*. Oxford University Press: Oxford.

Feller, W. (1971) *An Introduction to Probability Theory and Its Applications*, Vol. 2. Wiley: New York.

Hall, P. (1992) *The Bootstrap and Edgeworth Expansion*. Springer-Verlag: New York.

Spanos, A. (1986) *Statistical Foundations of Econometric Modelling*. Cambridge University Press: Cambridge.

White, H. (2001) *Asymptotic Theory for Econometricians*, second edition. Academic Press: London.

Zaman, A. (1996) *Statistical Foundations for Econometric Techniques*. Academic Press: London.

Index

For Product Safety Concerns and Information please contact our EU
representative GPSR@taylorandfrancis.com
Taylor & Francis Verlag GmbH, Kaufingerstraße 24, 80331 München, Germany

www.ingramcontent.com/pod-product-compliance
Ingram Content Group UK Ltd.
Pitfield, Milton Keynes, MK11 3LW, UK
UKHW020930280425
157818UK00025B/134